CHINUL

BERKELEY BUDDHIST STUDIES SERIES 6

CHINUL:

The Founder of the Korean Sŏn Tradition

Hee-Sung Keel

BERKELEY BUDDHIST STUDIES SERIES

1984

Produced under the editorial control of the Center for South and Southeast Asian Studies, University of California at Berkeley and the Institute of Buddhist Studies, Berkeley.

A publishing project of Po Chin Chai Ltd. 8, 5-Ga Dangsan-Dong Yeongdeungpo-Ku Seoul, Korea

Printed in Korea

ISBN   0   89581   1545

For Nam-Mee

Contents

Abbreviations

C   Pŏpchip pyŏrhaengnok chŏryo pyŏngip sagi   法集別行錄節要並入私記

CKC   Chosŏn kumsŏk ch'ongnam 朝鮮金石總覽. Seoul: 1974. Photographic reprint of *Chōsen kinseki sōran*. 2 vols. Keijō: 1919.

CKPN   Hyosŏng Cho Myŏng-gi Paksa hwagap kinyŏm Pulgyo sahak nonch'ong 曉星趙明基博士華甲紀念佛教史學論叢. Seoul: 1965.

CPT   Chosŏn Pulgyo t'ongsa 朝鮮佛教通史. 2 vols. Seoul: 1918.

CSS   Chŭngbo kyojŏng Chosŏn sach'al saryo 增補校正朝鮮寺刹史料. 2 vols. Seoul: 1972. Enlarged edition of *Chōsen jisatsu shiryō*. 2 vols. Keijō: 1911.

HTHK Han'gŭl taejanggyŏng, Han'guk kosŭng 한글대장경, 한국고승. Seoul: since 1969.

KFKK   Kōrai Fushō Kokushi no kenkyū—sono shisō taikei to Fushōzen no tokushitsu 高麗普照國師の研究—その思想體系と普照禪の特質. Seoul: 1974 (mimeographed).

Po   Hyŏnt'o yŏkhae Pojo pŏbŏ 懸吐譯解普照法語. Seoul: 1963.

PHPS   Sungsan Pak Kil-chin Paksa hwagap kinyŏm Han'guk Pulgyo sasangsa 崇山朴吉眞博士華甲紀念韓國佛教思想史. Iri, Chŏlla Pukto: 1975.

PKPN   Paek Sŏng-uk Paksa songsu kinyŏm Pulgyohak nonmunjip 白性郁博士頌壽紀念佛教學論文集. Seoul: 1959.

T.   Taishō shinshū daizōkyō 大正新修大藏經. 85 vols. Tokyo: 1914–1922.

Z.   Dai-Nihon zokuzōkyō 大日本續藏經. 750 vols. Kyoto: 1905 1912.

Notes on style

1. The Romanization of Korean words follows the McCune-Reischauer system, and the Romanization of Chinese follows the Wade-Giles system.

2. Names of Buddhist scriptures, unless popularly known in English or Sanskrit titles, are given either in Korean or Chinese, depending upon the context in which they occur. Names of Buddhist figures and denominations, including Sŏn (Ch'an) and Kyo (Chiao) in Korea, will also be given in either Korean or Chinese, depending upon the context.

3. Chinese characters for the Romanized Korean, Chinese, and Japanese words and names are provided in the glossary, except for those already given in the text itself.

4. Many non-English terms which are common in Buddhist studies have not been translated; e. g., *Tao, Dharma, saṁsāra, saṅgha, prajñā, samādhi, sūtra,* etc.

5. Some technical terms are capitalized in Enligh translation (e. g., *li* as Principle, *hsing* as Nature) in oder to differentiate their meaning from ordinary English usage, often with a hyphen in the case of a phrase or compound.

6. Page references to the two most often quoted works of Chinul, *Pojo pŏbŏ* and *Pŏpchip pyŏrhaegnok chŏryo pyŏngip sagi,* are often given at the end of the quotations in parenthesis, not in the footnote. In such cases, the former will be abbreviated simply as *Po* (followed by page number) and the latter as *C.* In the footnotes they will be abbreviated as *Pŏbŏ* and *Chŏryo.*

Preface

The present work is the outcome of my doctoral dissertation which I wrote at Harvard University in 1977. Some portions of the dissertation were left out and some altered here and there, but it remains substantially the same. For the sake of those who may have broader interest in Korean Buddhism, I have left the original bibliography intact, which covers the materials not merely on Chinul and the related topics but also on Korean Buddhism in general. Six years have elapsed since I have written the dissertation, but the situation of scholarship on Korean Buddhism has not changed very much at all. Korean Buddhism is still a virgin field as far as the Buddhist studies in the West are concerned. It is my hope that this book will contribute something to the wider interest in Korean Buddhism as well as to the deeper understanding of Sŏn (Zen) among the students of Buddhism.

Sŏn has often been described as esoteric, illogical and mystical. Whoever has the opportunity to read this book will find such a view seriously challenged. Sŏn, at least as far as Chinul understood and practiced it, is not inaccessible to intellectual comprehension. A great Sŏn master, Chinul wrote many theoretical works which guide us into the profound realm of Sŏn religious experience. This has to be regarded as a rather rare phenomenon and certainly a valuable contribution in the history of Sŏn Buddhism. It is true that Chinul's Sŏn thought was very much indebted to Tsung-mi, the ninth-century Chinese Hua-yen and Ch'an patriarch who wanted to harmonize Ch'an with doctrinal Buddhism, as well as to a host of other thinkers before him. Throughout this book I make reference to Tsung-mi and others whenever Chinul borrows significant ideas from them. But I must say that it is often difficult to distinguish Chinul's thought from Tsung-mi's for instance, or, for that matter, from Li T'ung-hsüan's, another Chinese Hua-yen master whose thought had greatly influenced Chinul's interpretation of Hua-yen philosophy. Chinul freely used their words verbatim in his writings without having any consciousness of "plagiarism" or anything like that. Their thoughts provided the threads with which he weaved a colorful fabric—a comprehensive approach to Sŏn, which eventually became the established tradition in Korean Buddhism.

I have to take this opportunity to express my gratitude to Professor Masatoshi Nagatomi at Harvard University who supervised my doctoral dissertation. My deep gratitude also goes to Professor John Carman and the Center for the Study of World Religions at Harvard which made my study there possible with its generous support, both financial and spiritual, for many years. I also thank Professor Lewis Lancaster and the editorial team of the Berkeley Buddhist Studies Series who had to do a laborious job to make a work by a nonnative English writer more readable.

Hee-Sung Keel

Department of Philosophy
Seoul National University
Seoul, December 24, 1983

CHAPTER I

THE LIFE OF CHINUL

INTRODUCTION

KOREAN BUDDHISM REACHED ITS APOGEE in the latter half of the seventh century A.D., when the Silla dynasty unified the Three Kingdoms into which the Korean peninsula had been divided for centuries. Under the general influence of T'ang China, Buddhism permeated and inspired every aspect of Silla social and cultural life—art, architecture, scholarship, the court and the nobility, popular faith, patriotism, foreign trade, and diplomacy. In the field of Buddhist doctrinal studies, a host of eminent scholars appeared representing the major schools of Chinese Mahāyāna Buddhism. The greatest and most creative among them was Wŏnhyo (617–686), who was a master in doctrinal harmonization and composed numerous important treatises and commentaries on various Mahāyāna Buddhist scriptures.

But from the end of the eighth century on, Silla politics began to betray serious internal conflicts within the ruling class, and Buddhism also began to lose much of its earlier vitality and creativity. It was during that time that Ch'an (Sŏn in Korean) Buddhism was introduced into Korea from T'ang China and began to take root in local areas such as the so-called Nine Mountains (*kusan*). Most founders of the monasteries of the Nine Mountains received the *Dharma* from the disciples of the famous Ma-tsu Tao-i (707–786). Their radicalism soon created tension and conflict with the old-established schools of doctrinal Buddhism (Kyo), posing a major problem in the Buddhist community of Korea thereafter. As we shall see, Chinul himself had to wrestle with this issue and made it the central concern of his thought.

In the final period of the Silla dynasty social turmoil and unrest prevailed. The authority of the central government collapsed due to the political struggle among the aristocrats of the capital, the poor administration of the kings, and the rise of powerful local warlords. Eventually order was restored out of this chaos by Wanggŏn, a local warlord who founded a new regime, the Koryŏ dynasty (918–1392). Even though the dynasty changed, however, there was no weakening of the intimate relationship that existed between Buddhism and the state. In fact, from the Koryŏ period on, Buddhism became even more solidly established as the state religion. Thus we see the foundation in the early tenth century of the monks' examination system, paralleling the civil-service examination, which had already been initiated by King Kwangjong after the Chinese model. Along with the monks' examination (sŭngkwa 僧科), a clerical ranking system (pŏpkye 法階) was devised. The monks who passed the examination began to climb the ladder of clerical ranks; those who did not pass the examination could not be appointed abbots of monasteries. Since the examination was taken separately for Sŏn and Kyo— indicating the polarization of Koryŏ Buddhism into two camps— the names of the ranks conferred were different, except for the highest two, which were common to both: royal preceptor (wangsa) and national preceptor (kuksa). These were bestowed only upon the most honored monks. Throughout the Koryŏ period, this system was a great incentive to advancement for Buddhist monks, and the higher ranks bestowed prestige on those who possessed them. Hence to be a monk was, in Koryŏ society, a respectable career for men of ambition.

As Buddhism flourished under the patronage of the state, monasteries became financially wealthy. Contributions from the court and the nobles, the privilege of tax exemption, the practice of lending money at interest, and various other commercial factors provided their economic prosperity. It is not hard to imagine that this lured many into the *sangha* who had material motives. Despite its external flourishing, Koryŏ Buddhism lacked the inner vitality demonstrated by Silla Buddhism, and there was no creative development that would set Koryŏ Buddhism apart from that of Silla. But with the appearance

2

of Ŭich'ŏn in the middle of the eleventh century Koryŏ Buddhism began to show its own dynamics. Ŭich'ŏn and his religious career are important for our understanding of Chinul and the religious movement he came to launch about eighty years after Ŭich'ŏn's death.[1]

Born in A.D. 1055 the fourth son of King Munjong, Ŭich'ŏn left home at the age of eleven years and entered a Hwaŏm (Hua-yen) monastery. At thirty-one he went to Sung China, where he met many illustrious Chinese masters of various schools and collected large amounts of Buddhist literature. While in China, Ŭich'ŏn showed a particular interest in T'ien-t'ai (Ch'ŏnt'ae) philosophy. He paid a visit to the pagoda of the T'ien-t'ai master Chih-i and made the following vow before it:

> Ŭich'ŏn, bowing down and taking refuge with the T'ien-t'ai master Chih-i, reverently announces: I was told long ago that you had completely expounded the sacred teachings of the Buddha that had flowed into the East by the "five periods and eight teachings" [T'ien-t'ai system of doctrinal classification], so that all students of Buddhism in later periods base themselves upon it. My patriarch, the master commentator of the *Hua-yen Sūtra* [Ching-yüan, a Chinese Hua-yen master (1011–1088)] said that the "five teachings" of Hsien-shou [Fa-tsang's Hua-yen doctrinal classification] are not much different from those of T'ien-t'ai.
>
> I recall that in the past our country had a master by the name of Ch'egwan [the author of the famous *Ch'ŏnt'ae sagyoŭi* (*T'ien-t'ai ssu-chiao-i*)] who had expounded your doctrinal study (*kyo* 教) and contemplation (*kwan* 觀) and had spread it overseas. But now both the transmitters and the students have ceased to exist. Therefore while I, with my heart aroused and my body forgotten, have searched for a mentor and asked the way, only now have I been in touch with the *kyo* and *kwan* at the lecture by Tz'u-pien of Chien-t'ang [Chinese T'ien-t'ai master Ŭich'ŏn met in China] and have found the bare knowledge of their outline.
>
> Later, when I return home, it is my vow that I will endeavor with all my life to repay the grace of the trouble you took to teach sentient

---

[1] On Ŭich'ŏn's life and thought, see Takahashi Tōru's "Daigaku Kokushi Giten no Kōrai Bukkyō ni taisuru keirin ni tsuite, "*Chōsen gakuhō* 10 (1956): 113–47; see also Cho Myŏng-gi, *Koryŏ Taegak Kuksa wa Ch'ŏnt'ae sasang* (Seoul: 1964).

beings by spreading them [*kyo* and *kwan*] far and wide.[2]

Several points deserve our attention in this vow: the idea of the basic harmony between Hwaŏm (Hua-yen) and Ch'ŏnt'ae (T'ien-tai) philosophies, the awareness of a previous tradition of Ch'ŏnt'ae in Korea, the earnest desire to learn the Ch'ŏnt'ae teachings of *kyo* and *kwan*, and finally his vow to propagate this teaching in Korea. We see here Ŭich'ŏn, a monk of the Hwaŏm School in Korea, committing himself to the new teaching of Ch'ŏn-t'ae. The reason behind this is his idea of *kyogwan kyŏmsu*, which means "parallel cultivation of doctrinal study and practical contemplation." Ch'ŏnt'ae's balanced emphasis upon *kyo* and *kwan* was Ŭich'ŏn's prescription for the major illness of the Buddhist community of his time, namely, the antagonism between Sŏn and Kyo.

Ŭich'ŏn's greatness as a Buddhist leader, however, was not so much this idea (the parallel cultivation of *kyo* and *kwan*) as the concrete actions he took to achieve the unity of the Koryŏ *saṅgha*. Upon his construction of the Kukch'ŏng Monastery (in memory of his deceased mother), he made it the center of the Ch'ŏnt'ae Order, and he himself became its first abbot. Royal support and Ŭich'ŏn's personal ability soon made Ch'ŏnt'ae the most flourishing order of the time. Significantly, it regarded itself as a Sŏn order—its monks received the titles of the Sŏn clerical ranks—and absorbed many brilliant monks from the Nine Mountains of Sŏn. Ŭich'ŏn persuaded able leaders of the Nine Mountains to join the new order. For a time it looked as if he might have actually accomplished the integration of Sŏn and Kyo under the Ch'ŏnt'ae ideal of *kyogwan kyŏmsu*; but he died at the age of forty-seven, too soon to give his ideal a more solid embodiment.

Thus eventually the Ch'ŏnt'ae Order became simply another sect in an already crowded field, and the distance between Sŏn and Kyo remained as wide as ever. Ŭich'ŏn's effort only helped to strengthen denominational self-consciousness on the part of the existing sects, particularly those of Sŏn, whose Nine Mountains now began to show

---

[2] *Taegak Kuksa munjip, Han'guk kosŭngjip: Koryŏ sidae* I (Seoul: 1974), pp. 167–68.

a movement of consolidation under the new name of Chogyejong. They adopted this name from the mountain where the Sixth Patriarch, Hui-neng, used to dwell, just as Ch'ŏnt'ae was the name of the mountain where Chih-i had resided. In this way a new and unified Sŏn order emerged.[3] But it had no Ŭich'ŏn yet; it had to wait about half a century for the appearance of Chinul, who became the first, and the last, in the history of Korean Sŏn Buddhism to give it a clear ideology and identity—hence the title of the present work, *Chinul, the Founder of the Korean Sŏn Tradition.* Before turning to study how Chinul accomplished this, we will review the social and religious circumstances that formed the immediate background of Chinul's life and thought; for many events of great consequence took place not long after Ŭich'ŏn's death.

When the Koryŏ dynasty was founded by the local warlord Wang-gŏn, he was assisted by many others like him. From the beginning the power of the warlords was strong. Though many of them were incorporated into the central aristocracy through intermarriage with the royal family, they were still a potential threat to the centralization of power around the throne. Boastful of their region or family, powerful aristocrats vied with each other in the expansion of their political and economic sway, particularly through marriage of their daughters into the royal family. The ever-growing power of some of the aristocrats finally led to open revolt against the royal authority. Yi Cha-gyŏm's uprising (1126), although unsuccessful, opened the door to the long period of turbulence that was to follow. Stimulated by this revolt, and by the threat from the new neighboring power of Chin (1115–1234), some in P'yŏngyang, including a Buddhist monk named Myoch'ŏng, insisted that the capital be moved from Kaesŏng to P'yŏngyang. The importance of this city had been recognized as early as the time of T'aejo, the founder of the Koryŏ dynasty. Myoch'ŏng strengthened his argument with the theory of geomancy,

---

[3] This is the usual view on the origin of the Chogye Order. Yi Nŭng-hwa, in his *CPT*, II, p. 336, expresses the view that it was owing to Chinul that the Chogye Order came into being. We will discuss this view, which we do not agree with, when we examine Chinul's life in the next chapter.

which considered Kaesŏng's earth-power (*chidŏk*) to be waning, whereas that of P'yŏngyang to be waxing. His opinion might have been followed by King Injong but for the opposition of the conservatives represented by Kim Pu-sik, the compiler of the *Samguk sagi* [*Chronicles of the Three Kingdoms*] and an able military leader. This opposition led Myochŏng to a revolt in 1135, which was put down by Kim Pu-sik.

Things grew still worse under King Ŭijong (1146–1170). Numerous insurrections arose throughout the country toward the end of his reign, and in the midst of this confusion the military seized power. The Koryŏ bureaucracy had been traditionally run by civil ministers, who held most of the political and economic power, and who despised the military officials. Even work properly belonging to the military had often been taken over by the civil ministers and the military degraded to mere bodyguards of the king and the civil ministers. Soldiers had been mobilized not only for military affairs but also for civil purposes. These factors finally caused the military officials to rise up in revolt in 1170. The powerful civil ministers were murdered and the king deposed. Thus began the long period of military rule which would have lasted even longer but for the Mongol invasions in the first half of the thirteenth century. An intense power struggle soon ensued among the military men to be settled eventually by the able Ch'oe brothers. The political confusion in the capital also offered a good opportunity for peasants and slaves to rise up against the local authorities and even the central government, in order to free themselves from their harsh burdens. "The opposition of the country against the capital, and the revolt of the lower classes against the higher society"[4] became the order of the day. It was in that period that Chinul spent the early part of his life.

The Buddhist community could not remain unaffected by this social and political upheaval. The monk Myoch'ŏng, as we have mentioned, was the leader of a revolt against the throne. As the military regime was established, many monks of the powerful mon-

---

[4] An expression of Yi Pyŏng-do's, *Han'guksa taegwan* (Seoul: 1964), p. 231.

asteries joined forces against the new political order to protect their privileged socioeconomic status, long associated with the court and the civil ministers.[5] Meanwhile, the court continued its lavish practice of "meritorious works." As the times became more restless, those works were carried out even more extravagantly. This was intended to ward off calamities and promote the welfare of the state, but it only drained the royal treasury and burdened the people. The monasteries grew richer, only to be spoiled by their enormous wealth. As early as the time of King Munjong, when Buddhism reached its peak, the corruption of the *sangha* became so serious that he had to proclaim the following edict to the monasteries:

> The teaching propounded by Śākyamuni aims at purity foremost; it moves far away from dirty baseness, and it removes avarice. These days, however, many who dodge the labor service, calling themselves monks, maintain their livelihood by increasing property; they make plowing [the field] and tending [the cattle] their job, and doing business is customary for them. Due to this, they deviate from [the Buddha's] precepts, and in their life they know no binding to purity. ... They are engaged in buying and selling with the merchants, and they are at one with the visitors in drunkenness and rolicking. The gardens of flowers [i.e. monasteries] are filled with noise, and an impure stench permeates the pots of orchids [monasteries]. ... It is my desire to distinguish between the good and the evil [monks] and to establish firm order. Let the monasteries in the capital as well as in the provinces carry out the purging, so that all those who cultivate the practice of the precepts with diligence may stay comfortably, while the transgressors should be ruled by the [civil] law.[6]

Monks of different denominations vied with each other in the quest for high clerical positions and the royal favor that would enhance the power and prestige of their sects and monasteries. The mutual antagonism between Sŏn and Kyo became even more aggravated because

---

[5] Also pointed out by Yi Pyŏng-do, p. 229; for a more detailed analysis of this significant phenomenon, see Kim Chong-guk, "Kōrai bushin seiken to sōto no tairitsu kōsō ni kansuru ichi kōsatsu," *Chōsen gakuhō* 21–22 (1961); 567–89.

[6] Translated from Kim Sang-gi, *Koryŏ sidae sa* (Seoul: 1961), p. 157; Kim's Korean translation consulted. The text is found in *Koryŏsa*, vol. 7, the 10th year of Munjong, September.

of Ŭich'ŏn's unsuccessful effort mentioned earlier. The world of peace and prosperity that Ŭich'ŏn had enjoyed in his time no longer existed as the eleventh century, the golden period of the Koryŏ dynasty, gave way to the twelfth; the mood of the times had changed. It was not a time for expansion, but a time for introspection; not a time to busy oneself with the external world, but a time for the quiet pursuit of the internal world. In the midst of an ever-darkening society, the Koryŏ Buddhist community was waiting for the appearance of a leader to represent the new spirit of the times and to suggest a new direction to pursue. But this could only be made possible by strong self-negation on the part of Koryŏ Buddhism—something it had never known before. It was Chinul who squarely faced the necessity of this painful act with firm determination. Eda Shunyū, a scholar of Korean Buddhism, puts the significance of Chinul's appearance as follows:

> Under these ecclesiastical and social circumstances, it was none other than Chinul who, walking Ŭich'ŏn's reformatory path reversely seventy or eighty years later, stood up for the purification of the Koryŏ Buddhist world and for the edification of Koryŏ society. He sought to harmonize Sŏn and Kyo, but always from the standpoint of "Sŏn the master and Kyo the servant."[7]

Let us first examine what kind of source materials are available concerning Chinul's life. The first and by far the most important source of information is the inscription written in 1211, i.e., the year following the death of Chinul, by Kim Kun-su, the grandson of the famous Kim Pu-sik who compiled the *Samguk sagi* [*Chronicles of the Three Kingdoms*][8]. Our knowledge of how it came to be composed

---

[7] "Chōsen zen no keisai—'Fushōzen' no seikaku ni tsuite," *Indogaku Bukkyōgaku kenkyū* V, 2 (1957): 353.

[8] The full name of the inscription is *Sŭngp'yŏngbu Chogyesan Susŏnsa Puril Pojo Kuksa pimyŏng pyŏngsŏ*. The original stele which had been preserved in the present Songgwang Monastery where Chinul spent the last period of his life was damaged during the Japanese invasion of Korea in 1597. Fortunately, however, before the damage, it was inserted into the *Tongmunsŏn*, a collection of Korean literary writings, compiled by Sŏ Kŏ-jŏng in 1478 (fascicle 117). Im Ch'ang-sun, in his article "Songgwangsa ŭi Koryŏ munsŏ," *Paeksan hakpo*, No. 11 (1971), p. 40, tells us that the monastery has a scroll which contains the text of the inscription; the scroll is said to have been written not earlier than 1221 (eleven years after Chinul's death). At any

is itself based upon the inscription.[9] When Chinul passed away, his *Dharma* heir Hyesim and others collected information on the life of their master and presented it to the court, beseeching King Hŭijong to erect a memorial stele to perpetuate the memory of their great master. The king, having also a deep respect for the master according to the inscription[10], granted their wish and ordered Kim Kun-su, a noted literary man of the time, to compose the inscription for the stele. Since it was written only a year after Chinul's death, it can be regarded as a very reliable source, despite the inevitable basic limitation that it was not meant to be a "biography" in our conception of the term.

The second source for our study of Chinul's life is the *Taesŭng Sŏnjong Chogyesan Susŏnsa chungch'anggi* [Record of the Reconstruction of Susŏnsa of the Mahāyāna Sŏn Order in Chogye Mountain]. Composed by Ch'ŏe Sŏn in accordance with a royal order in 1207 when Chinul was fifty years old,[11] the record is still preserved in Songgwang Monastery.[12] It gives us some information on how Chinul and his followers came to reconstruct an almost deserted monastery into Susŏnsa (the present Songgwang Monastery), the Society for the Cultivation of Sŏn.

The third indispensable material is one of Chinul's own writings,

---

rate, if this is true, when in 1678 the Sŏn Master Paegam Sŏngch'ong reconstructed the stele, the inscription must have been based upon either this scroll or the *Tongmunsŏn*. The new inscription, still preserved in the monastery, is slightly shorter than the original one. The text of the original inscription is given in *CPT*, II, pp. 337–42. It is also contained in the *Hyŏnt'o yŏkhae Pojo pŏbŏ* [*Discourses on the Dharma by Pojo*] which is currently the most widely circulated text of Chinul's works (not all of them) in Korea. Published in 1963 in Seoul with Korean translation by Kim T'anhŏ, it was originally edited by the Sŏn Master Pang Hanam in 1937. We will use this text in this book as far as the works contained in it are concerned. On the history of the stele, see *Taesŭng Sŏnjong Chogyesan Songgwangsa chi* (Songgwang Monastery, 1965) compiled by Im Sŏk-chin, pp. 60–61.

[9] *Pŏbŏ*, p. 143.

[10] *Pŏbŏ*, p. 141.

[11] We follow in this book Korean age, simply because the sources themselves use it; Chinul was born in 1158.

[12] The text is given in *CSS*, I, pp. 174–77. Only a record written on paper, it is not clear whether its text was actually inscribed (or meant to be inscribed) on a stele. Yi Chong-ik seems to think that it was inscribed on a stele; see his *KFKK*, p. 33.

Kwŏnsu chŏnghye kyŏlsamun [*Invitation to the Society for the Cultivation of* Samādhi *and* Prajñā] which was written when Chinul was thirty-three. As the first work of Chinul, this is an invaluable source which informs us about one of the most crucial events in his life, namely the formation of the Society for the Cultivation of *Samādhi* and *Prajñā*.

The preface of another work by Chinul, *Hwaŏmnon chŏryo* [*Condensation of the Treatise on Hua-yen*],[13] sheds light on how he came to discover Li T'ung-hsüan's *Treatise on Hua-yen*[14] which, as we shall see, constituted a tremendously important experience for Chinul.

These four are the primary sources for our study of Chinul's life. Besides them, there are two kinds of additional materials. The first category includes the various accounts of Chinul's life which are based upon the primary sources indicated above, particularly the inscription; hence their significance for our purpose is nearly negligible. To this category belong such works as *Haedong Pulcho wŏllyu* compiled by a monk named Saam in 1764 and *Tongsa yŏlchŏn* compiled by Pŏmhae in 1894. The second category of materials consists of various legendary stories associated with Chinul. But they are by no means full-fledged legends, nor are they focused on the figure of Chinul. Most of them appear to have been invented later simply to enhance the prestige of a particular monastery by associating Chinul with its foundation. A typical example is the story of Hyŏndŭng Monastery which associates its origin not merely with Chinul but also with other renowned figures in Korean Buddhism such as King Pŏphŭng, Tosŏn, and Hamhŏ.[15] These stories are collected in the *Song-*

---

[13] The existence of this work came to be known to the world by the discovery of a hand-written copy in the Kanezawa Bunko (Library) in Japan by Yi Chong-ik in 1942; see his "Pojo Kuksa ŭi sorok in 'Hwaŏmnon chŏryo' ŭi sin palgyŏn," *Pulgyo sin*, No. 27 (1942). Through the laborious work of editing the text by Kim Chi-gyŏn it was published in photographed edition as *Koryŏguk Chinullok Hwaŏmnon chŏryo* (Tokyo, 1968).

[14] The original name is *Hsin Hua-yen-ching-lun* [*New Treatise on the* Hua-yen *Sūtra*], T. 36, No. 1739. Chinul calls it simply *Hwaŏmnon* [*Treatise on Hua-yen*]. It was called "new" because it was a treatise based on the new translation of the sūtra by Śikṣānanda in eighty fascicles.

[15] See *Unak Hyŏndŭngsa sajŏk, CSS*, I, pp. 32–35.

gwangsa sago, Inmulp'yŏn which was compiled by Im Ki-san (Im Sŏk-chin) in 1935,[16] and their sources are identified there as well. We do not intend to examine them here at all; suffice it to say that they provide information not so much on Chinul himself as on his image—better, his popularity and prestige—at the time when they were invented. With this brief review of the source materials on the life of Chinul, let us now proceed to investigate the personal history of Chinul, which can be divided into four distinct periods.

1. *The First Period: Chinul leaves the capital*

Chinul was born in 1158 in Sŏhŭng District (its old name was Tongju)[17] of Hwanghae Province. His secular surname was Chŏng, Chinul being his Buddhist name. But he liked to call himeslf "Mo-guja" 牧牛子, his style meaning "one who tends cows."[18] Chinul is more popularly known as "Puril Pojo Kuksa" 佛日普照國師 (or simply Pojo Kuksa) which means "National Preceptor Universally Illuminating like the Sun of Buddha," the title conferred upon him posthumously by King Hŭijong in the year he died, i.e., 1210.

Chinul's father, Chŏng Kwang-u, was a *hakchŏng* at the Kuk-chagam or the National Academy.[19] Though not much is known in detail about the duty of a *hakchŏng*, we know at least that it was not a teaching position. Together with *hangnok* its ranking was *chŏng kup'um* which was one of the lowest government ranks in Koryŏ.[20] Perhaps *hakchŏng* was something like the present dean of students

---

[16] A fairly bulky volume, it is kept in the museum of Songgwang Monastery. Its essential content, what Im calls *chŏngsa* (proper history), is contained in his *Taesŭng Sŏnjong Chogyesan Songgwangsa chi* which we have already referred to.

[17] See "Sŏhŭng," *Han'guk chimyŏng yŏnhyŏk ko*, ed. by Kwŏn Sang-no (Seoul, 1961).

[18] We will see why Chinul liked to call himself so later on in our study. Tending cows symbolizes the diligent act of Buddhist cultivation of the mind; see, for instance, D. T. Suzuki's *Essays in Zen Buddhism*, First series (New York, 1961; hereafter to be referred to as *First Series*. Likewise, his *Second Series & Third Series*), pp. 369–76.

[19] About its structure, see "Kukchagam," *Kuksa tae sajŏn,* ed. by Yi Hong-jik (Seoul, 1971).

[20] On the government ranking system of Koryŏ, see "wigye," *Kuksa tae sajŏn,* or "Koryŏ sidae kwanjik p'yo" in the appendix.

and *hangnok* the registrar. Be that as it may, we can assume that Chinul's father was an educated man, though not a high bureaucrat, and that Chinul also received a decent education in his childhood. But at the same time we can tell that, seen from the literary Chinese of his writings which in both vocabulary and style was rather simple and limited, he did not receive the refined and aesthetic literary education available to the sons of high aristocratic families, such as Ŭich'ŏn seems to have received. According to the inscription, from birth Chinul suffered from many diseases, and his parents tried various medicines, to no avail. Finally they offered prayer before the Buddha (which Buddha, we have no way of knowing) with the vow to make their son *ch'ulga* (leave the home, *pravrajyā*), that is, to make him a monk if the disease were cured. The prayer was answered, and Chinul took refuge with the Sŏn Master Chonghwi of the Mt. Sagul branch of Sŏn who tonsured him and gave the *kugye* (or *kujok-kye*, the 250 precepts for *bhikṣu*). This was when Chinul was only eight years old, the inscription tells us.

Now, there are some problems about this age of Chinul's *pravrajyā*. First of all, it is not (and was not) customary that one receives the tonsure and the full precepts at the same time and at such an early age.[21] Thus, either the age of his tonsure must be later than eight if it was taken simultaneously with the reception of the full 250 precepts (even this is hard to believe, for one usually begins with receiving the ten precepts for *sami* first) or he received the *pigu* precepts much later. At any rate, the inscritption here is not clear at all. Second, the inscription gives the total span of Chinul's religious career as thirty-six years (*Po.* 142), which would make the span of his life forty-four if he had left home at eight; but this does not square with the other report in the inscription that Chinul died in 1210 at the age of fifty-three (*Po.* 142). Third, Chinul himself mentions at the beginning of his *Kwŏnsu chŏnghye kyŏlsamun* (*Po.* 1) that he

---

[21] The traditional ordination process in Korea generally followed that in China (and in Theravāda countries). At the time of tonsure one receives the ten precepts for *sami* (*śrāmaṇera*), and then only after the age of twenty is one allowed to receive the full 250 precepts for *pigu* (*bhikṣu*); see Takahashi, *Richō Bukkyō*, pp. 1006–18.

12

"threw himself into the realm of patriarchs" (i.e., Sŏn monastic life) when he was in "*myonyŏn*" 妙年, a term which refers to the age around twenty.[22] All these considerations lead us rather to conclude that Chinul left home when he was between fifteen and twenty, which is a more usual age for a person to think about his life and make fundamental decisions. Our supposition is in fact strengthened by the compiler of *Tongsa yŏlchŏn* who puts the age of Chinul's *pravra-jyā* as sixteen, not eight.[23] And if our supposition is correct, then the authenticity of the story of his illness and the prayer has to be called into question too. We are inclined to think that the story, by no means uncommon in the stories about great monks, was attached to Chinul to show that he became a monk by special destiny, what the Buddhist calls "*inyŏn*" 因緣 in the popular sense of the term.

What then, if the story is discredited, was the cause that led Chinul to give up secular life? Having no particular clue to it, we cannot but turn our eyes to the much confused social conditions that characterized the entire period of his life. The coup by the military officials took place when Chinul was twelve years old, and soon it was followed by a merciless power struggle among them. It is said that because of this coup many literary men of the time took refuge in the Buddhist monasteries to indulge in a quiet life of meditation and study, not necessarily as monks.[24] Numerous uprisings by the peasants and slaves followed one after another throughout the country, and the tremendous sufferings of life were to be seen everywhere. Normally Chinul, like his father, might have been expected to pursue a career of some kind of government service. Not that the career of a Buddhist monk was an unusual or a disreputable one as in the Yi dynasty, but it is not improbable that the harsh fate of the civil ministers plus the gloomy social conditions could have stimulated, if not caused, Chinul at an adolescent age to seek his identity in the

---

[22] See "myonyŏn," *Kugŏ tae sajŏn*, ed. by Yi Hŭi-sŭng.

[23] *Pulgyo munhŏn charyojip*, I (Seoul, 1972), p. 100; but the compiler does not give any explanation for this change. Most likely, it was because of the same difficulty as we have, namely the arithmatic one.

[24] Yi Pyŏng-do, *Han'guksa taegwan*, p. 233.

Buddhist path of liberation from the world. The worldly order had already broken down, and the social turmoil and the omnipresent misery of human life must have made the Buddhist promise of liberation sound more "real."[25] Certainly the way the world looked to Chinul was quite different from the way it did to Ŭich'ŏn about a century earlier, and the religious needs were different accordingly. A young man of sensitive religious mind would have found himself in no mood or leisure to be engaged·in time-consuming doctrinal studies nor to travel around in search of masters and new literature. Was it not perhaps for this reason that Chinul took refuge in Sŏn Buddhism rather than in a doctrinal school, if we are to suggest any particular reason as to why he chose Sŏn?

There is a significant qualitative difference between the voluntary *pravrajyā* done on the basis of individual decision, and the involuntary one which the story of his illness suggests, however fated or miraculous it may have been. On the one hand we see a child of only eight years old pushed by his parents into a Buddhist temple; on the other hand we see a lonely young mind disillusioned with the transient world of turmoil and longing for liberation through the Buddhist path. It is less likely that out of the former a new spiritual awareness would emerge to launch a movement of religious reform; a feeling of disappointment and disillusion, such as we find in Chinul later on, is more likely to arise in an individual who joined the *sangha* on a voluntary basis of conscious decision. Koryŏ Buddhism, as the established state religion of the time, had already enough of the monks who entered monkhood for a professional career, but ironically few for the genuine religious goal of salvation from the world.

Be that as it may, here is young Chinul whose official religious affiliation was as a member of the Mt. Sagul branch of the Sŏn Order, or the Chogye Order according to its new name. But this affiliation does not tell us much about Chinul's early spiritual back-

---

[25] Here we *may* be reading Chinul's later thought into his early life—an inevitable thing to a certain extent, for "life is understood backward."

ground or training, not simply because we happen to know little about the monk Chonghwi, Chinul's preceptor, but more significantly because the inscription tells us that Chinul, much like Wŏnhyo of Silla, "had no permanent master" and "only followed the *Tao*."[26] By this we are led to believe that sectarian identity did not mean much to Chinul from the beginning of his religious career. This independent spirit, fostered by his concern with the *Tao*, was to characterize the rest of his life, and out of this singular commitment to the *Tao* he was eventually to initiate a unique Sŏn tradition of his own at Chogye Mountain where he established a center for the cultivation of Sŏn and spent the last ten years of his life.

The inscription is silent about Chinul's life after ordination until we come to his taking the monks' examination at the age of twenty-five (1182). About this crucial event of his life Chinul himself gives us better information in his *Kwŏnsu chŏnghye kyŏlsamun*.[27] As he tells it, the examination was held at Poje Monastery in the capital, the examination site for Sŏn monks at the time, in the form of a *tamsŏn pŏphoe* (*Dharma* Meeting for the Discussion of Son).[28] Unfortunately we do not know much about this system, what preparations had to be made for it and how it was actually practiced. We merely know from the inscription that he successfully passed it. Since in those days no abbotship of a monastery or any state clerical appointment was given to a person who had not passed the examination, it must have been customary for any learned or ambitious monk to take it. So did Chinul too, and to this extent he followed the usual course; but the rest of his career had little in common with the direction followed by other monks. For, right at the place of the examination which was the way to honor and fame for his fellow monks, an entirely different type of concern was voiced by Chinul. He describes it as follows:

---

[26] *Pŏbŏ*, p. 140.

[27] Henceforth, we will call this work simply *Kyŏlsamun*.

[28] *Pŏbŏ*, p. 2. The examination was held every three years, but sometime after Chinul it was held more often and in other monasteries as well; see *CPT*, II, p. 10, and *Hanguksa*, 7 (Seoul, 1974), pp. 311–14.

One day I made a promise with about ten of my fellow students [of Sŏn] saying that: When this meeting is over, we should reject fame and gain, retreat to the mountains and woods, and form a common society, always making the balanced practice of *samādhi* and *prajñā* our task. If each of us carries out his work, from the worship of Buddha and the reading of *sūtras* down to our manual labors, nourishes his Nature according to various conditions, leads a carefree life, and follows from afar the high practices of the masters and true men, would it not be a joy(*Po. 2*)?

Here we can vividly see before our eyes a young monk possessed by the vision of an ideal religious life, a dream which is humble and yet lofty, concrete and yet liberating. Simple as this vision may appear, when we carefully analyze it—and the reality behind the ideal—we discover that there is hidden in it a series of revolutionary ideas, at least in the Koryŏ Buddhist world of Chinul's time. His ideal specifies the following actions: "reject fame and gain," "retreat to the mountains and woods," "form a common society," and "balanced practice of *samādhi* and *prajñā*." It further talks about such things as "the worship of Buddha," "reading of *sūtras*," and "manual labors." Let us now examine these ideas one by one more closely.

First of all, "reject fame and gain" was obviously an explicit indictment of the aberrations of the Koryŏ Buddhist world. It was above all by the acute awareness of this pursuit of "fame and gain" among the monks that young Chinul's vision was awakened. He deplores it as follows:

But, as I reflect on the traces of what we monks do morning and evening, [it is evident that] pretending to work for the cause of Buddhist *Dharma*, we display [the notion of] "self" and "other" and follow the trivial path of gain and benefit. Drowned in the world of wind and dust, we do not cultivate the *Tao* and virtue but merely squander clothes and food. Even if we have left home, what virtue is there in it? Alas, though desirous of transcending the three realms of existence [*kāmadhātu, rūpadhātu,* and *arūpa-dhātu*], we do not act to leave the dust [of mundane existence]; born as men, we do not harbor man's ambition. Above us [to the Buddha], we neglect to spread the *Tao*; below us, we do not benefit sentient beings; and in the middle [world of our own lives], we betray the four kinds of grace [the grace of king, teacher, parents, and friends]. Shameful truly it is, and I have deeply deplored this for long already(*Po.2*).

Here we can imagine what had been occupying Chinul's mind ever since he joined the *saṅgha*. It was a feeling of thorough disenchantment, frustration, and shame. What distressed Chinul's conscience so painfully was the ironical reality that monks, who should be least mundane, were the most mundane of all. This all too glaring contradiction young Chinul came to find in the *saṅgha*, and the self-awareness that he also belonged to this group called forth in him an overwhelming sense of shame and guilt as well as disenchantment and frustration.

But this absurd reality that had for such a long time been taken for granted by ordinary monks could only be disturbing problem to a person gifted with an exceptionally sensitive soul. In the following words we have a graphic account of the religious agony that agitated the mind of young Chinul:

If one is not stabilized in meditation and calm in thought, his karmic consciousness would become vague with no basis to rely on. At the time of death the wind and fire [i.e., the breath and heat of the body] would oppress him and the four elements will be scattered; his mind will be mad and agonized, and his views perverted and confused. There will be no device to ascend up to heaven above and no design to descend under the earth below; in horror and terror with nothing to rely on, his form will look forlorn like the exuviae cast off by a cicada. The path of delusion [i.e., the path of transmigration or *saṃsāra*] is far and distant, but the lonely spirit travels alone. Though he may have treasures and rare things, there is nothing he can take with him; though he may have relatives and a powerful family there is after all no one to accompany and help him. This is called "self-work self-earning" [reaping one's own karma], and there is no one to replace him. At this time, what eyes would there be to become the bridge to cross over the sea of suffering? Do not say that you can evade this calamity by virtue of a small amount of worldly [lit. conditioned; *saṃskṛta* or *yuwei*] merits (*Po.* 13).

For a person vexed with this kind of existential concern no ordinary answer was satisfactory. His disturbed self simply could find no easy accommodation in the self-complacent Koryŏ Buddhism of his time. The last warning not to count on "the small amount of worldly merits" is particularly revealing. For it was a clear challenge to the ceremonial and ritualistic Buddhism of his day which was busily engaged in all sorts of external activities supposed to generate "merit" for the sponsors but more obviously wealth for the monasteries. By this simple word of warning Chinul was exposing the hollowness of the current ceremonial Buddhism—the Buddhism which was believed to protect the state from various calamities, which catered to the tastes of the court and the nobles, but which failed to answer the spiritual need of a young man disenchanted with the world that he saw around him. In short, what we see here in young Chinul is truly an awakened *individual* who finds himself alienated from the comfortably established Buddhist community of his time.

To continue the discussion of the ideal Chinul proposed at the meeting, for Chinul rejecting "fame and gain" could only be done successfully in the quiet of the mountains and forests, far away from the bustle of the capital. The true significance of this proposal to "retreat to the mountains and woods" has to be measured in the light of the strong tendency of Korean Buddhism, ever since the Three Kingdoms period, to be oriented toward the capital and the towns, the seat of culture and political power. For most of the Yi dynasty, this option was denied to Buddhism, which had been forced to retire to the seclusion of the mountains, virtually losing all social relevance and influence. But this proposal of retreat by Chinul was something quite dissimilar to the retreat of Yi dynasty Buddhism, for there exists a profound qualitative difference between a voluntary retreat and a forced one. Had Koryŏ Buddhism at the height of its worldly involvement taken Chinul's advice more seriously, perhaps the Buddhism of the Yi dynasty might have been spared its harsh fate.

This retreat urged by Chinul had a definite aim; it was not meant for a mere enjoyment of carefree secluded life. It meant a positive step toward constructing an ideal *sangha* dedicated to the authentic goal of monks. For this Chinul proposed to "form a common

18

society," not just another monastery. This is a clear indication that from the beginning Chinul had no interest in a hermit's life. Rather his intention was to demonstrate to the misoriented Buddhist community of his time a true alternative model for monastic life. It goes without saying that it was by virtue of this concern that he was eventually to become a historic figure in Korean Buddhism.

The task of this common society is defined as "balanced practice of *samādhi* and *prajñā*" 習定均慧, a phrase used by Tsung-mi of China in his *Ch'an-yüan chu-ch'üan-chi tu-hsü* describing what he did for ten years after he had "left the people and entered into the mountain."[29] We defer a thorough discussion of Chinul's conception of *samādhi* (concentration) and *prajñā* (sapience) to the next chapter where we intend to examine Chinul's theory of Sŏn in detail. But we cannot but ask why Chinul particularly chose such a catchword to define the essential task of the new community he was envisaging. To this question the context in which Tsung-mi uses the phrases seems to provide a significant answer. Namely, Tsung-mi is talking about nothing other than the balanced study of both Sŏn and Kyo, asserting that one should avoid the two extremes of "idiotic Sŏn [*samādhi*] vainly keeping silence" and "crazy wisdom [*prajñā*] merely delving into texts." In fact, Chinul even quotes these phrases in his *Kyŏlsa-mun*.[30] Thus, in this proposal of the balanced cultivation of *samādhi* and *prajñā*, we see Chinul already dealing with the problem of the conflict between Sŏn and Kyo, the fundamental issue Ŭich'ŏn had to grapple with about eighty years earlier. The "balanced practice of *samādhi* and *prajñā*" was in a way Chinul's version of Ŭich'ŏn's "combined cultivation of *kyo* [doctrinal study] and *kwan* [contemplation]" (*kyogwan kyŏmsu*). It is in this that we have to discern the true significance of Chinul's proposal of the balanced or combined practice of *samādhi* and *prajñā*. As we shall see, ever since this expression of his concern, the problem of the harmonization of Sŏn and Kyo was to remain with him throughout his life as one of the most pressing issues he had to deal with.

---

[29] T. 48, No. 2015, p. 399c.
[30] *Pŏbŏ*, p. 10.

Another thing to be noted in Chinul's conception of the task of the new community is the fact that he, along with "the balanced practice of *samādhi* and *prajñā*," also recommended such activities as "worship of Buddha" and "reading of *sūtras*." The idea of exclusive cultivation, *senju* 專修, which was prevalent among his contemporary Kamakura Buddhist leaders in Japan, was foreign to Chinul despite the intensity of his religious quest. As we shall see, this comprehensive attitude, allowing even the recitation of the name of Amit'a Buddha, characterizes his approach to Sŏn Buddhism as much as it characterizes Korean Sŏn tradition in general after him.

Finally, we have to pay a particular attention to the fact that Chinul includes "manual labor" in the vision of the ideal *saṅgha*. There is hidden in it a protest against the contemporary wealthy monasteries where monks led a semi-aristocratic life surrounded by numerous temple serfs. Thus it was unmistakably a call to poverty as the essential virtue of a monk. From the pursuit of "fame and gain" to the pusuit of *samādhi* and *prajñā*, from the Buddhism of the capital and cities to the Buddhism of the mountains and forests, and from the Buddhism of "merit" and state-orientation to the Buddhism of individual salvation, such was the call Chinul sent out to his companions of the *Tao*.

Indeed, the invitation was not extended in vain, for we are told in the *Kyŏlsamun* that it found positive responses from his fellow monks at the examination site, leading them to make a record of vow that should they be able to achieve their goal some day and form a common society they would name it "the society of *samādhi* and *prajñā*." This endorsement of Chinul's proposal, however, did not come without some objections; it had to be preceded by a lengthy discussion of the various issues and doubts that arose in the minds of his friends. *Kyŏlsamun* is in fact nothing else than the report of this lively discussion as recalled later by Chinul. To be sure, it contains a lot of ideas which Chinul could only have acquired much later, and thus we should not uncritically take all those conversations and debates as having taken place at the meeting. Nevertheless, judging from their content, many of them appear to have been genuine lively discussions at the time, even though they were recalled and put into writing about ten years later. A summary of these discussions, if done with caution, is very worthwhile because it furnishes us with a rare insight into the thoughts and ideas prevalent among Koryŏ monks in the twelfth century. Furthermore, in these discussions already are found some of the essential aspects of Chinul's theory of Sŏn. Let us then consider briefly what the main points of debate between Chinul and his friends were.

First of all, some objected as follows:

> Our time is the period of degenerate-*dharma* [*malpŏp, mo-fa*], and so the right path is hidden; how can we attempt *samādhi* and *prajñā*? We had better recite the name of Amit'a Buddha and cultivate the works for the Pure Land (*Po.* 3).

This was indeed a serious challenge to Chinul's proposal, and a substantial portion of his *Kyŏlsamun* is devoted to the discussion of this view. As is generally known, there were in China roughly two ways of calculating the chronology of the three periods of right-*dharma*, counterfeit-*dharma*, and degenerate-*dharma*. Thus the period of degenerate-*dharma* was thought to begin either 1500 years after the birth of the Buddha (taken as 949 B.C. in China) or from 2000 years after his birth.[31] In China the former theory seems to have been more popular, for the idea of degenerate-*dharma* was widespread by the sixth century in China, particularly after the severe persecutions of Buddhism in the northern dynasties. But in Korea the sixth century was rather a blooming period for Buddhism. Thus we seldom find the idea of degenerate-*dharma* playing a significant role in Silla Buddhism. The story, however, becomes different when we look at twelfth-century Koryŏ society and Buddhism where the signs of the period of degenerate-*dharma* were surely omnipresent. Thus it is not hard to imagine how persuasively the theory of 2000 years after the Buddha could have appealed to the pious Buddhists of twelfth-century Koryŏ. More

---

[31] There were other variant theories too. For a general discussion of this problem, see Kenneth K. S. Ch'en, *Buddhism in China* (Princeton, 1964), pp. 297–98.

accurately the theory would have indicated the latter half of the eleventh century as marking the beginning of this period of degenerate-*dharma*. But it happened to be the time of King Munjong and Ŭich'ŏn, rather the climactic period of Koryŏ. Soon after this climax, however, the long turbulent period of social and political confusion began, as we have seen. Who in twelfth-century Koryŏ would have doubted that the last period had really set in for them? Yet Chinul's response to this prevalent idea was very poignant:

> Though time changes, our Mind-Nature does not. To see the rise and fall in the *Dharma* and the *Tao* is the view held by the expedient teachings of the three vehicles; a man of wisdom does not endorse it. You and I have come across this path of the highest vehicle, have seen and heard about it, and have been permeated [perfumed, *vāsanā*] by it; is it not the karmic result of our past lives? Yet, you do not have joy over this but, on the contrary, downgrade yourselves and are content to be the followers of the inferior vehicles. This is to betray the patriarchs of the past and become the final men to cut the seed of Buddhahood. Recitation of the name of the Buddha, reading the *sūtras*, and the myriad acts [of Bodhisattvas] are the regular things monks should follow; what harm would there be in them? Yet, if one does not thoroughly delve into the fundamental but merely is attached to the [superficial] Characteristics [*sang*, 相] and look for the external things, I am afraid that one should be laughed at by the man of wisdom (*Po*. 3).

"Though time changes, our Mind-Nature does not," Chinul's attitude was firm and clear; there is no such a thing as the period of degenerate-*dharma* in our Mind-Nature which transcends time.[32] To admit such a thing is the view held by the inferior vehicles. So do not be timid and downgrade yourselves, but have the courage to set your goal at the highest vehicle (i.e., the one vehicle or Buddha-

---

[32] It is interesting to note that Dōgen also sharply rejected the notion of degenerate-*dharma*. To accept it would violate the fundamental spirit of Sŏn Buddhism. But, on the other hand, both Chinul and Dōgen admit such a notion on the level of provisional truth, and they employ it rhetorically once in a while. About Dōgen's view, see Hee-Jin Kim, *Dōgen Kigen—Mystical Realist*, n. 17 on pp. 323–24.

vehicle). And do not be occupied with external world of *Characteristics* 相 but look inward to your own *Nature* 性.

Another serious objection was raised against the proposal of Chinul:

> If today's cultivators of mind, learned and erudite, teach the *Dharma* and deliver people, it would mean a loss in their internal illumination. If, on the other hand, there is no act of benefiting others, how could they be different from those addicted to quiescence (*Po.* 23)?

This was an implicit criticism of Chinul's ideal as selfish "addiction to quiescence." To this, Chinul says that if one is going to deliver others, one should first cultivate *samādhi* and *prajñā*, and it is easy to do so in quiet place (*Po.* 24). Once one has the power of *Tao*, then there will be the "gate of compassion like the spreading of clouds"; it surely does not mean being "addicted to quiescence" for oneself only (*Po.* 24). Nor does Chinul necessarily agree with the view that teaching other people would result in a loss in one's internal illumination. If one "realizes enlightenment on the basis of words" and "clarifies the fundamental [Mind-Nature] in reliance on Kyo"—an idea very important in Chinul's theory of Sŏn as we shall see later—one is never attached to the names and Characteristics (*Po.* 23). But if, on the other hand, one is unable to "forget the thought of fame and gain" and unable to distinguish between the "finger" and the "moon," such a person should not teach others at all; he had better save himself first (*Po.* 23).

Having thus addressed his companions, he finally was able to win their support for the ideal he proposed. But Chinul tells us that due to some unexpected "event of gain and loss in the meditation hall"—we do not know what it was—the companions were all scattered and their vow could not be carried out (*Po.* 36). Before it eventually came to be realized, Chinul was to undergo a long period of solitary religious struggles through which his spiritual experiences deepened and his intellectual understanding of the Buddhist path sharpened. Thus in 1182 lonely Chinul leaves the capital, abandoning the normal career expected of a monk who has passed the examination, such as working up the ladder of the clerical ranks or seeking an appointment to a position in a prestigious monastery. "If a man cultivating the *Tao*," says Chinul, "does not enter the mountains to cultivate this act [namely, the three learnings of *śīla*, *samādhi*, and *prajñā*], but falsely displays prestigious demeanor and defrauds the faithful to receive their offerings, he had better seek after fame, gain, and wealth, and indulge in wine and women, spending his life in futility with his body and mind wildly gone astray" (*Po.* 35). If leaving home was Chinul's first *pravrajyā*, this act of leaving the capital in a way amounted to his second *pravrajyā*,[33] not an uncommon phenomenon in the history of religion.[34]

2. *The Second Period: Ripening of religious experiences*

Leaving the capital behind him, Chinul went down to the south and came to dwell in a temple named Ch'ŏngwŏnsa in Ch'angp'yŏng, the present Ch'angp'yŏng-myŏn of Tamyang District in Southern Chŏlla Province.[35] Though deeply disappointed with the religious world of monks, he did not return back to the people and secular life. Longing for a quiet hidden life and perhaps vaguely hoping for the realization of the vow some day, he headed for a temple in a remote place far away from the capital, which he was never to see again. As a monk nurtured in Sŏn Buddhism, Chinul was not in any way close to being a popular religious leader among the masses—the masses who were in great suffering at the time. Withdrawing from the turbulent secular world as well as from the corrupt world of Koryŏ *saṅgha*, the only place left for him was the world of his inner self. Throughout his life Chinul always remained faithful to the monastic ideal, and in this sense he was undoubtedly a religious elitist. But, on the other hand, the real problem of Koryŏ Buddhism in Chinul's eyes was its excessive

---

[33] This has been well pointed out by Pak Sŏng-bae in his "Pojo," *Han'guk ŭi in'gan-sang*, III (Seoul, 1965), p. 147.

[34] Cf. the Kamakura Buddhist leaders leaving Mt. Hiei, which was roughly contemporary with Chinul's leaving the capital.

[35] See "Ch'angp'yŏng," *Han'guk chimyŏng yŏnhyŏk ko.*

closeness to the world. Too many monks were too busy trying to "save" others, but without saving themselves first. Thus the initial demand of Chinul's conscience was first to be true to himself. Young Chinul was clearly aware of what was wrong with the Buddhist community of his time, but he did not yet know how to take care of his own being.

It was while Chinul was in this state that, according to the inscription, an important experience of religious breakthrough occurred to him in the monastery:

> It came to pass that when Chinul was reading in the library the *Platform Sūtra of the Sixth Patriarch* his eyes were arrested by a passage: "The Self-Nature of Suchness gives rise to thoughts; though the six organs see, hear, perceive, and know, [you are] not stained by the myriad images, and the True Nature is always free." Chinul was surprised and caught by the joy. Having acquired what he had never had before, he stood up and walked around the Buddha hall, reciting and pondering over the passage, and the meaning was grasped of itself (*Po.* 140).

What in this passage made Chinul so overjoyed? The meaning of this passage will be made clear when we discuss Chinul's thought in the next chapter. Let it be simply pointed out here that the essential message is the idea that our ordinary thoughts, "the myriad images," and hence our daily life, have their origin in the ultimate reality of Self-Nature or Suchness; thus they cannot obstruct our freedom. The basic insight is none other than the classic Mahāyāna teaching that Form (*rūpa*) is Emptiness (*śūnyatā*) and the very Emptiness is Form, or in Hua-yen philosophical terms "the nonobstruction between Principle [*li* 理] and Phenomena [*shih* 事]." The meaning of the passage is further illumined by the next words that follow it in the *Platform Sūtra*:

> The *Vimalakirti Sūtra* says: "Externally, while distinguishing well all the forms of the various *dharmas*, internally he stands firm within the First Principle.[36]

---

[36] *The Platform Sutra of the Sixth Patriarch*, trans. by Philip B. Yampolsky (New York & London, 1967), p. 139. It is hard to tell what edition of the *sūtra* Chinul read;

The practical implication of this message was that one does not have to deny ordinary life in order to overcome the turmoil of life — the turmoil which was by no means easy for the people in twelfth-century Koryŏ to endure. This sudden discovery of the First Principle, or Self-Nature, was for Chinul tantamount to the sudden enlightenment of the mystery of True Self, what is called in Sŏn "seeing into Nature and becoming a Buddha."

One thing that has to be noted about this experience is the fact that Chinul's "sudden enlightenment" did not occur through a direct encounter with a living Sŏn master, but came about by an encounter with the *Platform Sūtra*, a book. Chinul simply did not have the proper master, Korean or Chinese; hence the book was an important medium of truth for him, and this throws much light upon why "genuine teaching in words" came to have so much value for him even later as a Sŏn master. At a time when it was customary for ambitious Korean monks to go to China to obtain "the seal of *Dharma*" or for further study, Chinul did not do so. "Though time changes, our Mind-Nature does not." This principle may well have been valid for Chinul in geographical matters as well. What counted most to Chinul was the straight cultivation of one's own Mind-Nature which transcends time and place.

The *Platform Sūtra* is supposedly the words of the Sixth Patriarch Hui-neng. But according to modern critical study, it is regarded as either a complete fabrication by Shen-hui and his group or as containing in part some authentic words of the Sixth Patriarch and additions by Shen-hui's people. At any rate, its close relationship to Shen-hui is undisputed.[37] What this suggests to us is that Chinul's first important religious breakthrough occurred through an indirect encounter with Shen-hui's line of Sŏn. This is significant in view of the fact that, as we shall see, Chinul has a high regard for Shen-hui's thought—and for Tsung-mi as well who was a follower of Shen-hui's Sŏn and who also introduced it to Chinul—in spite

---

see Yampolsky's discussion of the various editions of the *sūtra*, pp. 98–106.
[37] See Yampolsky, pp. 89–98.

of some reservations. The *Platform Sūtra* also continued to play an important role in Chinul's approach to Sŏn.

After this experience, we are told that Chinul became engaged in even more serious self-cultivation. Then in the year of 1185, after three years at the Ch'ŏngwŏn Monastery, he moved to Pomun Monastery at Haga Mountain (now Hakka Mountain) in the present Yech'ŏn District of Northern Kyŏngsang Province,[38] again nowhere near the capital. There another religious development of enormous significence took place. Concerning this, it is best to listen to Chinul's own testimony in the preface to his *Hwaŏmnon chŏryo*:

In the autumn of 1185, when I lived hidden in Haga Mountain, my heart was always upon the path of Sŏn, which tells us that our mind is none other than Buddha. I would say to myself that if one does not meet this path, one's effort for *kalpas* would be futile and never reach the state of sainthood. Yet I was not able to remove the doubt about what sort of thing Hwaŏm [Hua-yen] doctrine actually teaches about the path of entering enlightenment. Thus I once went to a lecturer to ask [about my doubt]. He told me to meditate on "nonobstruction between Phenomena and Phenomena" [*shih-shih wu-ai*]. Furthermore, he warned me saying: "If you merely meditate on your own mind and not on the nonobstruction between Phenomena and Phenomena, you will lose the perfect virtue of the fruit of Buddhahood." I did not answer, but said to myself silently that if one meditates on Phenomena with one's mind Phenomena would become obstacles and merely annoy one's mind endlessly; when would there be the time of enlightenment? But if one's mind is clear and one's wisdom pure, then even a hair and the world would interfuse without becoming an external event [to one's own mind]. Thus I returned to the mountains.

Sitting down, I surveyed the canon for about three years, seeking the words of the Buddha that would agree with the school of mind [i.e. Sŏn], until I found in the chapter "The Appearance of Tathāgatas" in the *Hwaŏmgyŏng* [*Hua-yen Sūtra*] the simile that one particle of dust contains fascicles of a *sūtra* as large as billions of worlds. Later on [the chapter] concludes that the wisdom of the

---

[38] See "Pomunsa," *Pulgyo sajŏn*, ed. by Unhŏ.

Tathāgatas is also like this; it is fully present in the body of sentient beings, but the foolish ones do not know and realize it. Thereupon, I put the fascicles of the *sūtra* upon my head, and the tears dropped unwittingly.[39]

Here we see Chinul wrestling with one of the most urgent and fundamental issues in the Buddhist world of his time: the conflict between Sŏn and Kyo. Despite Ŭich'ŏn's grand design a century earlier to unite the two in the system of Ch'ŏnt'ae teaching, the antagonism between them remained as severe as ever. In fact, as mentioned, the emergence of the Ch'ŏnt'ae Order merely produced the adverse effect of further stimulating their already serious confrontation—a confrontation which was not merely religious and institutional but at the same time economic and political. Thus no one who was concerned about the situation of Koryŏ Buddhism could bypass this problem. Nor could Chinul.

Having been convinced, through his ecounter with the *Platform Sūtra*, of the truth of Sŏn teaching that one's own mind is none other than Buddha, Chinul's loyalty to Sŏn was firm, as he tells us. He was not moved by the lecturer's routine presentation of Hwaŏm teaching. Yet despite this he was not able to stifle the voice of his conscience, doubting that Sŏn might not be the only truth, and that it would be able to find confirmation of its truth in the teaching of the Buddha. This is why he was deliberately seeking "the words of the Buddha that would agree with Sŏn." In a way, Chinul was seeking in Hwaŏm teaching exactly what he had already obtained from the *Platform Sūtra*. His determination to find it was so stubborn that he grappled with the vast corpus of Buddhist literature for three years, certainly a rare dedication for a student of Sŏn. The moment of breakthrough finally came when his eyes caught the following passage in the *Hwaŏmgyŏng*:

If a man whose wisdom is clear and without obstruction, and who is fully equipped with pure divine eyes, sees these fascicles of a *sūtra*

---

[39] *Hwaŏmnon chŏryo* (photographic edition of the Tokyo edition; Seoul: 1972), pp. 1–2.

contained in a particle of dust, its benefit to sentient beings would be not small. He would immediately think: "I will break open this particle of dust carefully and take out these fascicles of *sūtra*, and let all sentient beings be benefited by them." With this thought he would, using an excellent skill [*upāya*], break open the particle of dust and take out the enormous *sūtra*, and let the sentient beings acquire benefit universally. Not merely in one particle of dust but also in all dust, you should know, it is so. O Sons of the Buddha, the wisdom of the Tathāgatas is also like this; without limit and obstacles, it can benefit all sentient beings universally. It is fully present in the body of sentient beings, but the foolish do not realize it because of their attachment to deluded thoughts, and thus they do not acquire benefit from it.[40]

The simile was clear: The enormous *sūtra* is the wisdom of Tathāgatas, or the Buddha-Nature, and the dust refers to sentient beings themselves. Its message was not divergent from the cardinal teaching of Sŏn that one's own mind is none other than Buddha, and what really matters is whether we realize this or not. Thus came Chinul's assurance of the basic unity of thought between Sŏn and Hwaŏm. This discovery, Chinul tells us, caused such joy in him that tears dropped down from his eyes—a sign indicating to us how intense his search had been.

But the struggle was not yet over. As for the scriptural teaching of the *Hwaŏmgyŏng* itself, Chinul's mind was now clear. The further question he had, however, was how an ordinary being was to understand this wonderful truth of the *sūtra*, what the "initial gate of entrance in faith" 最初信入之門 is supposed to be in Hwaŏm teaching. In other words, what does Hwaŏm teach about the first step for an ordinary man to take in order to appropriate this truth? These were the questions which still assailed his mind. Thus Chinul continues to say in the preface:

Yet I was not clear about the initial gate of entrance in faith for sentient beings. I further read the interpretation of the first position of the ten faiths in the *Treatise on Hua-yen* written by the elder Li.

---

[40] *T.* 10, No. 279, p. 272c.

It said: "Kaksu Posal [Enlightenment-Head Bodhisattva] realizes three things. First, he realizes that his own body and mind are originally none other than the *Dharmadhātu*, being white and pure without defilement. Second, he realizes that the discriminating nature of his own body and mind is originally free from [the distinction of] subject and object, being itself the Buddha of Immutable Wisdom. Third, he realizes that the mysterious wisdom in his mind that well distinguishes good and evil is none other than Mañjuśrī Bodhisattva. [*Right*] *at the beginning of the mind of faith,* he realizes these three things, and [thus] is called Enlightenment-Head [Bodhisattva]." The treatise further states that the reason why it is difficult for ordinary beings to enter into the ten faiths is because one recognizes oneself as an ordinary being and does not recognize one's own mind as the Buddha of Immutable Wisdom.[41]

Again, a full discussion of the idea expressed in this passage has to be deferred to the next chapter. But the basic message of Li T'unghsüan's interpretation of faith above was clear: The first position of ten faiths, which constitutes the beginning of the long process of spiritual progress—fifty-two positions in Mahāyāna teaching[42]—is nevertheless the place where one realizes and recognizes oneself as Buddha. Faith consists in the courageous act of affirming one's own ordinary state of being, with all its imperfections, as Buddhahood, transcending in one leap all the numerous positions and grades to be passed through in order to reach it. This, for Chinul, was none other than the very spirit of sudden enlightenment in Sŏn, and this was what

---

[41] *Hwaŏmnon chŏryo*, p. 2. The passage is found in Li's treatise on pp. 814c–15a, *T.* 36. Enlightenment-Head Bodhisattva is the name of the Bodhisattva residing in the southern world mentioned in the chapter "The Names of Tathāgatas" of the *Hua-yen Sūtra*; the Buddha of Immutable Wisdom is the name of the Buddha residing in the eastern world together with Mañjuśrī.

The word *Dharmadhātu*, which appears often throughout this book, has basically two meanings in Hua-yen as well as in Chinese Mahāyāna thought in general. When *dhātu* is understood as meaning Nature, *Dharmadhātu* refers to the Nature of *dharmas*, i.e. *dharmatā* or *tathatā* (Suchness); in this sense, it could be roughly translated as "The World of Reality" or simply "Reality." But when *dhātu* is taken as meaning "world," "realm," or "boundary," it refers to the world of *dharmas* (things), namely the entire world or cosmos in ordinary sense of the word. See "hokkai," *Bukkyōgo daijiten*, ed. by H. Nakamura (Tokyo: 1975).

[42] About ten faiths (ten pious thoughts of faith) and the fifty-two positions, see "gojūnii" in Mochizuki's *Bukkyō daijiten*.

made him so impressed with Li's interpretation of Hwaŏm. Thus Chinul "put down the book and said with a deep sigh":

> What the Buddha said through his mouth is Kyo, whereas what the patriarchs transmitted to the mind is Sŏn. The mind and mouth of the Buddha and the patriarchs should not be at odds. How can it be right that people do not penetrate to the very root but squander their time in futile arguments and disputes, each feeling comfortable in what he is accustomed to.[43]

This was a hard-won conclusion after three years of intensive study and struggle. Together with this conclusion, Chinul uttered a word of reproach against the "futile arguments and disputes" with which Koryŏ Buddhism was wasting its time and energy. Now, at least for Chinul, the issue was settled; Sŏn and Kyo are one at the "root and spring." It was more than a personal religious victory for Chinul. For out of this experience Chinul was to initiate a unique approach to Sŏn that eventually came to be the established tradition of Korean Sŏn Buddhism.

It was already six years since Chinul had left the capital. Now it looked as if his personal religious problems were largely settled and his spiritual identity established. He was in his thirties, and it was time for this period of solitary religious struggle to be concluded, time to pull himself out of this seclusion and move forward to share with others what he had learned through this series of exciting religious experiences. About the circumstances of Chinul around that time, the stele with the inscription on which we based ourselves in this study says:

> ... Acquiring the elder Li's *Treatise on Hua-yen*, once again the mind of faith was generated in Chinul. He searched and dug into it and found out its hidden [meanings]; he chewed and tasted and relished its feeling. His previous understanding grew clearer and his mind was immersed in the complete-sudden [Hwaŏm] gate of contemplation. At the same time he wanted to guide erring future

---

[43] *Hwaŏmnon chōryo*, pp. 2–3.

generations by removing their nails [passions] and uprooting their stakes [illusions].

This tells us how much Chinul cherished Li's treatise. It also indicates Chinul's eagerness by this time to conclude his solitary life of seclusion. The inscription continues:

> Just at this time his old acquaintance Tŭkchae, a veteran in Sŏn, was residing in Kŏjo Monastery at Mt. Kong,[44] and he invited Chinul with such sincerity that he finally moved to that place (*Po.* 140).

It was a timely call from an old friend in the vow, a call perhaps much awaited and yet unexpected. Here is Chinul's own account of it:

> In the early spring of 1188, Venerable Chae [Tŭkchae], who was my elder brother in Sŏn as well as a friend in the vow, came to dwell in Kŏjo Monastery at Mt. Kong. Not oblivious of the old vow, he was planning to form the Society for *Samādhi* and *Prajñā*. Thus he sent cordial letters several times to invite me in Pomun Monastery at Mt. Haga. Although I had long been dwelling in the mountains and forests and was just preserving "foolishness" [peaceful life] with nothing to care about, I had longing for the old promise as much as I was moved by his sincerity. Thus in the spring of that year I moved to that monastery with Hang, a student of Sŏn who accompanied me (*Po.* 36).

With this move in 1188 at the age of thirty-one, the second period of Chinul's life is concluded, and a new positive and active life opens up for him.

3. *The Third Period: The Society for* Samādhi *and* Prajñā *is established*

One may temporarily withdraw from the world to lead a hermit's life, but often it is only to return to the world with even greater commitment. Had Chinul retreated from the world for good he would not have become a historic figure in Korean Buddhism. On the other

---

[44] In the present Northern Kyŏngsang Province. See "Kŏjoam," *Pulgyo sajŏn.*

hand, if Chinul had never known the agony of solitary religious struggle, he could never have become what he was, one who broke a new ground in Korean Sŏn tradition.

From the beginning, it was not Chinul's concern to indulge in a life of personal contentment. Suddenly a seemingly dormant longing for the ideal monastic life became aroused by this unexpected call from his friend. A confident and mature man, he set about to form the Society for *Samādhi* and *Prajñā* as soon as he moved to Kŏjo Monastery. He sent out an invitation to his old friends who had shared the vow with him at the place of the examination. But to his disappointment, he could assemble only a few of them; some had died, some were ill, and some had gone after "fame and gain" (*Po*. 36). This led Chinul in 1190 to send out an open invitation to the entire Buddist community of his time, and this famous imvitation, his first work, the *Kwŏnsu chŏnghye kyŏlsamun* [*Invitation to the Society for the Cultivation of* Samādhi *and* Prajñā], became one of the historic writings of Korean Buddhism. It was a bombshell thrown into the languid world of Koryŏ Buddhism, which suffered from the burden of tradition; but at the same time it was a seed of hope. An invitation as well as an indictment, a persuasion as well as a protest, it sketched the noble ideal as much as it touched the painful reality. In the following words we can glimpse the mood and spirit in which the invitation was sent out:

> As I reflect thus, since the remote past we have received to no purpose the great sufferings of the body and mind without any benefit; in the present there is an incalculable amount of oppression, and the future suffering knows no bound either, being hard to remove or escape from, and yet we do not realize it. What is more, the birth-and-destruction of this bodily life is impermanent and this life is difficult to preserve even for a moment. It cannot even be compared to the fire of a flint, a lamp before the wind, or to the flowing stream and the sunlight about to disappear. Time is swift and sudden, and it silently spurs our aging; yet we are gradually approaching the gate of death with the ground of our mind uncultivated. As I recall my old friends, wise and foolish all mixed, and count them this morning, only one out of ten survives. And even the survivors fade away one after another like them. How much

33

of a future do we have left for us, that we still loosen our will and indulge in avarice, anger, jealousy, arrogance, and laxity, seeking fame and gain to squander our time, and discussing the affairs of the world with aimless talk; that some without the virtue of precepts unduly receive the offerings of the faithful and accept service from the people, and yet have no shame and guilt? (*Po. 5–6.*)

The theme of death, impermanence, and suffering in Koryŏ society at the time was a reality right in front of people's eyes that required no reminder: They witnessed a merciless power struggle among the military leaders, peasant uprisings throughout the country, and the clash of the monks with the military regime. Nor could the theme of corruption and deviation in the Buddhist community escape people's notice. While the monasteries and monks were busy scrambling to maintain and protect their wealth and power in the sociopolitical upheaval, the masses were suffering in poverty and starvation.

It appears that Chinul circulated copies of the text, probably hand-written, for others to sign their names to; for near the end the text says:

I humbly express my wish: If there are men of high aim in Sŏn and Kyo or in Confucianism and Taoism who feel averse to the world and have shaken off the mundane dust, who roam aloft outside earthly things and solely concentrate on the path of inner practice, and who share this opinion, I allow them to sign their names at the end of this text, though they may have not previously shared the vow with me (*Po. 36*).

Chinul extended his invitation not merely to the students of Sŏn and Kyo but even to those of Confucian and Taoist learning. His belief that the Mind-Nature does not change may have worked here also. In fact, we find no inkling of any sectarian bias in this invitation; it is not even a document of Sŏn Buddhism. Rather it was a straightforward universal appeal—phrased and expressed, to be sure, in Buddhist and Sŏn terms—to the common spiritual need of the people, regardless of their religious affiliations. Perhaps Chinul felt even closer to those Confucian scholars and Taoist hermits who

34

were disenchanted with the world than to the fellow Buddhist monks addicted to the worldly life. At any rate, Chinul's universalistic spirit seems to have worked. The inscription gives us the following pithy account of Chinul's activity in Kŏjo Monastery from 1188 to 1197:

> Chinul welcomed hosts of men of high aim belonging to various sects [chong, tsung] who had deserted fame, and exhorted them with sincerity. Practicing samādhi and prajñā day and night, he spent many years without being tired of them (Po. 140).

Even the Ch'ŏnt'ae Master Yose, later called National Preceptor Wŏnmyo, came to Chinul to participate in the society. The inscription of National Preceptor Wŏnmyo records as follows:

> At that time, Moguja of Chogye Mountain [Chinul] was dwelling at Hoebulgap of Mt. Kong, and he heard of the master's [Yose] style, which fitted in with his own. Thus he sent a verse to the master, urging him to cultivate Sŏn:
>
> *Waves roar and the Moon is hard put to appear;*
> *The hall is deep, but the lamp shines even more.*
> *I urge thee to order the receptacle of the mind;*
> *Do not spill out the sauce of the sweet dew.*
>
> The master saw this and it suited his heart; he immediately went to follow him, to become Chinul's friend in the *Dharma*, helping him to spread the edification of the *Tao*. He resided there for several years.[45]

Although Yose later parted with Chinul and formed an independent movement of Ch'ŏnt'ae called the White Lotus Society[46] (Paengnyŏn-sa; not to be confused with the Chinese one), this incident demonstrates the universalistic, open spirit of Chinul and the society he founded. Yose's religious movement, also very powerful, was indebted to Chinul's influence.

We do not know much about Chinul's activity during this period

---

[45] *CKC*, I, pp. 590–91.
[46] For brief information on this society, see *Han'guksa* 7, pp. 322–25.

of almost ten years except that the cultivation of *samādhi* and *prajñā* was the main concern of Chinul and the society. The first six years after he had left the capital were the period of Chinul's discovery of "sudden enlightenment" through his encounter with the *Platform Sūtra* and the *Treatise on Hua-yen*; whereas this period of ten years at the Society for *Samādhi* and *Prajñā* was the time of his "gradual cultivation" following the experience of sudden enlightenment. All this, as we shall see, becomes reflected in his theory of Sŏn.

Kŏjo Monastery turned out not to be spacious enough to accommodate the large crowd flowing into the society; so Chinul decided to search for a new place for the cultivation of Sŏn. In 1197, when he was forty, he sent his disciple Suu to the south to look for such a place. Suu spotted on Mt. Songgwang an almost deserted monastery by the name of Kilsang, which had about one hundred rooms. Since "its scenery was superb, the land fertile, the water sweet, and the wood flourishing," he started to reconstruct the monastery. Chinul too left Kŏjo Monastery in 1197, heading for the new place. With this, the third period of his life comes to the end.[47]

After six years of solitary religious quest in mountain and forest, and after a long process of self-cultivation in the ideal community he had longed for, Chinul's religious personality must have fully matured and his religious views been firmly established. It looked now as if no more spiritual problems were left for him. One would expect that all he had to do now was to find a more effective channel to get across what he had learned to as wide a group of people as possible, to embody and institutionalize his ideal more firmly in contemporary Koryŏ Buddhist society. Yet this was not to be. He still had to undergo another spiritual trial, and eventually another religious breakthrough.

Despite the long period of hard spiritual training, Chinul, in his forties, was still a student, not a master of Sŏn. For one thing, he had not yet sung the song of final triumph, of absolute freedom, with which we are so familiar from the stories of the illustrious Sŏn

---

[47] *Taesŭng Sŏnjong Chogyesan Susŏnsa chungch'anggi, CSS,* I, p. 275.

masters before and after him. Chinul also had had moments of dramatic breakthrough, but they were followed by long and rather dull periods when nothing significant seems to have happened. Chinul is still in the *process* of Sŏn, and has not yet *mastered* it. He did not yet have the confidence, exuberance, and virtuosity that are the hallmarks of Sŏn masters. Until he attained these, he needed another withdrawal from the world, "a third *pravrajyā*", one that had a different meaning and consequence for his life from the previous ones. By the initial awakening of his religious mind, his *bodhicitta* (the thought or desire of enlightenment), he left the secular world, and in the same spirit he had to negate the Buddhist world of his time as well, "the group of the capital."[48] By the establishment of the Society for *Samādhi* and *Prajñā*, however, Chinul was reapproaching the world, this time on a new level. But this movement back to the world required another step, just as his desertion of the world needed two steps. This last step to reintegrate himself more closely with the world inaugurates the fourth period of Chinul's life, the period of his Bodhisattva activities for sentient beings. Paradoxically, this step began with another retreat.

4. *The Fourth Period: Another Retreat and the Susŏnsa* (*The Society for the Cultivation of Sŏn*)

When Chinul was on his way to the new monastery found by Suu, accompanied by a few companions in Sŏn, he passed a place of retreat called Sangmuju-am at Chiri Mountain. Its atmosphere attracted him, so he decided to stay there some time for meditation. "Pushing aside external conditions," says the inscription, "he became solely involved in internal contemplation" in this place (*Po.* 140). The inscription also tells us that many good omens occurred during this stay, substantiating Chinul's spiritual attainment, but stories about them are not in the inscription. More important than the good omens, however, was his new breakthrough in religious experience

---

[48] An expression used by *Susŏnsa chungch'anggi*, p. 276.

through his encounter with the Sŏn of Ta-hui (1089–1163), the Chinese Lin-chi master of "*kōan*-watching" or *kanhwa* Sŏn.[49] Here is what Chinul says about the experience, as told in the inscription:

> The master once said: "For more than ten years, since my days at Pomun Monastery, I never wasted time but was engaged in diligent cultivation with proper understanding. Yet the illusory views were not removed from me. Something was still sticking to my heart as an obstacle, as if I were staying with an enemy. But when I came to dwell in Chiri Mountain I acquired a copy of the *Words of Ch'an Master Ta-hui, the Possessor of Universal Enlightenment*, which said, 'Sŏn does not exist in a quiet place, nor does it exist in a noisy place; it does not exist where one responds to daily affairs, nor where thought and discrimination occur. Nevertheless, above all you should study Sŏn without leaving such places—quiet places, noisy places, the places where one performs daily task, and the places where thought and discrimination occur. Once your eyes are opened, suddenly you will realize that this is just like things happening inside your own house.' Upon this I acquired an understanding. Naturally the obstacle no longer stuck to my heart, and the enemy was gone; and I felt comfortable immediately."[50]

How should we understand this event? What was the thing that was "sticking" to him like an enemy? Whatever it was, it is clear that despite such a long period of rigorous self-cultivation Chinul did not possess perfect freedom but still had something bothering him. Thus it was not by mere chance nor by the attraction of the scenery of Sangmuju-am alone that he decided to stay at Chiri Mountain; rather it was meant to be another retreat, designed to solve his own problem away from others. Perhaps a doubt arose in his mind about

---

[49] "*Kanhwa*" (*k'an-hua* or *kanna*) literally means "watching of *hwadu*," *hwadu* being identical with *kōan* (*kung-an*). *Hwadu*, or simply *hwa* (*du* being an expletive), means story or dialogue. About *kung-an*, Suzuki says:

Kung-an is a question or theme given to the student for solution. It literally means "public document," and, according to a Zen scholar, it is so called because it serves as such in testing the genuineness of enlightenment a student claims to have attained. The term has been in use since the early days of Zen Buddhism in the T'ang Dynasty. The so-called "case" or "dialogues" (*mondō*) are generally used as kōans (*First Series*, p. 333).

[50] *Po*. 140. Ta-hui's work is *T*. 47, No. 1998A; and the passage is found in pp. 893c–894a.

the efficacy of the path he had been following for ten years, a path that looked like an unending process, producing no experience of final consummation. It is in this light that we should understand his delay in joining the reconstruction works begun by his disciple Suu at Kilsang Monastery, for Chinul only came to the new place in 1200, that is, about three years after he had left Kŏjo Monastery at Mount Kong. Facing an even greater task and responsibility ahead, Chinul concluded that it was now time for him to clear away the last impediment that had been afflicting him.

To understand the nature of this obstacle we have to reexamine his encounter with the *Platform Sūtra*. As we have mentioned, it was not a personal encounter face to face with a living Sŏn master; it was only an encounter with the truth as presented by a text, and hence was inevitably intellectual and abstract. We have also construed the event as an indirect contact with Shen-hui's Sŏn. Now, in an important work written in 1209, Chinul states that Shen-hui, despite his clarity of thought, is not "the proper heir of the Sixth Patriarch," and that he is only a "Sŏn master of intellectual understanding."[51] To remove this "disease of intellectual understanding" Chinul recommends the *kanhwa* Sŏn of Ta-hui.[52] Thus we are led to believe that the obstacle that was bothering him like an enemy was most likely the "disease of intellectual understanding," which not merely spoils the perfect spontaneity of mystical experience but also causes attachment to what one has grasped intellectually.

The passage that liberated Chinul seems to have served for him as a *kōan*. Again, having no master, Chinul had to receive the *kōan* from a book. Nevertheless, it worked just as powerfully for Chinul, for it liberated him from the problem that had been bothering him "from the days at Pomun Monastery" for more than ten years. Although the realm of experience accessible through *kanhwa* Sŏn is supposed to lie beyond intellectual comprehension, we still have to attempt an intellectual analysis to see at least why the passage worked so powerfully to shatter Chinul's "disease of intellectual understand-

[51] *Chŏryo, Sajip happon*, ed. by An Chin-ho (Seoul: 1957), p. 680.
[52] *Ibid.*, p. 681.

ing," his hitherto intellectual orientation to Sŏn. First, the passage says that Sŏn does not exist in a quiet place. This remark alone was enough to shake Chinul, for it directly challenged his predilection for "mountain and woods" (and not because the remark was in any sense logically incomprehensible). Then this injunction is followed by another remark, "nor does it exist in a noisy place," which certainly was baffling in its logic. Chinul now does not know what to do: "If neither a quiet place nor a noisy place, then where am I supposed to cultivate Sŏn?" Then another logical shock strikes him: "Nevertheless, above all you should study Sŏn without leaving such places." We should stop our analysis here. This much at least shows how the passage baffles the logical mind and how it could possibly shatter an intellectual orientation in Sŏn. But the crucial thing, of course, is the fact that this logical absurdity became for Chinul a powerful medium to call forth a profound experience of freedom. Chinul's problem seems to have been the very preoccupation with Sŏn itself through an intellectual understanding of it—which, in turn, probably had its origin in his encounters with texts. Now this encounter with Ta-hui's words, though again an encounter with the written word, removed this last vestige of imperfection from Chinul. Now he is truly a master of Sŏn, who knows what the absolute freedom is that makes one free even from the very act of striving for freedom, namely Sŏn. Now Chinul can "live" Sŏn, not merely understand and cultivate it.

As in the first retreat, this second one did not prevent Chinul from going back to the world again. Thus in 1200 he joined the work of reconstruction of the newly found monastery where he was to spend the most fruitful period of his life. But once again we have to note the direction of his reintegration with the world. "Sŏn does not exist in a quiet place," Chinul was told, "nor does it exist in a noisy place." Why then did Chinul particularly choose the "quiet place" of another monastery, and not the "noisy place" of the people? Perhaps for him even the monastery was a "noisy place." Be that as it may, Chinul was once again able to overcome his own spiritual crisis. Armed with his new discovery of the power of *kanwha* Sŏn, he was now better prepared than ever to lead the community he had founded.

Spanning nine years from 1197 to 1205, the reconstruction work was finished in the year King Hŭijong ascended the throne, still under the military regime of the Ch'oe family, who took power in 1196. In this work Chinul was helped by many pious laymen and lay women; some donated money and goods, and some assisted with their skill and physical labor.[53] We have no indication that Chinul had recourse to the court or the nobles for this work; he might have received some help from them, but at least he does not seem to have approached them on his own initiative. But now when the work had been completed, King Hŭijong, who is said to have had a great respect for Chinul even before his enthronement by the Ch'oe family, sent congratulations along with a fully embroidered clerical robe for Chinul. The king also ordered to change the name of the monastery from Kilsang to Susŏnsa (Society for the Cultivation of Sŏn) and the mountain's name from Songgwang to Chogye,[54] the latter being the name of the mountain where the famous Sixth Patriarch used to dwell. When Chinul moved to this new center for Sŏn, he continued to use the name of the Society for *Samādhi* and *Prajñā* (Chŏnghyesa). But, since there was nearby another monastery of the same name already, the king bestowed the new name Susŏnsa. As the inscription tells us (*Po.* 141), this change of name did not imply a change of spirit. Of more symbolic significance, however, was the change in the name of the mountain from Songgwang to Chogye—a change which indicates that the Susŏnsa now had become the center of Koryŏ Sŏn Buddhism. But the name Chogye, as has been indicated already, does not suggest that Chinul founded the Chogye Order of Koryŏ; Chogye Mountain should not be confused with the Chogye Order. We have no indication that either Chinul or his followers understood his religious movement as establishing a new Buddhist order such as Ŭich'ŏn had done a century earlier. The successors to Chinul of the Susŏnsa were called, for instance, "X X generation of the Susŏnsa of Chogye Mountain," not "X X generation of the Susŏnsa of the Chogye

---

[53] *Susŏnsa chungch'anggi*, p. 276.
[54] *Pŏbŏ*, p. 141.

41

Order."[55] The *Taesŭng Sŏnjong Chogyesan Susŏnsa chungch'anggi* [*Record of the Reconstruction of the Susŏnsa of the Mahāyāna Sŏn Order in Chogye Mountain*], which was composed in 1207 while Chinul was the leader of the Susŏnsa, does not mention the Chogye Order. Moreover, the name Chogye Order had already been in use before Chinul, representing along with Ch'ŏnt'ae the two branches of Sŏn Buddhism.[56] Chinul simply established another "mountain," just like the traditional Nine Mountains, and through this new center of Sŏn Chinul was able to give to the Chogye Order, which was in need of a spiritual renewal, a new ideology and identity so that the spirit of the Chogye Order after Chinul came to be no longer the same as before. The central purpose of the present study is to elucidate how Chinul came to initiate this new species of Sŏn in Korea, what its characteristics are, and what its meaning and consequences were in the history of the Korean Buddhist tradition.

Now it is time to examine Chinul's activites in this new center for Sŏn, the Susŏnsa. A succinct and instructive account of his activities is provided in the inscription:

1) Whether he discussed the *Tao* or cultivated Sŏn, whether he stayed for *uposatha* or cultivated purity (*dhūta*), everything was done based upon the precepts of the Buddha. Both monks and laymen from the four quarters heard of his style and poured in to form a flourishing gathering. Some relinquished their names and positions, some left their wives and children; they dyed their clothes, shaved their heads, and invited their friends and came together. Also, king, nobles, literati, and ordinary men registered their names and joined the society by the hundreds.
2) The master committed himself to the Tao, his mind being unmoved by the praise and blame of others. His character being

---

[55] See for instance the inscription of the stele for Hyesim or Chin'gak Kuksa, the immediate successor of Chinul, *CPT*, II, p. 351; see also pp. 366, 368, 370.
[56] This has been pointed out by many. See Kim Yŏng-su, "Chogyejong kwa chŏndŭng t'onggyu," *Pulgyo sin* 43 (1943); Kwŏn Sang-no, "Han'guk Sŏnjong yaksa," *PKPN*, and "Chogyejong," *Pulgyo* 58 (1929).

compassionate and persevering, he was good and kind in guiding younger followers. Though perverse persons sometimes deviated from his will, he still embraced them with compassion, having abiding affection for them such as a loving mother would have towards her beloved son.

3) When he exhorted students to recite, he always recommended the *Diamond Sūtra*; when he established the *Dharma* and expounded its meaning, it was always found in the *Platform Sūtra of the Sixth Patriarch*; and he further elucidated it with Li's *Treatise on Hua-yen* and the *Words of Ta-hui*, which are like the two wings of a bird.

4) He opened the path in three ways: the path of parallel keeping of quiescence and wakefulness, the path of complete-sudden faith and understanding, and the path of direct cutting. Cultivating [Sŏn] on the basis of [these paths], a great many entered into [the truth] in faith. Never before, has the study of Sŏn been so flourishing (*Po.* 140–41).

We have conveniently divided the passage into four parts (with our own numbering), each of which tells us about a different aspect of Chinul's activity at the Susŏnsa. Let us examine them one by one.

1) When Chinul talks about *samādhi* and *prajñā*, he also has *sīla* (precepts) in mind, for these three together constitute the "three learnings" (*samhak*).[57] As Chinul saw the problems of the Buddhist community of his time, the loosening of the precepts was the most serious of all. He despised those who "receive the offerings of the faithful unduly without the virtue of precepts." No antinomian or libertine attitude (so easily associated with spiritual freedom) is found in Chinul. Strict adherence to the precepts was the essential precondition for the cultivation of *samādhi* and *prajñā*. This must be why Chinul, as soon as the busy reconstruction work was completed in 1205, composed his *Kye ch'osim hagin mun* [*Admonitions for beginning students*]. As the title indicates, this work gives concrete rules and exhortations to the novice in Sŏn—but in fact to every student.[58]

---

[57] See *Pŏbŏ*, pp. 11–12, where he says that the two words *samādhi* and *prajñā* are an abbreviated name for the three learnings.

[58] Traditionally, it has been interpreted as addressed to three groups: novices (*śrāmaṇera*), all the monks, and the monks of the meditation hall (*sŏnpang*) in particular. See Yi Chi-gwan, *Han'guk soŭi kyŏngjŏn yŏn'gu* (Seoul; 1969), p. 31.

43

It sets forth the daily rules that monks should observe in this new community (the Susŏnsa), much like the Pure Rules of Pai-chang Huai-hai in ninth-century China. As a reformer of Koryŏ Buddhism deeply fallen into moral deterioration, Chinul saw it as the most urgent task to set up firm guidelines to govern monastic life. Once a person joined the Susŏnsa, no matter what his social position may have been, he was supposed to abide strictly by the uniform rules; it was in this sense truly an egalitarian society.

What was the relationship between Chinul's Susŏnsa and the king and the nobles who "threw in" or registered their names as its members? The reconstruction of the monastery itself, as we have said earlier, seems to have been accomplished without any particular support from the ruling classes, be it the court or the military junta led by Ch'oe Ch'ung-hŏn. But the maintenance of the society was another matter, for it needed continuous sources of support, particularly for such a large community.[59] For this, the society must have had a large endowment, and it is possible that most of it came from those supporters who registered their names as members of the society (without actually becoming monks).[60] Thus it seems evident that, like most of the other Koryŏ monasteries, the Susŏnsa does not appear to have drawn its financial resources from the common people, nor was it self-supporting—which tells us something about the nature of the religious movement led by Chinul. As far as the economic aspect of the Susŏnsa was concerned, it did not depart from the way of the other established monastic communities of the

---

[59] Im Sŏk-chin, in his *Songgwangsa chi*, says that there were about five hundred people in the society at the time of Chinul, which is likely in view of what the inscription tells us (p. 161).

[60] Im Sŏk-chin also gives in the same book the size of the endowment at the time of Chinul, based upon a Koryŏ document preserved in the present Songgwang Monastery. But this document, as Im Ch'ang-sun points out ("Songgwangsa ŭi Koryŏ munsŏ," *Paeksan hakpo* 11 [1971]: 48), dates from 1221 at the earliest (11 years after Chinul's death); thus it informs us on the financial condition of the society at the time of Hyesim rather than at the time of Chinul. Nevertheless, from it we can have a rough idea of the size of the endowment (at the time of Chinul), which was quite substantial, and which mostly came from the contributions of high officials, particularly military; see the article by Im Ch'ang-sun for the details.

time, and it is worth pondering how close the Susŏnsa was to the ideal *saṅgha* young Chinul had envisaged.

It is not known why King Hŭijong showed such concern for the society; it is not even certain whether this concern was voluntary on the part of the king or whether he followed the will of the Ch'oe family to whom the throne *de facto* belonged. On the other hand, we have a significant clue pointing to a keen interest on the part of the Ch'oe family in this new Buddhist movement by Chinul. In 1207, when Chinul was fifty years old, the *Taesŭng Sŏnjong Chogyesan Susŏnsa chungch'anggi*, to which we have referred several times, was composed to commemorate the reconstruction of the Susŏnsa. It was written by Ch'oe Sŏn (no relationship to the ruling Ch'oe family), a high government official and a man of literary fame. But it was composed under some kind of supervision by Ch'oe U, the son of powerful Ch'oe Ch'ung-hŏn. The exact nature of the supervision depends on the meaning of the word "*kamjip*" 監集 which literally means "supervisory collection."[61] Whatever it may mean, this fact clearly suggests that the Ch'oe family had a strong interest in what Chinul was doing in a remote corner of the peninsula, and this fact is important because Ch'oe U's son Ch'oe Hang, who later succeeded his father, was initially a monk in the Susŏnsa. Moreover, Ch'oe U himself maintained a close relationship with Chin'gak Kuksa (Hyesim), Chinul's successor as the leader of the Susŏnsa.[62] Perhaps the Ch'oe family's interest in this new Buddhist movement was based on its clean other-worldly orientation that was in such contrast with that of the old ecclesiastical world, deeply involved in the political and economic power of the court and the old aristocrats. In this context, it is important to remember the serious clashes between the Ch'oe family and the monks of the powerful monasteries, culminating in 1217 when about 800 monk-soldiers are said to have been

---

[61] Morohashi's *Dai kanwa jiten* does not list the word; but it gives the word "kamch'an" (Jap. "kansen"), which means "supervisory composition." It appears likely, therefore, that *kamjip* means "supervisory collection [of materials]."

[62] To be discussed further later in Chapter IV.

killed by the private military force of Ch'oe Ch'ung-hŏn.[63] One such conflict resulted in the ousting of King Hŭijong by Ch'oe in 1211, the year following Chinul's death. Ironically, the purist and transcendental character of the Susŏnsa movement attracted the interest of not merely the Ch'oe family, the new holders of political power, but also the king and the nobles, who witnessed the collapse of the old social and political order. It is also ironical that a society founded on the idea of transcending the world was being drawn into the world, already in Chinul's time, but even more so after he passed away.

2) This passage tells us about Chinul's personality as a Sŏn master. Unlike the typical Sŏn master, who is popularly known as radical, uncouth, eccentric, and hard to approach, Chinul seems to have been a kind man. As one who had to struggle alone to find the path without a permanent master, he had great compassion for those who were still in the searching period of their spiritual life. Just as his quest for the truth was dictated by an uncompromising respect for the *Tao*, without personal loyalty to any particular Sŏn master or sect, so were his interpersonal relationships in the Susŏnsa unswayed by private feelings. Firm yet free, strict yet compassionate, demanding as well as forgiving: such seems to have been Chinul's manner as he guided people in this new center for Sŏn.

3) A Sŏn master relying on texts and prescribing them to students is an uncommon phenomenon in Sŏn Buddhism. Nevertheless it is a true picture of Chinul. All these texts, we remember, were those which had once touched his heart and given him liberating experiences. Why could they not (Chinul may have thought) do the same for others? He did not have a negative attitude toward "letters." There was nothing wrong with texts in themselves; what mattered was how one approached them, and what effect they produced on a person individually. Chinul knew from his own experiences that they could bring about a revolutionary effect upon a person's re-

---

[63] Concerning the clash between the monks and Ch'oe Ch'ung-hŏn, see *Han'guksa* 7, pp. 293–95, and Kim Chong-guk's article cited already on this matter.

ligious orientation, as well as become constant guides for the fruitful practice of Sŏn. For Chinul, who had no mentor, the weight that "letters" carried was naturally much greater than for other Sŏn masters. Furthermore, this situation led Chinul to reflect deeply concerning the proper method to cultivate Sŏn. What is the most efficient way of studying Sŏn for ordinary people? What constitutes the first step in the quest for enlightenment? How important is doctrinal study (Kyo) for the students of Sŏn? And why is the laborious process of spiritual cultivation still needed even after the experience of liberating enlightenment? Such were the questions he had to answer. Also, the environment of the Susŏnsa, where all sorts of people with diverse religious backgrounds and with various levels of spiritual attainment were gathered together, may well have been another stimulating factor for Chinul's development of methodological reflections on Sŏn, what we call his theory of Sŏn. It was in this living context that most of Chinul's writings were composed. It may be helpful here to make a brief survey of his writings, for it will throw light on how Chinul instructed his students of Sŏn in the Susŏnsa and serve as a good preparation for our study of his theory of Sŏn in the next chapter.

It is not known when Chinul composed his *Susimgyŏl* [*Key to the Cultivation of Mind*].[64] From its basic content, it is possible that it was written at about the same time as his *Kye ch'osim hagin mun*, that is, around 1205, when the busy work of reconstruction was finished. If the latter was meant to provide the students of Sŏn with the rules to govern their daily life, *Susimgyŏl* seems to have been designed to give them a pithy introduction to the essence of the cultivation of Sŏn. It mainly clarifies the relationship between sudden enlightenment and gradual cultivation, an issue that must have been one of the most hotly debated problems of the day and that, more significantly, has close bearing upon the conflict between Sŏn and Kyo. *Susŏnsa chungch'anggi* says:

---

[64] *T*. 48, No. 2020.

As a result of the hardening of conflicts in the course of two thousand years since the death of the Buddha, most monks follow the names and Characteristics of "sudden" or "gradual," being attached to what they are good at. They argue about the positions [they take] and fight against each other, racing to seek fame and gain and spending their time in futility. Therefore the path of total engagement in contemplation and [inner] illumination and the path of seeing into Nature by the cultivation of mind have completely disappeared from the land. The Master [Chinul] alone turned his back to the stream of the world, and even forgot to eat in indignation. He turned the wheel [of the *Dharma*] that never rolls back, having engaged in meditation in the mountains for more than twenty years.[65]

In contrast with the *Susimgyŏl* is Chinul's masterpiece, *Chinsim chiksŏl* [*Direct Exposition of the True Mind*]. Praised by Nukariya Kaiten as the finest piece of Sŏn literature in Korea,[66] it systematically elucidates the various aspects of the True Mind, the ultimate reality in Sŏn. Whereas *Susimgyŏl* concerns man's path to this ultimate reality, *Chinsim chiksŏl* is a direct attempt to disclose it. In its preface, Chinul says:

What can we do in the face of the great *Tao*, which is mysterious and empty, neither existent nor nonexistent, the True Mind, which is profound and subtle, transcending thinking and discussion? Therefore, if one cannot find the way to enter it, even reading the five thousands works of the *Tripiṭaka* would not be counted as much. Whereas if one who has the bright insight into the True Mind utters even a word of reasoning it is already superfluous. Yet I would not spare my eyebrows [based upon a story that someone's eyebrows fell off due to his reckless discourse on the *Dharma*], but venture to write some chapters expounding the True Mind, intending them to be the basis and order for entering enlightenment (*Po.* 60).

The preface of Chinul's next work, *Hwaŏmnon chŏryo* [*Condensation of the Treatise on Hua-yen*], is dated January of 1207 and is

---

[65] *CSS*, I, p. 275.
[66] *Chōsen zenkyōshi*, p. 183. It is *T.* 48, No. 2019B.

signed by "Chinul, a monk of Korean Chogye Mountain."[67] How much Chinul valued Li T'ung-hsüan's treatise is once again demonstrated by the enormous time and effort that must have been required to complete this work, which, though a condensation, is still very massive (about 450 pages in Chinese). The purport of the condensation is stated in the preface:

> Whenever I found leisure while sitting in meditation, I used to explain the treatise for my companions. Because the treatise is coarse and not smooth, and too lengthy and expansive, it was difficult for me to expound it. Also, due to its critical spirit that is not bound by ordinary norms, it has not been popular among the people. Nevertheless, it is the best mirror of the mind for sentient beings of great mind who enter the gate of complete-sudden [Hwaŏm] enlightenment. Thus making a sincere vow, burning incense, and beseeching the grace of the Buddha, I abstracted the essentials out of the forty fasicles and edited them into three volumes. I entrusted my student Ch'ungdam, a man of Sŏn, to gather artisans and make engravings and impressions of them in order to transmit them [to posterity] forever.[68]

Here again we are struck by this picture of a Sŏn master who, from time to time whenever he found leisure, lectured on a text. Certainly the kind of Sŏn Chinul practiced and taught was different from the kind that shouts for the "nonreliance on letters." But at the same time Chinul clearly regarded the text as a mirror for the act of contemplation, which he never intended to sacrifice or replace by intellectual studies.

The identical attitude governed Chinul when he composed his *Pŏpchip pyŏrhaengnok chŏryo pyŏngip sagi* [*Condensation with Comments of the Pŏpchip pyŏrhaengnok*]. Written in 1209, a year before his death, this is a condensation of *Pŏpchip pyŏrhaengnok*, a work by Tsung-mi,[69] supplemented by Chinul's own lengthy comments

---

[67] *Hwaŏmnon chŏryo*, p. 4.

[68] *Ibid*, p. 3.

[69] Since this work is not extant, and since no catalogue of Buddhist literature mentions this book, some have questioned if Tsung-mi ever wrote a book by this name. Ui Hakuju,

and discussions. This is his most comprehensive work setting forth his theory of Sŏn. At the outset of the work Chinul states:

Hat'aek Sinhoe [Ho-tse Shen-hui] is a master of intellectual understanding. Although not the proper heir of the Sixth Patriarch, his

---

for instance, asserts that the title was given by Chinul himself to another work of Tsung-mi, *Ch'an-men shih-tzu ch'eng-hsi-t'u*. Ui argues that Chinul separated out from this work (hence *pyŏrhaeng*, meaning separate circulation) only the portions dealing with the teaching (hence *pŏpchip*, meaning collection of *Dharma*) of the four sects of Ch'an (Shen-hsiu, Niu-t'ou, Hung-chou, and Shen-hui), disregarding the lineages of their *Dharma* transmission. Ui also says that Chinul at the same time shortened it (hence *chŏryo*, meaning condensation), leaving out particularly those parts which suggest a strong sectarian bias of Shen-hui's (Tsung-mi's) sect against the view of other sects. Ui's view is based on the unmistakable and striking agreement, almost *verbatim*, of the two texts; for his view, see *Dai san zenshūshi kenkyū* (Tokyo: 1943), pp. 477–506. Yet there are serious problems in his view. His explanation of *chŏryo* (condensation) is not satisfactory, for Chinul's subtraction—if he ever did it—is only minor and looks rather casual, and so does not justify the word *chŏryo*, which he uses in the case of his condensation of Li's treatise; what is more, there are not only minor subtractions but also minor additions as well. But the most serious objection to Ui's view is the fact that Chinul himself often refers to this work of Tsung-mi calling it simply *Nok* (Record), the last character of the title. It is absurd to think that Chinul is quoting from a work to which he himself had provided the title,.as if it were a separate work that has nothing to do with him. Moreover, Chinul quotes its full name in his *Kyŏlsamun* (*Po.* 19), which is his earliest work at the age of thirty-three; it is unlikely that he made that "condensation" and comments on it before this work.

The view, with which I agree, of Korean scholars (for instance, Yi Chong-ik, *KFKK*, pp. 78–81) is that *Pŏpchip pyŏrhaengnok* is an independent work of Tsung-mi. Unlike his *Ch'an-yüan chu-ch'üan-chi*, which is a collection of the words of numerous masters and sects on the *Dharma*, it is a separate collection of the teachings of only the four sects (hence *pyŏrhaeng*). Thus its content, almost identical as it is with *Ch'an-men shih-tzu ch'eng-hsi-t'u*, is from *Ch'an-yüan chu-ch'uan-chi* (not extant today). Being works by the same author, the agreement between *Pŏpchip* and *Ch'an-men* is not that striking. In fact, Tsung-mi "often repeats his own words in different books" (Jan Yün-hua, "Two problems concerning Tsung-mi's Compilation of Ch'an-tsang," *Transactions of the International Conference of Orientalists in Japan*, XIX [1974]: 42; this article refutes the view that Tsung-mi never wrote the *Ch'an-yüan chu-ch'üan-chi*, his *magnum opus*). Kamata Shigeo is uncertain about this problem, although he points out that Tsung-mi, in his *Yüan-chüeh-ching ta-shu-ch'ao*, refers to another work of his, calling it a "separate volume," for further information about the teaching of the Northern Sect (Shen-hsiu's); Kamata speculates that this "separate volume" might refer to the *Pŏpchip pyŏrhaengnok*. See his *Shūmitsu kyōgaku no shisōshi teki kenkyū* (Tokyo: 1975), p. 330; on pp. 391–410, Kamata gives the textual comparison of the corresponding portions between Chinul's *Chŏryo* and the *Ch'an-men*. We conclude this lengthy discussion by saying that Chinul condensed (with comments of his own) a work of Tsung-mi called *Pŏpchip pyŏrhaengnok*, and that this condensation came close to Tsung-mi's other work *Ch'an-men* for the reasons mentioned above, and possibly due to Chinul's skillful condensation as well.

enlightened understanding is high and bright, and his decisions are clear-cut. Tsung-mi, who inherited Shen-hui's views, expatiates and clarifies it in this *Record* [a clear indication that Chinul is refering to another work upon which he is now working] to make it clearly comprehensible. Now, *for the sake of those who realize Mind on the basis of Kyo*, I remove the superfluous words from it and abstract the essential parts, designing it to be the *mirror for the act of contemplation*. As I see today's people cultivating mind, they do not rely on what letters point to, but simply regard the place of mutual esoteric transmission [of the *Dharma*] as the *Tao*. Thus in obscured manner they work in vain and fall asleep while sitting in meditation. Some even lose their minds and get confused in the act of contemplation. If, therefore, they rely upon the *genuine teaching in words* and differentiate the root and branch of enlightenment and cultivation reflecting upon their own minds, they will not make distorted efforts in their contemplation and illumination.[70]

The spirit and intention of the work is made clear; it is a sharp criticism of "idiotic Sŏn." In spite of his awareness of the danger of the "disease of intellectual understanding" in Sŏn, Chinul is convinced that the study of Sŏn should be solidly grounded on "genuine teaching in words."

Two of Chinul's works, the *Wŏndon sŏngbullon* [*Treatise on the Complete-sudden Attainment of Buddhahood*] and the *Kanhwa kyŏrŭiron* [*Treatise for the Settlement of Doubts on* Kanhwa], were found after Chinul's death in a wooden box by his *Dharma* heir Hyesim, who published them in 1215, five years after Chinul died.[71] Based upon the Hua-yen thought of Li T'ung-hsüan, the *Wŏndon sŏngbullon* elucidates the Hwaŏm version of the idea of sudden enlightenment in Sŏn, or more precisely, a Sŏn version of Hwaŏm thought. The *Kanhwa kyŏrŭiron* discusses the efficacy and significance of the *kanhwa* method in Sŏn, particularly as taught by Ta-hui, and defends it against skeptical attacks. Whereas the *Wŏndon sŏngbullon* was

---

[70] *Chŏryo*, p. 680; my own italics.

[71] This information is given in the postscript written by Hyesim which was included in the first publication of the texts. It is given in *Han'guk kosŭngjip: Koryŏ sidae* II (Seoul: 1974), pp. 627–28.

composed with the idea of the fundamental unity of Sŏn and Kyo (particularly Hwaŏm), the *Kanhwa Kyŏruiron* emphasizes the uniqueness of the enlightenment experience accessible through the *kanhwa* method and the idea of a "separate transmission [of the *Dharma*] outside of Kyo."

Chinul was also concerned with the Pure Land practice of reciting the name of Amit'a Buddha, *yŏmbul* (*nien-fo, nembutsu*) 念佛. Thus he composed his *Yŏmbul yomun* [*Essential Path of* Yŏmbul][72] where he warns againt blind faith in rebirth in the Pure Land while ignoring moral law, and recommends ten kinds of *yŏmbul* as a means of attaining *samādhi*. Also extant is the postscript Chinul wrote for a new publication of the *Platform Sūtra*.[73] Written in 1207, here his view on the value of the *sūtra* is clearly expressed.

Thus far we have examined Chinul's writing activity at the Susŏnsa, and we believe that his attitude toward "letters" and Kyo has been revealed here to some extent as well. Certainly Chinul was a *writing* Sŏn master as well as a practicing Sŏn master, and this is why we are able to talk about his theory of Sŏn, as we will do in the next chapter. In addition to the works enumerated above, the inscription mentions the *Sangdangnok* (most likely the records by his disciples of Chinul's sermons) and the *Kasong* (which must have been a collection of his verses and poetry). Had these works been extant, we would have known more about Chinul's *style* of Sŏn; perhaps it would be more casual, free, and lively than it now looks to us.

---

[72] There is some confusion concerning the exact name of this book, but there seems to be no doubt that this is an authentic work of Chinul; see Yi Chong-ik's discussion of this matter, *KFKK*, pp. 92–99.

[73] It is not clear again what edition of the *sūtra* it was for which Chinul wrote the postscript; it was written at the request of his disciple Tammuk, who brought a copy of the *sūtra* to Chinul in 1207 and asked him to write the postscript for its publication, saying that it was a "recently acquired copy"; it was probably a copy of the Northern Sung edition of 1153 (see Yampolsky, pp. 98–104). The earliest edition of the *sūtra* extant in Korea is the so-called Tei-i edition of 1290, published in 1316 in Koryŏ; see the text and its discussion by Ōya Tokujo in *Zengaku kenkyū* 23 (1935); see also Yampolsky, p. 107 and n. 52. For a discussion of the various editions of the *sūtra* in Korea, see Kuroda Akira, *Chōsen kyūsho kō* (Tokyo; 1940), pp. 93–111; Chinul's postscript is given in this book, pp. 104–05, as well as in *Hyŏnt'o pŏnyŏk Yukcho tan'gyŏng*, trans. Kim T'anhŏ (Seoul: 1960), pp. 5–7 of the appendix.

Nevertheless, we are fortunate to have so many extant works (a rare occurrance for a Sŏn master) that are of greater significance for those of us who strive for the intellectual understanding of Sŏn. The inscription also mentions the *Pŏbŏ*, which probably refers to works like the *Susimgyŏl* and the *Chinsim chiksŏl*.

4) The last part of the quotation describes the system of Chinul's instruction in Sŏn. A detailed study of this is found in the next chapter. But we may note here, in advance, that in view of our study of Chinul's Sŏn thought in general, the three paths mentioned by the author of the inscription sum up the essentials of Chinul's theory of Sŏn. This is why our discussion of Chinul's theory in the next chapter will be structured according to these three paths, that is, "the path of complete-sudden faith and understanding" 圓頓信解門 (what we call "the beginning of Sŏn"), "the path of parallel keeping of quiescence and wakefulness" 惺寂等持門 ("the process of Sŏn"), and "the path of direct cutting" 徑截門 ("the perfection of Sŏn").[74] Our study of Chinul's theory of Sŏn will be a close examination of these three paths in Sŏn, plus a study of Chinul's conception of the ultimate reality, the True Mind 眞心 (what we call "the source of Sŏn").

These paths in turn have their origin in Chinul's own religious experiences. Just as Chinul recommended to his students only those texts with which he had once had fruitful contact, so did he teach the paths which he himself had gone through already. Chinul taught what he had experienced. Through his encounter with the *Platform Sūtra* and the *Treatise on Hua-yen*, Chinul had an experience of what sudden elightenment, or the path of complete-sudden faith and understanding, was; the path of parallel keeping of quiescence and wakefulness, or the gradual cultivation of *samadhi* and *prajñā*, was his life-time concern; and finally, the power of the path of direct cutting was dramatically revealed to him through his encounter

---

[74] In this respect, my presentation of Chinul's thought will be different from the way Yi Chong-ik presents it in his *KFKK*, where he discusses Chinul's thought under seven separate headings, without much organic interrelationship between them.

with Ta-hui's *kanhwa* Sŏn. In the tightly integrated, existentialist personality of Chinul, no gap existed between theory and practice, or between doctrine and experience; and it is this quality that attracts us so much in our study of his life and thought.

In February of 1210, at the occasion of the memorial service for his deceased mother, Chinul told the gathering: "Since I will not long dwell in this world and discourse on the *Dharma*, you should each exert your own effort" (*Po.* 141). On the twentieth of March by the lunar calendar, he suddenly fell ill; eight days afterward he quietly passed away, sitting on the platform with the stick in his hand, after having exchanged questions and answers on the *Dharma* with his disciples. We are inclined to attribute his illness to overwork at the Susŏnsa. The writing activity alone would have been more than an ordinary man could accomplish in such a short time (most probably, from 1205 to 1210). Chinul's life may well have ended without regret just after his encounter with Ta-hui's Sŏn, for in that moment the world of freedom, where life and death no longer counted, was opened up to him. Thus in a sense his life after that event was for him nothing but the compassionate activities of a Bodhisattva for the sake of sentient beings.

Chinul's life was relatively short; he died at the age of fifty-three. So was the life of Ŭich'ŏn, the other great leader of Koryŏ Buddhism, who died at the age of forty-seven (1055–1101). Beyond this coincidance, however, their lives were widely different. Unlike Ŭich'ŏn, Chinul left the capital permanently. His interest was not divided: His sole concern was the single-minded pursuit of the goal of liberation from the world. He did not go to China, but to the mountains and forests of Korea. He did not collect thousands of Buddhist literature and catalogue them, though he composed some works of his own; he did not publish texts, nor did he establish institutions, except for the humble Society for *Samādhi* and *Prajñā*; he did not create a new religious order by state power, but simply tried to reform the old tradition by a new spirit; he did not attempt to unify Sŏn and Kyo artificially, but verified their fundamental unity through his own searching. Compared with the glorious and colorful life of Ŭich'ŏn, Chinul's life looks rather monotonous. Yet, monotonous as it was, it was a profound life marked by the ceaseless quest for perfect freedom.

After Chinul's death, his devotees served him with incense and lights. For seven days, it is said, his countenance did not change, and the beard and hair continued to grow. It is also said that when they culled the remains after the cremation they were able to gather about thirty large pieces of relics (sari), a phenomenon believed to occur only with deceased monks of the greatest virtue. They erected a pagoda for him at the northern side of the Susŏnsa. King Hŭijong, distressed by his death, bestowed the name Kamno (Sweet Dew) on the pagoda, and conferred upon Chinul the posthumous title of Puril Pojo Kuksa, "National Preceptor Universally Illuminating like the Sun of Buddha." As mentioned at the beginning of this study, Chinul's disciples, headed by Hyesim, collected materials on their master's life and presented them to the king, asking him to set up a memorial stele. Thus was erected the stele with the inscription, upon which we have mainly based ourselves in this study of one of the greatest personalities in the history of the Buddhist tradition.

CHAPTER II
CHINUL'S THEORY OF SŎN

INTRODUCTION

CH'AN MAY BE CALLED THE FLOWER of Chinese Buddhism; but the flower blossoms only on the basis of the root and the branches. According to recent critical studies of the history of Ch'an Buddhist thought, such principal mottoes as "direct pointing to the Mind of man," "seeing into Nature and becoming a Buddha," "nonreliance on letters," and "separate transmission [of the *Dharma*] outside of doctrinal teaching [*chiao*]" came to be firmly established within Ch'an Buddhism rather late, perhaps in the ninth century at the earliest.[1] On the other hand, we know that in early Ch'an such texts as the *Laṅkāvatāra Sūtra* and the *Diamond Sūtra* played an important role.[2] There are yet other links between early Ch'an and the doctrinal schools. Important concepts such as "Mind" and "Nature," had already been highly developed in the philosophical systems of Ti-lun, San-lun, T'ien-t'ai, Fa-hsiang, and Hua-yen, before they were common in Ch'an. In its philosophical substance, therefore, Ch'an contributed virtually nothing new to Chinese Buddhist thought.

It is often pointed out that, after all, only the two so-called "practical schools," that is Ch'an and Pure Land, survived in China. This seems to be true particularly after the severe Hui-ch'ang persecution of Buddhism (A.D. 841–845).[3] But the seemingly highly theoretical

---

[1] In fact, according to Sekiguchi Shindai's study, even the name "Ch'an-tsung" (Ch'an School) was not in use in the early history of Ch'an; instead, such names as "Leng-chia-tsung," "Tung-shan-tsung," and "Nan-tsung" were used up until late T'ang; see his *Zenshū shisōshi* (Tokyo: 1964), pp. 1–4 for a brief information, and pp. 189–238 for more details.

[2] See *ibid.*, pp. 43–74.

[3] Many reasons are given for the better survival of Ch'an, such as less reliance on

systems of philosophical thought such as T'ien-t'ai and Hua-yen were also aimed at the practical religious act of contemplation 觀行. In T'ien-t'ai such an act was called "*chih-kuan*" (*śamatha-vipaśyanā*), expounded in works of Chih-i such as the *Mo-ho chih-kuan* and the *T'ien-t'ai hsiao-chih-kuan*, and its influence on Ch'an was considerable.[4] In the Hua-yen School it centered on the contemplation of the *Dharmadhātu* as first defined and formulated by Tu-shun, and further developed by Chih-yen, Fa-tsang, and Ch'eng-kuan.[5] Seen from this perspective, Ch'an Buddhism, both in its thought and practice, was the culmination of the Chinese Buddhist spirit rather than a novelty in Chinese Buddhism; it is, indeed, the flower.[6]

Ch'an Buddhism, particularly the so-called Southern Sect, went through its most creative development in eighth-century China, the period when the lavish support of Buddhism, particularly of the Hua-yen School, by Empress Wu disappeared at the restoration of the T'ang dynasty,[7] and when a profound change in the political and economic structure was taking place in the powerful and ancient state system of T'ang.[8] It was in this period that groups of creative minds in the local provinces started to propagate vigorously a more radical form of Ch'an. Shen-hui and his followers were perhaps the

---

"external paraphernalia of religion," and economic self-sufficiency based on the "Pure Rules" of Pai-chang Huai-hai (710–814); see K. Ch'en, *Buddhism in China*, p. 363.

[4] See Sekiguchi Shindai, *Daruma Daishi no kenkyū* (Tokyo: 1969), pp. 270–94, as well as his "Zenshū to Tendaishū to no kōsō," *Taishō Daigaku kenkyū kiyō* 44 (1959): 39–75.

[5] Both Fa-tsang and Ch'eng-kuan composed separate works devoted to the elucidation of the act of contemplation. Fa-tsang's work is *Hsiu-hua-yen ao-chih wang-chin huan-yüan-kuan* (*T*. 45 No. 1876), and Ch'eng-kuan's work is *San-sheng yüan-jung-kuan-men* (*T*. 45, No. 1882).

[6] In his "Ch'an (Zen) Buddhism in China: Its History and Method," Hu Shih properly states: "The Ch'an (Zen) movement is an integral part of the history of Chinese Buddhism, and the history of Chinese Buddhism is an integral part of the general history of Chinese thought. Ch'an can be properly understood only in its historical setting just as any other Chinese philosophical school must be studied and understood in its historical setting." *Philosophy East and West*, III, 1 (1953): 3.

[7] On this issue, see Stanley Weinstein, "Imperial Patronage in the Formation of T'ang Buddhism," *Perspectives on the T'ang*, ed. by A. Wright and D. Twitchett (New Haven: 1973), pp. 265–306.

[8] For a historical survey of the social change in this period, see Reischauer and Fairbank, *East Asia: The Great Tradition* (Boston: 1958), pp. 183–93.

most instrumental in the popularization and establishment of the Southern Sect by their sharp and vigorous attacks against the Northern Sect represented by P'u-chi, Shen-hsiu's disciple, in the capital.[9] Yet eventually Shen-hui's line of Ch'an came to be overshadowed by the appearance of more prominent masters, most notably Ma-tsu and Shih-t'ou, in the lines of the other disciples of the Sixth Patriarch, such as Nan-yüeh and Ch'ing-yüan. With the emergence of the more radical form of Ch'an thought and practice, the conflict between Ch'an and Chiao (doctrinal Buddhism) became more pronounced. Nevertheless, it was from the ninth century—with the formulation of the famous "Pure Rules" by Pai-chang Huai-hai at the turn of the eighth century, after the Hui-ch'ang persecution—that Ch'an Buddhism began to have a more solid institutional basis, and became more independent of, and antagonistic toward, doctrinal Buddhism, putting forth such idiosyncratic slogans as "nonreliance on letters" and "separate transmission outside of doctrinal teaching."

Meanwhile, under the influence of this new development within Buddhism as well as within T'ang society in general, there appeared in the doctrinal schools the trend of adjusting doctrinal thought to this new spirit, which was increasing in popularity. Thus such great figures as Chan-jan (711–782) in the T'ien-t'ai School and Ch'eng-kuan (738–839)[10] in the Hua-yen School emerged. Ch'eng-kuan in particular was a good representative of this new trend.[11] By interpreting Hua-yen doctrine in the light of Ch'an thought, he gave a strong practical bent to the former. He was especially influenced by the Ch'an thought of Shen-hui,[12] and it was he who definitely identified Ch'an with the fourth teaching, that is, the "sudden

---

[9] About Shen-hui's activity, see the cited article by Hu Shih, pp. 4–17.

[10] There is some uncertainty about the year of his birth and death; see Kamata Shigeo, *Chūgoku Kegon shisōshi no kenkyū* (Tokyo: 1965), pp. 159–69.

[11] About the social circumstances surrounding the formation of Ch'eng-kuan's thought, see *ibid*, pp. 221–33.

[12] This has been the generally held view. See, for instance, Takamine Ryōshū, *Kegon shisōshi* (Kyoto: 1942), p. 272, or his *Kegon to Zen to no tsūro* (Nara: 1956), pp. 89–98. Kamata, while admitting this, attributes this view to Tsung-mi's influence and emphasizes the influence of the Niu-t'ou Sect upon Ch'eng-kuan; see *op. cit.*, pp. 475–500.

teaching" in the Hua-yen doctrinal classification system established by Fa-tsang.[13]

It was in this context that Tsung-mi appeared, the heir of Ch'eng-kuan's Hua-yen thought as well as of Shen-hui's Southern Ch'an,[14] and who, more significantly for our purpose, was the most influential man in the formation of Chinul's theory of Sŏn. Whereas Ch'eng-kuan still stood firmly within the Hua-yen School in spite of his considerable interest in Ch'an, Tsung-mi simply put Ch'an and Chiao on a par, each with its particular function and characteristic, while on the other hand he tried to demonstrate their fundamental underlying unity of thought. In his *Ch'an-yüan chu-ch'üan-chi tu-hsü*[15] he made a concrete attempt to harmonize Ch'an and Chiao by matching the teachings of the three major branches of Ch'an with the three basic types of doctrinal thought.[16] At the beginning of the work Tsung-mi states:

> *Sūtras* are the words of the Buddha, whereas Ch'an is the mind of

---

[13] See, for example, Kamekawa Kyōsin, *Kegongaku* (Kyoto: 1949), p. 83. By "sudden teaching" Fa-tsang had in mind the teaching of the *Vimalakīrtinirdeśa-sūtra*, which emphasizes the ineffable nature of truth.

[14] For an English article on Tsung-mi, see Jan Yün-hua, "Tsung-mi, His Analysis of Ch'an Buddhism," *T'oung Pao* LVIII (1972): 1–54. The most complete study of Tsung-mi, his thought and biography, is Kamata Shigeo's *Shūmitsu kyōgaku no shisōshi teki kenkyū* (Tokyo: 1975).

[15] *T.* 48, No. 2015; hereafter, this work will be referred to as *Ch'an-yüan*.

[16] The three major branches of Ch'an are: the sect that taught the stopping of falsity and the cultivation of mind (Northern Sect), the sect which taught absolute annihilation (Niu-t'ou or Ox Head Sect), and the sect which taught direct revelation of the Mind-Nature (Hung-chou [Ma-tsu] and Shen-hui's Sect); see Jan Yün-hua, note 14, pp. 37–40. The three types of doctrinal thought are, according to Jan's translation: esoteric teaching on the Characters as based on their Nature, esoteric teaching of revealing Nature itself by negation of the Characters, and the exoteric teaching revealing that the True Mind itself is the (Buddha) Nature. Jan's translation is misleading, especially as to the first two types. Both from the structure of the phrases and from Tsung-mi's own explanations, one discerns that in the first case "esoteric" does not modify teaching itself but the words "basing upon Nature." Hence, the correct rendering would be "the teaching which discourses on Characteristics basing itself upon Nature esoterically." In the second case, "esoteric" does not modify teaching itself but the words "reveal Nature." Hence, the correct rendering would be "the teaching which esoterically reveals Nature by destroying Characteristics." These translations bring out the meaning more clearly and are more in line with the harmonizing spirit of Tsung-mi's work itself, for his basic idea is that *all* three teachings ultimately teach about Nature; see pp. 28–29 for Jan's translation.

the Buddha; the mind and mouth of the Buddha should not be divergent.[17]

As Kamata Shigeo points out,[18] Tsung-mi was a representative of the transitional period from Chiao (doctrinal Buddhism) to Ch'an in the history of Chinese Buddhist thought. He was perhaps the last great figure in the doctrinal study of Buddhism in China for some time. Significantly, his death took place in A.D. 841 just when the terrible Hui-ch'ang persecution, which dealt such a fatal blow to the doctrinal schools of Buddhism, was about to start. His idea of the unity of Ch'an and Chiao did not find much support in later generations, particularly among the followers of Ch'an, who took an increasingly more radical course, ignoring his harmonizing approach to Buddhist thought and the kind of nonexclusive Ch'an he represented.

The situation was different in Korea, where Tsung-mi's thought was to receive a positive response and to leave a lasting effect. As we have already seen, the confrontation between the two camps of Buddhism had been severe and tense, and neither side was able to get the upper hand decisively. Even Ŭich'ŏn's grand design to embrace Sŏn and Kyo within the single system of Ch'ŏnt'ae was not successful. By his time Sŏn Buddhim was already too strong and independent to be absorbed into a new order that lacked a deep root in Korea. Moreover, Sŏn was as flourishing as ever it had been in China. On the other hand, however, neither was Sŏn able to dominate Kyo, which had a continuous and long tradition behind it; there had been nothing like the Hui-ch'ang persecution in Korea. It was in this situation that Chinul appeared from within the Sŏn camp and tried in his own way to integrate Sŏn and Kyo. For this task, he found not only Tsung-mi's thought appealing, but he also showed sympathy for Yung-ming Yen-shou (904–975), another Chinese master who emphasized the unity of Sŏn and Kyo, and whose thought had once been promoted by King Kwangjong (950–975) in early Koryŏ.[19] We have already considered Chinul's struggle with Hwaŏm

---

[17] *T*. 48, p. 400b.
[18] *Shūmitsu kyōgaku*, p. 233.
[19] On the introduction of Yen-shou's thought into Koryŏ and King Kwangjong's

thought and his discovery of the significance of Li T'ung-hsüan for the problem with which he was wrestling. But in the over-all scheme of Chinul's approach to Sŏn it was Tsung-mi to whom he was most indebted, and it was through Chinul that Tsung-mi's thought came to have a lasting effect on the Korean Sŏn tradition.

Chinul does not regard Shen-hui as the proper heir of the Sixth Patriarch, as Tsung-mi does. Chinul knew the later development of the history of Sŏn Buddhism, and therefore his historical perspective was different. Furthermore, he had encountered the *kanhwa* Sŏn of Ta-hui, a radical line of Sŏn, of which Tsung-mi could never have thought.

Nonetheless, for several important reasons, Chinul decided to condense, and comment on, the work of Tsung-mi as we have already seen. First, Shen-hui's "enlightened understanding is high and pure, and his decisions are clear-cut." Second, Tsung-mi's presentation of his thought in this work can provide those "who realize Mind on the basis of Kyo" with a good "mirror for the act of contemplation." Third and most important, Chinul thought it crucial even for the students of Sŏn to base themselves on "what letters point to," that is, on "the genuine (*yathābhūtam*) teaching in words" 如實言教, if they are to carry on a fruitful practice of Sŏn without falling into "idiotic Sŏn."[20] And he warns them against the preoccupation with "the mutual esoteric transmission as the *Tao* [enlightenment]." Chinul was convinced that the practitioners of Sŏn should first have clear intellectual guidance about the nature and method of Sŏn. It was for these reasons that he decided to condense Tsung-mi's work, which he regarded as an excellent "mirror for the act of contemplation." The same motivation, we recall, governed him when he condensed Li T'ung-hsüan's *Treatise on Hua-yen*. And it was in the same spirit that he composed most of his other works, in which he elucidates various facets of Sŏn.

Buddhist policy, see Kim Ch'ŏl-chun's important study, "Koryŏch'o ŭi Ch'ŏnt'aehak yŏn'gu," *Han'guk kodae sahoe yŏn'gu* (Seoul: 1975).

[20] An expression which, as we have seen already, Chinul borrows from Tsung-mi (*T*. 48, p. 399c) to describe the type of Sŏn that ignores intellectual understanding; its opposite is "crazy wisdom," which ignores the cultivation of *samādhi*.

To this extent, Chinul's approach to Sŏn was Kyo-oriented and clearly intellectual. The fact that Chinul, as a Sŏn master, recognized "those who realize Mind on the basis of Kyo" is a clear indication that Chinul wanted to draw the students of Kyo into the act of contemplation, that is, Sŏn. But on the other hand, in this recognition of realizing Mind on the basis of Kyo Chinul had another purpose in mind: to provide the students of Sŏn with intellectual guidance for their act of contemplation. In this sense, "Kyo" does not have to be taken in the narrow sense (of doctrinal Buddhism as opposed to Sŏn); it is virtually identical with any intellectual and verbal expression of the Buddhist truth, with any "genuine teaching in words." Of this, according to Chinul, there are two kinds: Kyo (in the narrower sense), which is "expansion," and Sŏn, which is "concision."[21] Chinul was primarily concerned with the latter kind of "genuine teaching in words," still Kyo (in the broader sense). The titles of his works often suggest that his main interest lay in "concision"—hence such words as "key" (kyŏl), "direct exposition" (chiksŏl), and "condensation" (chŏryo). Chinul's conception of verbal expression was functionalistic; words are merely the "finger pointing to the moon," no more than an upāya (Po.23). But for him this finger was truly important, for he himself experienced the power of "the genuine teaching in words" through his encounter with the Platform Sūtra, the Treatise on Hua-yen, and even the Words of Ta-hui. And from this recognition of the power of verbal expression in Sŏn came Chinul's freedom to use it whenever necessary; he calls this attitude chagyo myŏngjong 藉教明宗, meaning clarification of the fundamental (i.e. Mind) in reliance on or by borrowing Kyo (Po.23). It was because of this attitude that Chinul did not shun Shen-hui and Tsung-mi, in spite of his knowledge that they did not belong to the authentic line of Southern Ch'an. He had no qualm about verbal and theoretical discussions of Sŏn. It is certainly due to this exoteric and intellectual aspect of Chinul's Sŏn that we can have access to the esoteric world of Sŏn, although by way of theoretical understanding.

By "theory of Sŏn" we mean something broad and general. It

---

[21] Chŏryo, p. 694. This is originally the idea of Tsung-mi; see T. 48, p. 399c.

refers to Chinul's view of Sŏn—its nature and essence, its method and practice—as expressed through the "genuine teaching in words" of his, and to some extent of others as well, with whom he identifies himself, notably Tsung-mi and Li T'ung-hsüan.

To be sure, Chinul admits "the separate transmission outside of Kyo." While freely engaged in intellectual discussion of Sŏn, Chinul was clearly aware of its danger. It was, we remember, none other than "the disease of intellectual understanding" that disturbed his mind for such a long time like an "enemy," and it was through his encounter with the *hwadu* Sŏn of Ta-hui that he was finally able to overcome it. Thus when Chinul talks about the "separate transmission outside of Kyo," he has above all *hwadu* Sŏn in mind, which according to him opens up the spiritual realm, where no intellectual exercise or verbal communication could ever hope to reach. Here a sharp division exists between Sŏn and Kyo. Yet for Chinul, this *hwadu* Sŏn is really meant for people of the highest mental capability, not for ordinary practitioners of Sŏn. Moreover it is the last gate to enter (except for some gifted with "supercapability"). Thus he sets at the end of his *Chŏryo* a guideline that one should first develop the "genuine intellectual understanding" of the truth, and then go on to take *hwadu* to remove the disease of intellectual understanding (C. 814). In this sense, Chinul was not an unconditional supporter of *hwadu* Sŏn. He knew both its value and its limitation. Furthermore, even about this *hwadu* Sŏn, the nature of which is presumed to lie beyond any theoretical understanding, Chinul did not abstain from intellectual reflections; his *Kanhwa kyŏrŭiron* was an apology for *hwadu* Sŏn. This is why we are justified in including even his view of the "separate transmission outside of Kyo," that is, even the esoteric aspect of his approach to Sŏn, in this chapter discussing his theory of Sŏn.

Chinul's theory of Sŏn is most comprehensively set forth in his *Chŏryo*. Particularly in the following excerpt, which is near the end of this work, we find all major aspects or categories of his thought concerning Sŏn well outlined.[22] Borrowing the words of Tsung-mi,

---

[22] This is a judgment reached at the *end* of my study.

Chinul says by way of summary:

> The gate of the *Dharma* that has been elucidated thus far is all for
> the sake of those who enter enlightenment by the arising of under-
> standing based upon words. It sets forth in detail that the *Dharma*
> has two aspects, viz., Unchanging and Changing; whereas *man*
> has two paths to follow: the path of sudden enlightenment and the
> path of gradual cultivation. With the two aspects [of the *Dharma*]
> we know that the purport of the entire scriptures and treatises is
> none other than the Nature and Characteristics of one's own mind;
> with the two paths [for man] one can see that the footprint of all
> the wise and the holy is none other than the beginning and end of
> one's own action. It [the above "gate of *Dharma*"] is in this way so
> clear in discerning what is the primary and the secondary that it lets
> people not err but progress from the expedient to the real and
> promptly attain enlightenment.[23]

The structure of the present chapter is based on the framework provided in this passage. Thus section one in the present chapter, entitled "the source of Sŏn," discusses the objective side of Sŏn by in-
vestigating "the two aspects" of the *Dharma,* namely "Unchanging and Changing"; it is a study of Chinul's view of the nature of
Mind, the ultimate reality in Sŏn, and its two aspects called "Nature and Characteristics." Next, we will examine Chinul's theory
of the subjective side of Sŏn, "the two paths" for man, what Tsung-
mi calls "the *act* of Sŏn" 禪行, as distinct from "the *source* of Sŏn"
禪源;[24] it is a study of the path of sudden enlightenment (or, according to the inscription we have examined already, the path of complete-
sudden faith and understanding) and of the path of gradual cultivation (or the path of parallel keeping of quiescence and wakefulness).
We call the path of sudden enlightenment "the beginning of Sŏn"
and the path of gradual cultivation "the process of Sŏn," and these
constitute the subject matter of sections two and three of this chapter. But the inscription mentions another path, namely the path of
direct cutting (*hwadu* Sŏn); we gave it the title "the perfection of

---

[23] *Chŏryo*, p. 804; my own italics.
[24] *T*. 48, p. 399a; more will be said about this distinction later.

Sŏn," and its study constitutes the fourth section of this chapter. It is a path Tsung-mi did not discuss. So for Chinul "the act of Sŏn" consists of three paths, as the inscription informs us, instead of the two for Tsung-mi. This is why Chinul continues, after the previously quoted passage, as follows:

> If one produces understanding based upon words, and does not know the way to turn one's body [to be liberated], though he may contemplate all day long he will be bound by intellectual understanding, finding no time to rest. Therefore, for the sake of the monks today who enter [enlightenment] by transcending words and suddenly get rid of intellectual understanding, I briefly adduce words and phrases by which the learned patriarchs led the students of Sŏn in the method of direct cutting—although it was not respected by Tsung-mi. In this way the outstanding students of Sŏn may know the existence of one living path to pull their bodies out [of birth and death].[25]

1. *The Source of Sŏn: True Mind*

The most important concepts of Sŏn are Mind (*sim* 心) and Nature (*sŏng* 性). Often these two concepts combine to form one word, Mind-Nature (*simsŏng*). Their importance is attested by such cardinal principles of Sŏn as "direct pointing to the Mind of man" and "seeing into Nature and becoming a Buddha." This is why Sŏn Buddhism is also called the school of Mind. At the beginning of his *Ch'an-yüan chu-ch'üan-chi tu-hsü* [*General Preface to the Collection of Discourses on the Source of Ch'an*], Tsung-mi states that "the source of Sŏn" refers to "the true Nature of Original Enlightenment possessed by all sentient beings," and that it is also called the Buddha-Nature or Mind-ground.[26] Tsung-mi further says that this source of Sŏn is the *principle* of Sŏn as distinguished from the *act* of Sŏn, which he says is an act to "fit in with [the principle or the source of Sŏn] by forgetting passions."[27] In other words, what we have called the objective side of

---

[25] *Chŏryo*, pp. 804–05.
[26] *T.* 48, p. 399a.
[27] *Ibid.*

Sŏn, the *Dharma* or Mind,[28] is the source of Sŏn, whereas the act of Sŏn corresponds to the subjective side of Sŏn.[29]

The objective side of Sŏn, the *Dharma*, always exists, whether man recognizes it or not. When Chinul discusses it, however, he does so as a man who has already gone through the act of Sŏn. Thus in accordance with the order of *knowing*, it is proper that we begin our study with the investigation of the subjective side of Sŏn, namely, the three paths to which we have referred several times. But in accordance with the order of *being*,[30] the objective side comes first, and so it is legitimate to begin with its study. Here, let us follow the order of being and consider the ontological aspect of Chinul's Sŏn thought first, remaining aware that the order of knowing and the order of being are inseparable, like the two sides of a coin. Let us also keep in mind that if a Sŏn master distinguishes between the "*Dharma*" (the objective side of Sŏn) and "man" (the subjective side), it is done merely as an *upāya* on the lower level of truth—an indication that no more than a *theory* of Sŏn is meant here. Once one has entered into the so-called objective side of Sŏn or "the source of Sŏn," such a distinction, Chinul would say, may no longer be legitimate.

Every Sŏn master would agree that Mind, the ultimate reality in

---

[28] As we shall see, "Mind" here does not mean the mind as opposed to the body. It is a term referring to the ultimate reality in Sŏn; hence, it is capitalized when used in this sense, though often the distinction is hard to make. Tsung-mi distinguishes between four different meanings of the Chinese word *hsin*. 心: 1. Physical heart; 2. Eight consciousnesses; 3. The eighth consciousness, i.e. the *ālayavijñāna*; 4. The Real or True Mind, or the *Tathāgatagarbha* (*T*. 48, p. 401c). It is in the fourth sense that Mind is used throughout this study. Quoting from the famous passage in the *Kisillon* (*Ch'i-hsin-lun*), Chinul says: "What is called the *Dharma* refers to the Mind of sentient beings; this Mind embraces all the *dharmas*, mundane and supramundane; it is on the basis of this Mind that the aspects of the Mahāyāna are revealed" (*Pŏbŏ*, p. 16).

[29] The distinction between the subjective side and the objective side of Sŏn is my device for comprehending the structure of Chinul's theory of Sŏn. But it is based on Chinul's own distinction between "*Dharma*" 法 and "man" 人. I derived the title of the present section, "the source of Sŏn," from Tsung-mi, but not necessarily in strict agreement with his thought.

[30] Again, this distinction between the order of knowing and the order of being is my own; it corresponds to the above distinction between the subjective side and the objective side of Sŏn.

67

Sŏn, is a mystery and basically ineffable. Yet, every Sŏn master has tried to express it in some fashion, verbal or nonverbal, regular or irregular. Chinul says that the meaning of entire *sūtras* and treatises is nothing but the Nature and Characteristics (*sŏng* 性 and *sang* 相) of Mind.[31] For that matter, it is no exaggeration to say that the entire works of Chinul are no more than an exposition, direct or indirect, of Mind. Yet one of them, *Chinsim chiksŏl* [*Direct exposition of True Mind*], addresses itself specifically to this topic, as the title indicates. "At the top of Myogobong [Mysteriously High Mountain; refers to Mount Sumeru]," says Chinul in the introduction, "they have not allowed cogitation traditionally, but at the top of the second highest peak the patriarchs have allowed verbal understanding succinctly." Then follows a typical passage on the inadequacy of verbal expression in Sŏn:

> Someone said: I dare to pray that you let down succinctly a temporary means from the second highest peak. Response: Your words are correct. What can we do in the face of the great *Tao*, which is mysterious and empty, neither existent nor nonexistent, the True Mind, which is profound and subtle, transcending thinking and discussion (*Po.* 60).

The second chapter of this work enumerates the different names of True Mind in Sŏn and Kyo.[32] In Kyo, it is called Mind-Ground because it produces myriad good things, *Bodhi* because it has enlightenment as the essence, *Dharmadhātu* because things interpenetrate and embrace each other, Thus-Come because it originates from nowhere, *Nirvāṇa* because it is where all the saints return, Thusness because it is true and constantly unchanging, *Dharmakāya* (Buddha's Body of Truth) because *sambhogakāya* (Body of Enjoyment) and *nirmāṇakāya* (Body of Transformation) rely on it,[33] Suchness because it is unborn and undestroyable, Buddha-Nature because it is the original

---

[31] See p. 65 of this study.
[32] The following explanations, all Chinul's own, are excerpts from *Pŏbŏ*, pp. 63–64. All words expressing the absolute or ultimate reality are capitalized.
[33] On these three kinds of body of Buddha, *trikāya*, see Suzuki's short but il-

essence of the three kinds of body [of the Buddha], Dhāraṇī because merit flows out of it, *Tathāgatagarbha* because it hides, covers, contains, and embraces [Buddhahood], and Complete Enlightenmnnt because it destroys darkness and illumines alone. Chinul goes on to say:

> Under the gate of the patriarchs, names and words are discontinued; not a single name is established, not to mention many. Yet responding to and following capacities [of people], its names are numerous. Sometimes it is called "self," because it is the original nature of sentient beings; sometimes "right eye," because it reflects various characteristics; sometimes "subtle mind," because it is empty, spiritual, quiescent, and illuminating; sometimes "old master" because it has carried the burden from old.[34]

The names given above are various symbols pointing to the same ultimate reality; it is only that Chinul chooses from them one particular symbol, True Mind. "True" means "without falsity," and Mind means "spiritual mirror."[35] Chinul concludes:

> If one is conversant with True Mind, all the names will be completely understood; but if one is ignorant about True Mind, all the names will be obstructive (*Po.* 65).

It is obvious from the enumeration of the different names of True Mind that "Mind" does not refer to the mind as contrasted with the body, or to the subject as opposed to the object. Rather, it refers to the nature of reality as it is, and hence it is given such names as "Thusness" and "Suchness" (*tathatā*). In Mādhyamika philosophical terms, it means Emptiness (*śūnyatā*), not understood as some metaphysical reality underlying the phenomenal world but as denoting the way things (*dharma*) are in reality. In other words, Mind is not a psychological concept but is ontological. As the nature of all *dharmas*

---

luminating explanation in his *Third Series*, pp. 338–39. Suzuki's explanation is closely related to what Chinul is saying here.

[34] *Pŏbŏ*, p. 64; there are other names such as "Bottomless Bowl," "Rootless Tree," "Inexhaustible Lamp."

[35] *Ibid.*, p. 63.

(*dharmatā*), it is immanent in all *dharmas* while at the same time transcending them all. Not "a" *dharma*, it is "the" *Dharma*. With regard to ordinary sentient beings, it is called the Buddha-Nature or the *Tathāgatagarbha* (Womb of the Tathāgata), that which makes Buddhahood possible for us. And with regard to the phenomenal forms and appearances of Buddhas, talked about in Mahāyāna *sūtras*, it is called the *Dharmakāya* (Body of *Dharma*).[36]

After the enumeration of the different names of True Mind, which gives us a general idea of what Chinul is going to talk about, he elucidates it in its two aspects, "the mysterious Essence" (*myoch'e* 妙體) and "the mysterious Function" (*myoyong* 妙用). These two aspects of True Mind are what Tsung-mi and Chinul mean by "the two aspects of the *Dharma*," namely "Unchanging" 不變 and "Changing" 隨緣. They are also called Nature 性 and Characteristics 相, or Principle 理 and Phenomena 事. In this differentiation of the two aspects of True Mind, both Tsung-mi and Chinul are indebted to the classical example set up in the *Taesŭng kisillon* (*Ta-ch'eng ch'i-hsin-lun*),[37] where the *Dharma* as the Mind of sentient beings is said to have the three aspects of Essence, Characteristics, and Function, or where One Mind is considered in its two aspects, namely Suchness (Essence) and Birth-and-Destruction (Function and Characteristics). Tsung-mi employs various metaphors to explain the relationship of these two aspects. For instance, gold has the unchanging aspect of gold nature as well as the changing aspect of various golden orna-

---

[36] That this ultimate reality is called "Mind" in Sŏn indicates that Sŏn thought is deeply rooted in the Mind-only idealistic teaching of Hua-yen thought (not the *vijñapti-mātra* of the Yogācāra School). The *locus classicus* where the Mind-only (*yusim*) teaching occurs is the *Daśabhūmika-sūtra* incorporated into the *Avataṁsaka-sūtra*. There it is said that the three worlds are Mind-only (*citta-mātra*). At first, *citta* was understood as meaning our ordinary mind or thought; but later by Vasubandhu, and particularly by the Ti-lun School of China, it was interpreted as referring to the True Mind, an important development in Mahāyāna doctrinal thought. On this and its role in Hua-yen thought, see Kamata Shigeo, *Chūgoku kegon shisōshi no kenkyū*, pp. 502–09.

[37] It is obvious from his works that Chinul is at home in the thought of the *Kisillon*. Chinul quotes directly the *Kisillon's* words about the two gates, Suchness and Birth and Destruction, of One Mind; see *Chŏryo*, p. 786, and *Pŏbŏ*, pp. 16, 103, 104. On the central position it occupies in Tsung-mi's thought, see Araki Kengo, *Bukkyō to jukyō* (Kyoto: 1963), p. 98.

ments.[38] Later we will consider another metaphor, that of the clear jewel. Here is what Chinul says about these two aspects of True Mind. First the mysterious Essence:

The *Panggwang panyagyŏng* [*Prajñāpāramitā-sūtra*] says that *prajñā* has no characteristics at all and hence no characteristics of birth-and-destruction. The *Kisillon* says that Suchness itself neither increases nor decreases, whether in ordinary beings, *śrāvakas*, *pratyekabuddhas*, Bodhisattvas, or in all the Buddhas ... According to this *sūtra* and the treatise, the original Essence of True Mind transcends cause and effect, runs through the past and present, and does not distinguish between ordinary beings and saints; like great space it knows no contrasts and pervades everywhere. The mysterious Essence is unmoving and quiescent, and defies all idle talk about it. ...

Chinul continues:

Yen-shou's *Yusimgyŏl* says that in this Mind is gathered myriad mysteries and hosts of spiritual things, it is the king of *dharmas;* it is where the three vehicles and five natures return quietly, it constitutes the mother of a thousand saints; it alone is sublime and precious, having no peer and equals; it truly is the origin of the great *Tao* and the essence of the true *Dharma*. If you believe this all the Bodhisattvas of the past, present, and future have studied this Mind together, and all the Buddhas of the past, present, and future have realized this Mind together. The entire *Tripiṭaka* sets forth this Mind; all the sentient beings' delusions err with regard to this Mind, and the arising of enlightenment in the practioners is enlightened in this Mind. The mutual transmission [of the *Dharma*] by all the patriarchs transmits this Mind, and all the monks of the whole world seek this Mind. If one is conversant with this Mind, every item is proper and every thing is luminous; but if one is lost from this Mind, one stumbles everywhere and every thought is stupid and mad. This Essence is none other than the Buddha-Nature originally possessed by all sentient beings, and it is the source from which the entire world originates. Therefore, the Buddha kept silence at Gṛdhrakūṭa, Subhuti forgot words under the rock, Bodhidharma gazed at the wall in Shaolin cave, and the

---

[38] *T.* 48, p. 401b.

layman Vimalakīrti shut his mouth in Vaiśālī; all these were expounding the mysterious Essence of this Mind. Those who enter the garden of the patriarchs for the first time should know this Essence of Mind above all.[39]

Eloquent as these words are, they hardly explain the True Mind for us. For a more substantial explanation of the Essence of True Mind we have to refer specifically to the view held by Shen-hui and Tsung-mi, which Chinul adopted because of its clarity.

According to Tsung-mi's version of the Ch'an tradition, True Mind had been silently transmitted by the patriarchs in China from mind to mind until Shen-hui had to break the silence by enunciating "one word 'knowing'" as "the gate to myriad mysteries." Here is Tsung-mi's account of the story as found in Chinul's *Chŏryo*:

[I have previously mentioned that the transmission of Mind in India was mostly combined with *sūtras* and treatises, and that they were not two different paths.] But in this country [China], people erred from Mind and attached themselves to texts, and took the name to be the essence. Bodhidharma, as an excellent means of expediency (*upāya*), rejected the texts and transmitted the Mind; he suggested the name—Mind being the name—but silently showed its Essence —knowing being the Essence. He taught [Hui-ko, the second Chinese patriarch] [the exercise of] gazing at the wall, leading him to cut off all other conditions. When all the conditions were cut off, he asked him whether it meant complete annihilation or not. [Hui-ko] answered, "Though all conditions are cut off, it does not mean complete annihilation." "How do you prove," asked Bodhidharma, "that it is not complete annihilation?" "I know it clearly myself, but words cannot reach it." The master then confirmed it saying, "This is the pure Mind of Self-Nature; do not have doubt any more." If the answer had not fit, Bodhidharma would have merely prevented misunderstanding and would have required further contemplation, but he would not say in advance the word "knowing." He would wait until other people become enlightened by themselves,

---

[39] *Pŏbŏ*, pp. 66–67. "Five natures" refers to the five kinds of predetermined spiritual capacity with one of which each human being is born, according to Fa-hsiang philosophy: *srāvaka*, *pratyekabuddha*, Bodhisattva, undetermined nature, and the sentient beings with no nature (who thus can never attain Buddhahood). For the stories about Subhuti, Vimalakīrti, and Bodhidharma, see Suzuki, *Second Series*, p. 26.

and then would verify its truth. He confirmed it only after they personally had realized the Essence [of the Mind], thereby making them get rid of further doubts. This was called the silent transmission of Mind-seal. What is called the "silent" meant silence with regard to the word "knowing," it did not mean complete silence. The mutual transmission had been in this manner up to the sixth generation. When it came to the time of Ho-tse [Shen-hui], however, because sects competed with each other, and since, seeking the silent transmission, he could not find the proper capacity [of man] and conditions, he finally taught that the one word "knowing" is the gate to myriad mysteries, lest the essential teaching should perish. He also had the prophecy of Bodhidharma in mind. "The life of my *Dharma* would be like a hanging thread in six generations after me."[40]

According to Tsung-mi, Shen-hui was deserving of special credit in that he, going beyond mere negativistic expressions, clearly identified "knowing" as the Essence of True Mind just as liquidity is the essence of water.[41] Here is another passage by Tsung-mi regarding Shen-hui's view:

All saints agree that all *dharmas* are like a dream; thus deluded thoughts are originally quiescent and the world of dust originally empty. The empty quiescent Mind is spiritually knowing and never darkens; this empty quiescent Mind is none other than the pure Mind transmitted by Bodhidharma. No matter whether deluded or enlightened, Mind is knowing in itself; it is not born on the basis of conditions, nor does it arise on account of external objects. When deluded, there are mental defilements (*kleśa*), but knowing is not

---

[40] *Chŏryo*, pp. 801–02. The sentence in brackets at the beginning of this quotation is from Tsung-mi, *T*. 48, p. 405b, from where Chinul is quoting this passage. "The gate to myriad mysteries" is the famous expression occurring in the first passage of the first chapter of the *Tao-te-ching*. Hu Shih, *op. cit.*, p. 15, translates *chih* 知 as "knowledge." Suzuki, despite his criticism of this—he proposes "*prajñā* intuition" instead—himself uses the word "knowledge," which is misleading; see his *Second Series*, p. 34. "*Prajñā* intuition" may well express the meaning of "knowing" but is not suitable as a translation of the Chinese word *chih*; see his, "Zen, A Reply to Hu Shih," *Philosophy East and West* III, 1 (1953): 31ff.

[41] *T*. 406c., and *Chŏryo*, pp. 703–04. The idea is that "knowing" directly reveals the Essence of Mind, whereas such terms as "nonaction," "no-Characteristics," and others are merely negative descriptions.

mental defilements; when enlightened, there are miraculous transformations, but knowing is not miraculous transformations. The one word "knowing", however, is the source of myriad mysteries.[42]

Chinul also says basically the same thing:

> All *dharmas* are like dreams and hallucinations; deluded thoughts are originally quiescent, and the dust world is originally empty. Where all *dharmas* are empty, there is spiritual knowing never darkening. This Mind of empty quiescence and spiritual knowing is the original face [本來面目] of yourself. It is also the seal of the *Dharma* that has been esoterically transmitted by all the Buddhas of the three worlds, by the patriarchs throughout the generations, and by all the people of great learning in the world (*Po.* 45).

Further:

> Where all *dharmas* are empty, there is spiritual knowing never darkening, and thus it is not like nonsentient beings. Nature itself has divine understanding; this is the empty, quiescent, and spiritually knowing Essence of pure Mind. And this pure Mind of empty quiescence is the excellent pure and clear Mind of all the Buddhas of the three worlds, and it is the original enlightenment-nature of sentient beings (*Po.* 47).

These statements are saying that the Essence (*ch'e* 體) of this ultimate reality, True Mind, is not merely empty and quiescent but also has the positive aspect of spiritual knowing, so that Mind is not like the state of insentient beings.[43] It is *śūnyatā* or *dharmatā* plus something

---

[42] *Chŏryo*, p. 683. Tsung-mi explains that "empty" means to empty away all Characteristics, "quiescence" means the unchanging Real Nature, and "knowing" reveals directly the Essence itself; see *ibid.*, p. 704.

[43] Suzuki tells us the following interesting story:
A teacher of the *Avataṁsaka* came to see Hui-hai and asked, "Master, do you believe that nonsentient beings are Buddhas?" "No," said the master, "I do not believe so. If nonsentient beings are Buddhas, living beings are worse off than the dead; dead donkeys, dead dogs will be far better than living human beings. . . . If nonsentient beings are Buddhas, you, Reverend Sir, had better pass away this moment and attain Buddhahood" (*Second Series*, pp. 85–86).

Significantly, Shen-hui also, quoting from the *Nirvāṇa-sūtra* (of Mahāyāna), clearly

74

luminous called "knowing"; hence it is the Buddha-Nature or the enlightenment-nature that is originally in sentient beings,[44] and is said to be our "original face", that is, our authentic self.[45] Further, these two aspects, quiescence (*chŏk* 寂) and knowing (*chi* 知), *within* the Essence of True Mind are again construed by Chinul as having the relationship of essence and function (*ch'e* and *yong*).[46] According to Chinul, the empty-quiescent aspect is the *samādhi* inherent in our Self-Nature, and spiritual knowing corresponds to the *prajñā* of the Self-Nature. And the relationship between *samādhi* and *prajñā* is that of inseparable essence and function:

> If we establish the *Dharma* and its aspects, the thousand ways to enter into the truth do not go beyond *samādhi* and *prajñā*. If

---

says that nonsentient beings are devoid of Buddha-Nature; see J. Gernet, trans. *Entretiens du Maître Dhyāna Chen-Houei du Ho-Tsö* (Hanoi: 1949), p. 66. There was also the doctrine in Chinese Buddhism that even nonsentient beings have the Buddha-Nature; concerning this, see Kamata, *Chūgoku kegon shisōshi no kenkyū*, pp. 440–65. The crucial thing is the idea that if Suchness or Buddha-Nature is simply identified with emptiness, then it may well be the state of nonsentient beings. But Suchness or True Mind does not merely mean emptiness, but also has a positive *nonempty* aspect. The following words of the *Ch'i-hsin-lun* are important as forming the background of Chinul's (and Tsung-mi's) conception of the Essence of True Mind: "Next, Suchness has two aspects if predicated in words. One is that it is truly empty (*śūnya*), for [this aspect] can, in the final sense, reveal what is real. The other is that it is truly nonempty (*a-śūnya*), for its essence itself is endowed with undefiled and excellent qualities." *The Awakening of Faith*, trans. by Y. S. Hakeda (New York: 1967), p. 34. And, concerning this positive "nonempty" aspect of Suchness, it says: "From the beginning, Suchness in its nature is fully provided with all excellent qualities; namely, it is endowed with the *light* of great wisdom, [the qualities of] *illuminating* the entire universe, of true cognition and mind pure in its self-nature; of eternity, bliss, Self, and purity; of refreshing coolness, immutability, and freedom." Hakeda, p. 65 (my italicizing). As the last part of this quotation shows, this positive conception of Suchness is derived from the positive conception of *nirvāṇa* set forth in the *Nirvāṇa-sūtra*.

44 It is what is called in the *Ch'i-hsin-lun* "Original Enlightenment" 本覺, as distinguished from the "Enlightenment-to-be-realized" 始覺. See Hakeda, pp. 37–38.

45 A famous story about Hui-neng when he fled from the Fifth Patriarch after he had received the *Dharma* says that Hui-ming, who was pursuing Hui-neng, got enlightened when he was asked by the latter, "Not thinking of good, not thinking of evil, just at this moment, what is your original face before your mother and father were born?" See Yampolsky, pp. 109–10. Tsung-mi uses the word "true Self," *T.* 48, p. 406b.

46 This relationship of essence and function (not capitalized) should be clearly distinguished from the initial distinction of the two aspects of True Mind: mysterious Essence and mysterious Function. We are presently examining mysterious Essence which is again said to have two aspects, essence and function.

we take their essence, they are simply the two aspects, essence and function, of Self-Nature; what we have previously called empty quiescence and spiritual knowing is this. *Samādhi* is the essence, and *prajñā* the function; the function is the function of the essence, and so *prajñā* is not separate from *samādhi*; the essence is the essence of function, and so *samādhi* is not separate from *prajñā*. *Samādhi* being *prajñā*, it is quiescent and yet always knowing; *prajñā* being *samādhi*, it is knowing and yet always quiescent. It is as Ts'ao-ch'i [Hui-neng] says: "The ground of the mind without confusion is the *samādhi* of Self-Nature, and the ground of the mind without stupidity is the *prajñā* of Self-Nature (*Po*. 51).

It is possible, as the last part of this quotation suggests, that Chinul picked up this important idea of the inseparable unity of *samādhi* and *prajñā* as two aspects of the Essence of True Mind (Self-Nature) from the *Platform Sūtra*.[47] But this *sūtra*, on the other hand, is closely related to Shen-hui's thought, where a similar idea is found. Shen-hui says:

Nondwelling is quiescence, and quiescent essence is called *samādhi*. From above the essence, natural wisdom comes into being, and it knows the originally quiescent essence; it is called *prajñā*.[48]

---

[47] It is said in the *Platform Sūtra*:
Good friends, my teaching of the Dharma takes meditation (*ting*) and wisdom (*hui*) as its basis. Never under any circumstances say mistakenly that meditation and wisdom are different; they are a unity, not two things. Meditation itself is the substance of wisdom; wisdom itself is the function of meditation. At the very moment when there is wisdom, then meditation exists in wisdom; at the very moment when there is meditation, then wisdom exists in meditation. Good friends, this means that meditation and wisdom are alike. Students, be careful not to say that meditation gives rise to wisdom, or that wisdom gives rise to meditation, or that meditation and wisdom are different from each other (Yampolsky, p. 135).

Ting 定 (*samādhi*) should rather be translated as "concentration." than "meditation." Suzuki's *The Zen Doctrine of No Mind* (New York: 1972) is devoted to the elucidation of the significance of this idea of the unity of wisdom and concentration (he also uses "meditation" for *ting*) in Zen; see also his article cited already, "Zen: A Reply to Hu Shih." For a similar passage in Shen-hui, see Gernet, p. 50. Gernet translates *ting* as "concentration" and *hui* as "sapience." The significance of this idea in terms of Sŏn cultivation will be discussed later in section three of this chapter.

[48] Translated from Kamata's *Shūmitsu kyōgaku*, p. 376.

Further:

> The original essence is quiescent, and from this quiescent essence arises knowing, and it discriminates the various colors of the world such as blue, yellow, red, and white; it is called *prajñā*.[49]

Ch'eng-kuan, the famous Hua-yen master, says the following about Shen-hui's thought:

> The learned Shui-nan [Shen-hui] says: Function attached to essence is called knowing, and essence attached to function is called quiescence. Attached to the lamp, it is the light, and attached to the light, it is the lamp. If the lamp is taken as the essence and the light as the function, they are two without being two. That the one word "knowing" is the gate to myriad mysteries is also the word of Shui-nan.[50]

This idea of quiescence is based upon the philosophy of Emptiness (*śūnyatā*), and it is assumed to be readily understandable. But the aspect of knowing, the functional aspect of the Essence of True Mind, demands closer attention and examination. Thus Chinul tries to explain this mysterious reality through the following dialogue:

> Although there exist many clues for entering into the truth, I will point out one path for you that you may return to the origin [of your own being]: Do you hear the crows crying and the magpies twittering? "Yes, I do," answered [the person]. Listen again, then, to the nature of your hearing; are there still various sounds? "When

---

[49] *Ibid.* Suzuki's *No Mind* as a whole is an exploration of this mystery of the arising of *prajñā* (knowing) in the state of quiescence (*samādhi*), which he calls Unconscious. He says:

> In this Self-Nature [Essence of True Mind] there is a movement, an awakening, and the Unconscious becomes conscious of itself. This is not the region where the question "Why?" or "How" can be asked. The awakening or movement or whatever it may be called is to be taken as a fact which goes beyond refutation. The bell rings, and I hear its vibrations as transmitted through the air. This is a plain fact of perception. In the same way, the rise of consciousness in the Unconscious is a matter of experience; no mystery is connected with it, but, logically stated, there is an apparent contradiction, which once started goes on contradicting itself eternally. Whatever this is, we have now a self-conscious Unconscious or a self-reflecting Mind. Thus transformed, Self-Nature is known as Prajñā (*No Mind*, p. 124).

[50] Translated again from Kamata, p. 374.

it comes to this," replied he, "all the sounds and distinctions are not there." Wonderful, wonderful! This is the path of entering into the truth by Kwanŭm [Kuan-yin 觀音]. I ask you further: you say that when it comes to this all the sounds and distinctions are not there; but, at such a moment, does it mean emptiness? "Originally it is not empty," answered he, "it is very clear and not dark." What, then, is this non-empty Essence? "Also, having no form, words cannot reach it." This is none other than the very life of all the Buddhas and patriarchs; have no further doubt (*Po.* 45–46).

This fascinating conversation, which reminds us of the conversation of Bodhidharma with Hui-ko—or even of an Upanishadic dialogue— is an example of what Chinul calls the act of *panjo* 返照 (inward illumination).[51] It is an act designed to reach the deep inner reality through the introspective method. We have said that True Mind is not a mere psychological concept. Nevertheless, as is evident in the use of the word Mind, it is related to psychic phenomena, or it is some kind of reality that can be known through the deep introspective act. In the conversation above, hearing manifold sounds refers to our ordinary psychic activities. When we further "hear the nature" of our hearing, however, the quiescent and empty state is said to appear; and, what is more important, Chinul says that it does not mean a mere empty state, but that there is present in it something luminous, something "nonempty."

Could it mean that it is the mind itself that lies behind all our psychic activities, some kind of mental substance, perhaps the soul? In fact, Chinul sometimes comes close to suggesting this view—which has been regarded as heretical in Buddhist doctrine, particularly in the Theravāda tradition—in his *Susimgyŏl*, where he contrasts *ponsim* 本心 (original mind) with *saeksin* 色身 (form-body, *rūpakāya*) and attributes all our activities to the former as the agent or the subject.[52] But we must be cautious. First, as we shall see when we consider the

---

[51] More fully, it is called *hoegwang panjo* 廻光返照, which means "turning the light back and illuminating inward"; it is a common term in Ch'an, not particularly Chinul's own. We will come back to this again later. This approach to truth is given in the *Nŭngŏmgyŏng* (*Śūraṅgama-sūtra*). "Kwanum" literally means "contemplation of sound."

[52] See *Pŏbŏ*, pp. 40, 45.

mysterious Function of True Mind, Chinul says that all our psychic activities are simply the Function of True Mind, and that "one who knows [the True Mind] calls it [the agent of psychic activities] the Buddha-Nature, whereas one who is ignorant calls it soul [*chŏnghon* 精魂]."[53] Second, Chinul is clearly aware of the dualistic view of body and mind. Thus in his postscript written for the reengraving of the *Platform Sūtra*, he indicates that the *sūtra* is not free from the dualistic view that the body is impermanent whereas the mind is permanent.[54] But he says that this apparent dualistic view should be understood merely as an *upāya* designed to lead people to the highest truth where no distinction between body and mind exists. The following remarks of Chinul make this point clear and also have a direct bearing on the conversation above:

> In short, the *Platform Sūtra* makes the students of the *Tao* or lay people understand Suchness by inwardly illuminating the nature of their bodies' seeing and hearing; only then it lets them see the secret of oneness of body and mind. If it said directly without this good expediency that body and mind are one, then even the cultivators of

---

[53] *Pŏbŏ*, p. 40. In other words, what we call "mind" or "soul" is for the enlightened person the Buddha-Nature; but the reverse of this statement, that is, to say that Buddha-Nature is the mind or soul would not hold true for Chinul, unless this statement is made by an enlightened person as an *upāya* on the level of expedient truth. As we shall see, this is, according to Chinul, exactly what the *Platform Sūtra* does.

[54] It is a charge originally made by Hui-chung, a disciple of Hui-neng, and it is to this charge that Chinul is replying in the way of an apologetic for the *sūtra*. According to Chinul's postscript, Hui-chung's charge is as follows:

> These days, for me the mind and body are alike so that there is no room outside of Mind and there is completely no birth-and-destruction; but you in the south say that while body is impermanent the divine Nature is permanent so that half has birth-and-destruction while the other half does not.

Now, to this charge Chinul admits that the *sūtra* actually has such a dualistic view, and cites as evidence the passage which once captivated him so powerfully: "The Nature of Suchness itself gives rise to thoughts, and neither eyes, ears, nose, nor tongue can think." Here Chinul seems to be taking Nature of Suchness as the permanent mind (agent) behind our ever-changing mental activities through the organs of the body. But, as the next quotation from Chinul's comments show, for him, Nature or Suchness knows no distinction of body and mind; it is only as an *upāya* that the *sūtra* identifies Nature with the mind. It is interesting to know that Dōgen was also aware of Hui-chung's criticism; see Hee-Jin Kim, *Dōgen Kigen*, p. 216. Also, see Suzuki, *No Mind*, p. 80 on this issue.

the *Tao* who have left home would beget doubts, for they see with their eyes the impermanence of the body; how much less would the thousands of lay people be able to believe and accept the secret? It is for this reason that the patriarch made discourses to lure people in accordance with their capacity.[55]

Accordingly, we have to be careful and should not simply identify True Mind (its knowing aspect particularly) with the soul or some sort of psychic center. Here is what Chinul further says about it:

Now, what we are saying is that the Mind-Nature of all sentient beings, no matter whether foolish or wise, good or evil, fowl or beast, is by nature always aware so that it is different from trees and stones. But it is not the consciousness making distinctions according to the objects, nor is it identical with wisdom realizing enlightenment. It simply means that the Self-Nature of Suchness is not like lifeless empty space, because Nature itself is always aware (*C.* 766).

Here Chinul clearly says that this "knowing" does not mean knowledge based upon our ordinary consciousnesses. And it is not even to be confused with the "wisdom realizing enlightenment."[56] Yet it is knowing, hence it is knowing that is not knowing:

The deluded mind, when faced with objects, knows with knowing. Faced with objects, favorable or adverse, it gives rise to avarice and anger, or with regard to the objects of neutral nature it produces stupidity. Once the three poisons of avarice, anger, and

---

[55] *Hyŏnt'o pŏnyŏk Yukcho tan'gyŏng*, p. 6 of the appendix.

[56] Here, two kinds of *prajñā* should be distinguished, one the *prajñā* of Self-Nature (what we are considering now), namely "knowing," and the other the *prajñā* realizing enlightenment, namely "wisdom"; the first would be equivalent to the Original Enlightenment of the *Ch'i-hsin-lun* and the second to the Enlightenment-to-be-realized. In other words, one belongs to the "source of Sŏn" and the other to the "act of Sŏn." The second is ontologically based upon the first, but they should be distinguished. Suzuki makes a good point when he says: "*Chih* [knowing] is the absolute object of *prajñā* and at the same time *prajñā* itself. The Chinese Buddhist philosophers frequently call it, tautologically, *pan ju chih chih-hui* 般若之智慧 (*hannya no chiye* in Japanese), for they want to have *chih-hui*, as it is ordinarily understood, sharply distinguished from *prajñā* (*pan-ju*)." See his article cited already, p. 33. But in his *No Mind*, Suzuki himself often does not differentiate the two—perhaps deliberately, but causing confusion for us—when he discusses Hui-neng's "seeing into Nature"; see particularly pp. 41–42.

80

stupidity arise in relation to the objects, it is recognized as the deluded mind. A patriarch said that the conflict of the adverse and the favorable is the disease of the mind. Know, therefore, that to be faced with the proper and the improper is called deluded mind. True Mind, on the other hand, knows without knowing; roundly illuminating with the equanimity of thought, it is different from grass and trees, and it does not generate hate or love; thus it is different from the deluded mind. Faced with objects, it is empty and clear without hatred and love; knowing without knowing, it is True Mind (*Po.* 85).

Chinul continues with the words from the *Chao-lun* of Seng-chao, the famous disciple of Kumārajīva:

Therefore it is said in the *Chao-lun* that the Mind of the saint is subtle and without Characteristics, and hence cannot be regarded as a being; but when one uses it, it is all the more diligent, and so it is not to be taken as nonbeing. Since it is not a being, it knows and yet does not know; and since it is not nonbeing, it does not know and yet knows. For this reason, the knowing which is not knowing cannot be said to be different from the Mind of the saint.[57]

In short, Chinul says that the Essence of True Mind, quiescent and yet knowing, is different from ordinary consciousness, which may be knowing but is not quiescent. It is also different from the inanimate state which may be quiescent but is not knowing.

Yet, according to Chinul, this knowing, though not consciousness or even wisdom (realizing enlightenment), is nevertheless the basis and origin of our every empirical thinking and knowledge. And here we come to the other aspect of True Mind, its mysterious Function. Chinul says:

The empty, quiescent, and spiritual knowing that I have elucidated, though not the consciousness making distinctions nor wisdom realizing enlightenment, can *produce both the consciousness and the*

---

[57] *Pŏbŏ*, pp. 85–86. Seng-chao's *Pan-jo wu-chih-lun* 般若無知論 in particular is a discussion of this subtle truth; see W. Liebenthal, trans. *On Prajñā not cognizant, Chao Lun: The Treatises of Seng-chao* (Hong Kong: 1968).

wisdom; it can become ordinary beings as well as saints, practice good as well as evil. Its Functions, favorable and adverse, are ever changing with myriad aspects. The reason is *that its Essence is knowing*. When faced with various conditions, it is able to distinguish all kinds of right and wrong, like and dislike etc.[58]

This says that the quiescent and unchanging Essence of True Mind has at the same time the dynamic changing aspect where all particulars and distinctions of our ordinary empirical life come alive again. The basic philosophy underlying this view, as we have mentioned, is provided in the *Ch'i-hsin-lun*, where the *Tathāgatagarbha* as Suchness is identified with the *ālayavijñāna* as Birth-and-Destruction in the Essence-Function (*t'i-yung* 體用) relationship,[59] so that the former is given the attribute of dynamic character and is conceived of as the very principle of the development of the phenomenal world. This development is called in technical terms *yǒraejang yǒn'gi* 如來藏緣起. This system of thought was more fully developed by the Hua-yen philosophy of the famous Fa-tsang. The crux of the matter is how we view the nature of the phenomenal world. If ignorant, we see it as independent of the Absolute so that *saṃsāra* is no more than *saṃsāra*; if enlightened, however, we see it as the functional aspect of the Absolute, or Suchness, so that *saṃsāra* is *nirvāṇa*. The dichotomy of *saṃsāra* and *nirvāṇa*, sentient beings and Buddha, time and eternity, and Becoming and Being is closed in interpenetration. To use the Hua-yen philosophical expression, between the Principle (*li*) and Phenomena (*shih*) there is no obstruction (*wu-ai*). According to Chinul, the reason why this interpenetration is

---

[58] *Chǒryo*, p. 768; italics mine.

[59] On the development of these two concepts in Mahāyāna Buddhism, and about how these originally two separate ideas came to be related in this way, see Katsumata Shunkyō, *Bukkyō ni okeru shinshikisetsu no kenkyū* (Tokyo. 1961), pp. 513–637. Also, concerning the early development of this thought in China, see the remaining chapter of the book. Hui-yüan of the Ti-lun School (Southern) was one of the conspicuous early promoters of this idea. Tsung-mi, in the same place where he distinguishes the four different meanings of the word *hsin* (mind), compares the relationship of *Tathāgatagarbha* and *ālayavijñāna* to that of gold and golden things like rings, T. 48, pp. 401c–402a. For a study of the history of the concepts, *t'i* and *yung*, in Chinese philosophy, see Shimada Kenji, "Tai-yo no rekishi ni yosete," *Tsukamoto Hakushi shōju kinen Bukkyō shigaku ronshū* (Kyoto: 1961), pp. 416–30.

possible, why the unchanging Essence is able to assume the changing functional aspect, is the luminous and knowing character of the Essence itself of True Mind. But before going into this problem, let us see how Chinul describes this mysterious Function of True Mind:

The mysterious Essence of True Mind is originally unmoving; it is comfortable, calm, true, and constant. *Upon this true and constant Essence, however, the mysterious Function appears and does not prevent [us from] obtaining subtleties according to the stream.* Thus a verse by a patriarch says, "Mind moves with the myriad circumstances, and yet wherever it may revolve it can really keep profundity; when you *recognize Nature while following the stream*, you have neither joy nor sorrow." Thus at all times no matter whether you move, use, give, or do; whether you go to the east or west; whether you eat food or wear clothes, take spoon or move chopsticks, or look to the right or left; all these are the appearances of the mysterious Function of True Mind. Ordinary beings, deluded and perverted, merely think of wearing clothes when they wear clothes, merely think of eating when they eat food; whatever they may do, they move *merely following the Characteristics.* This is why they do not realize [the True Mind], though it is present in everyday life, and do not know it, though it is present in front of their eyes. If they are the *knowers of Nature*, they never become darkened in moving, using, giving, and doing. Thus a patriarch said: "If in the womb, [True Mind] is called spirit; if in the world, it is called man; if in the eyes, it sees and illumines; if in the ears, it hears; if in the nose, it smells; if in the mouth, it talks; if in the hands, it grasps; if in the feet, it travels around; if present everywhere, it embraces the whole *Dharmadhātu*, and if withdrawn, it exists in a tiny particle of dust. Those who know it call it the Buddha-Nature, and those ignorant of it call it soul.[60]

Our daily life and world are themselves regarded as the Function of True Mind *if* we "recognize Nature while following the stream." The "stream" here, of course, refers to our daily life and the world ever-changing, and "Nature" refers to the Essence of True Mind, the quiescent and knowing Mind. In other words, if we carry out our everyday affairs with reference to the Essence of True Mind, they are

---

[60] *Pŏbŏ*, pp. 67–68; I have italicized several key passages.

mysteriously transformed or elevated—or may we use the term "sanctified"?—into the Function of True Mind (Suchness, Buddha-Nature, *Tathāgatagarbha*). By contrast, "merely following the Characteristics" is the way ordinary beings live who are not "knowers of Nature." Not simply to deliver ourselves to the ever-changing Characteristics, not to live unreflectively involved in the worldly life at the mercy of manifold circumstances, and not to be forgetful of one's true self, that is, True Mind, is what is meant by "recognizing Nature while following the stream." So long as we do so, there is no need to leave or reject the "stream," to negate our ordinary empirical life, history, and world. For *samsāra*, with its myriad aspects of ever-changing particularities, is the functional manifestation of True Mind. To recognize Nature while following the stream—or to recognize Form (*rūpa*) as Emptiness (*śūnyatā*) to use the famous expression in the *Heart Sūtra*—does not mean reducing rich phenomenal diversities to the empty and abstract principle of Nature. On the contrary, all particulars of the empirical world are there in their sheer irreducible particularity, and this is what Chinul calls the mysterious Function of True Mind.

Now this recognition of Nature while one follows the stream of life, is possible because, ontologically, Nature (the mysterious Essence) itself gives rise to the stream of *samsāra*, the mysterious Function of True Mind. Or, rather, Suchness itself is not an abstract rarefied world but has the aspect of fullness and diversity of particulars. To borrow from the *Heart Sūtra* again, Form is Emptiness but Emptiness is Form; 'true Emptiness" (*chin'gong* 眞空) is "mysterious existence" (*myoyu* 妙有). Nature giving rise to Characteristics (Phenomena, Functions) is called in Hua-yen doctrine Origination-by-Nature (*sŏnggi* 性起) as distinguished from Origination-by-condition (*yŏn'gi* 緣起).[61] To see a phenomenon from the vantage point of Origination-by-Nature means to understand it in its phenomenality, in its conditioned nature, and thus in its Emptiness. So long as a thing is seen in its Nature of Origination-by-condition, it is Origina-

---

[61] Concerning the distinction between these two ideas, see Kamekawa Kyōshin, *Kegongaku*, pp. 103–27.

tion-by-Nature at the same time. Further, so long as one sees a phenomenon in this way, it is seen as a Function of the Essence of True Mind. Thus, for Chinul, the logic of Origination-by-Nature underlies the truth of the mysterious Function of True Mind. Every phenomenon, seen in this way, no longer becomes an obstruction to our spiritual freedom but is affirmed plainly as it is.[62] This, we recall, is exactly the truth that Chinul realized through his encounter with that crucial passage in the *Platform Sūtra*:

> The Self-Nature of Suchness gives rise to thoughts; though the six organs see, hear, perceive, and know, [you are] not stained by the myriad images, and the True Nature is always free.

The words immediately preceding this passage in the *Platform Sūtra* put the matter in a clear manner: "Suchness is the Essence of thoughts; and thoughts are the Function of Suchness."[63] In short, the mysterious Function of True Mind or Origination-by-Nature is a paradoxical reality; it is origination without origination, or "history" without "history." Once we know Origination-by-Nature, once we know the mystery of the Function of True Mind, we are already at the other shore of birth-and-destruction, because Function is the Function of the eternal Essence, and origination is the origination of the unchanging Nature:

> Now when we attain True Mind and fit in with the enlightenment-nature without birth-and-destruction, then we give rise to the mysterious Function without birth-and-destruction. The mysterious Essence is true and constant and has no birth-and-destruction, yet

---

[62] It is in this sense that the following words of Suzuki are to be understood:

Both in Te-shan and Huang-po, Zen is taught to be something in direct contact with our daily life; there are no speculations soaring heavenward, no abstractions making one's head reel, and no sentimental sweetness which turns religion into a love drama. Facts of daily experience are taken as they come to us, and from them a state of no-mind-ness is extracted. Says Huang-po in the above citations: "The original Mind is to be recognized along with the working of the senses and thoughts; only it does not belong to them, nor is it independent of them." The Unconscious, the recognition of which makes up *mushin* [no-mind], lines every thoughts (*No Mind*, pp. 132–33).

[63] Translated from the Chinese text in Yampolsky, p. 7.

the mysterious Function following the [changing] conditions [of life] may seem to have birth-and-destruction. Since, however, it is the Function born out of the Essence, it is none other than the Essence; how could there be birth-and-destruction? One who has attained [True Mind] realizes the true Essence, and so how could birth-and-destruction bother him? In the case of water, liquidity is its Essence and the waves its Function; since the liquidity has originally no birth-and-destruction, how could it have birth-and-destruction even if it were the liquidity of the waves? Yet, there being no waves apart from the liquidity, waves also have no birth-and-destruction (*Po.* 89).

Despite our foregoing discussion, we have not yet touched the core of the issue, namely, how the Essence of True Mind is able to assume the dynamic functional aspect, how Nature can give rise to various Characteristics. According to Chinul, it is because of the luminous knowing character of the Essence itself. It is this aspect of knowing that makes all the distinctions and diversities of the empirical world mysteriously reappear in the quiescent emptiness of True Mind. Here we should have recourse to the fine metaphor of the *maṇi* jewel that Tsung-mi employs in order to explain the different teachings on True Mind by the various sects of Sŏn:

> Just like a *maṇi* jewel, which is only round, pure, and clear, and has no Characteristics of different colors at all, the One Spiritual Mind-Nature is empty, quiescent, and constantly knowing; originally it has no distinctions whatsoever, not even the distinction of good and evil.
>
> Since the Essence is clear, it can manifest Characteristics of all the different colors when it comes into contact with external things; since the Essence is knowing, when it comes into contact with various conditions, it can distinguish all kinds of right and wrong, like and dislike, and carry out all kinds of activities mundane and supramundane. This is the changing aspect.
>
> Although the Characteristics themselves have distinctions, the clear jewel itself has never changed; although stupidity and wisdom, and good and evil, may have distinctions, and although worry and joy, and hatred and love, rise and disappear, the Mind that is knowing never ceases. This is the unchanging aspect (*C.* 695).

The core of this metaphor is that the jewel is not merely pure but also clear (the Essence of True Mind is not merely quiescent but also knowing), for due to this aspect of clarity, the jewel takes on and reflects various colors, while it itself does not undergo any change.[64] We have already mentioned that Chinul, following Shen-hui and the *Platform Sūtra*, construes the relationship between quiescence and knowing (purity and clarity of the jewel) as essence and function *within* the Essence of True Mind. Thus, it is this *unchanging function* within the Essence that gives rise to the *changing Function* of True Mind (clarity reflecting various colors). This is why it is crucial to recognize this knowing character of True Mind; it is "the gate to myriad mysteries." Also, this is why Tsung-mi, with his intellectual clarity, makes the distinction between two kinds of function, one changing and the other unchanging:

> The original Essence of True Mind has two kinds of function: One is the original function of Self-Nature, and the other is the function according to external conditions. If we compare them to copper, the quality of copper is its Essence of Self-Nature, its brightness the function of Self-Nature, and the reflections appearing on it the Functions according to conditions. ... Analogously, the constant quiescence of Mind is the Essence of Self-Nature, the constant knowing of Mind the function of Self-Nature, and to talk, to speak, and to distinguish are the Functions according to conditions.[65]

According to Tsung-mi, the Hung-chou (Ma-tsu Tao-i) Sect of Ch'an is well acquainted with the aspect of the Function according to conditions.[66] Hence it recognizes all our everyday activities as true, being the Function of True Mind (reflections on the clear jewel). But it is ignorant of the function of Self-Nature, that is, of

---

[64] Another popular metaphor is that of the mirror (its purity, clarity, and reflections); see Gernet, *op. cit.*, pp. 31–33.

[65] *Chŏryo*, p. 706. Suzuki does not clearly point out the distinction between these two kinds of function (which he translates as "Use") in his *No Mind*, so that often we are not certain to which of the two he is referring.

[66] This and the following view of Tsung-mi concerning the positions of various sects of Ch'an is taken from *Chŏryo*, pp. 694–707. How Chinul accepts Tsung-mi's evaluations will be discussed more fully later when we consider Chinul's theory of sudden enlightenment.

the knowing aspect of the Essence of True Mind, so that it is unable to distingusih the clear jewel from the colored one, being accustomed to the latter only. Chinul does not entirely agree with this view of Tsung-mi, but he agrees that it was Shen-hui who brought out the knowing aspect most clearly. The Northern Sect of Shen-hsiu, on the other hand, is ignorant even of the Function according to conditions, so that it regards various colors as real dirt, which has to be removed or cut off diligently in order for the clear jewel to appear brightly.[67] The Niu-t'ou Sect is so preoccupied with the idea of Emptiness that it even regards the pure and clear jewel itself as empty; hence its view is only half true, insofar as it recognizes the emptiness of the reflections. Again Chinul does not entirely agree with this judgment of Tsung-mi. Still, in terms of clarity and balance of view, it is Shen-hui's that Chinul recommends:

> Therefore, one who cultivates mind in this period of degenerate-*dharma* should first decide and discern the Nature and Characteristics of one's own mind according to the words and teaching shown by Ho-tse [Shen-hui] and should neither fall into quiescence [the particular tendency of the Niu-t'ou Sect] nor be bound by the changing conditions [Hung-chou Sect].[68]

---

[67] This popular view of Northern Sect is discredited by modern critical studies which attribute it largely to the propaganda of Shen-hui's line. See, for instance, Ui Hakuju, *Zenshūshi kenkyū* (Tokyo: 1939), pp. 269–75, 344–75.

[68] *Chŏryo*, p. 693. It must be clear by now that, ontologically, "knowing" occupies the middle position between Emptiness (quiescence) and Function (changing conditions); it is a mediator between these two. The significance of this view in Chinese Buddhist thought is that it transcends the polarity of Emptiness (*k'ung* 空) and Being (*yu* 有). This is made clear when Tsung-mi talks about three levels of truth instead of the two levels of truth taught by the School. of Emptiness (Mādhyamika or San-lun School): the first level of truth is concerned with the world of manifold diversity (Characteristics, Function, and Form), the second level is concerned with the world of Emptiness (Essence, quiescence), and the third level is the world of "knowing" (which forms, along with quiescence, the two aspects of Essence). This third level of truth concerns neither Emptiness nor Form, and both Emptiness and Form; thus it is the supreme truth of the middle path. Tsung-mi compares these three levels to the three aspects of a mirror: emptiness, clarity, and reflections. As Tsung-mi himself indicates, the three levels of truth correspond to the T'ien-t'ai doctrine of three levels of truth (which originally was derived from the philosophy of *prajñāpāramitā* literature): truth of Emptiness (*k'ung* 空), temporary existence (*chia* 假), and the supreme middle truth (*chung* 中). See *T.* 48, p. 407a for Tsung-mi's view above. The so-called School of

Thus far, we have studied Chinul's view of True Mind, the ultimate reality in Sŏn, in its two aspects of Essence and Function. Depending on which aspect we emphasize in our discussion of True Mind, there are two modes of discourse, called "the gate of total exclusion" 全揀門 and "the gate of total inclusion" 全收門, according to Chinul. Thus he says:

> This Essence of Mind, free from thoughts, which is to be realized, is none other than the Nature of all *dharmas*; it contains numerous mysteries and yet transcends words and speech. Since it transcends words and speech, it fits in with the path of sudden realization, forgetting mind; since it contains myriad mysteries, it has the aspect of the abundant prosperity of Characteristics and Functions. Therefore, this Mind-Nature has the gate of total exclusion and the gate of total inclusion. The cultivators of Mind should examine it carefully. As the Sŏn master Tsung-mi says, when One True Mind-Nature is set over against all *dharmas*, pure and impure, there are total exclusion and total inclusion. Total exclusion, penetrating into the Essence, straightforwardly points out the spiritual knowing as the Nature of Mind, and all the rest as empty delusion. ... Total inclusion says that all the *dharmas*, pure and impure, are nothing else than this Mind.[69]

To use different expressions, we may as well say that total exclusion refers to "world denial" and total inclusion to "world affirmation." But world affirmation here does not imply a shallow, one-dimensional affirmation. For Phenomena (*shih*) are affirmed only in their relationship with Principle (*li, śūnyatā*). This is what Chinul means when he says that only when Origination-by-condition is understood as

---

Nature (*hsing-tsung* 性宗) of Tsung-mi is the culmination of the tendency in Chinese Buddhism to go beyond the "negativistic" attitude of the *prajñāpāramitā* philosophy ever since its introduction to China. The role of the *Nirvāṇa-sūtra* and the *Ch'i-hsin-lun* in this tendency was crucial; see our previous discussions on pp. 74–75 of this book. The above difference of two levels of truth and three levels of truth is but one of the ten differences Tsung-mi points out with regard to the School of Nature and the School of Emptiness; see *T*. 48, pp. 406–407a.

[69] *Chŏryo*, pp. 778–79. According to Tsung-mi's *Ch'an-yüan*, from which Chinul is quoting this passage, by the gate of total exclusion the "School of Nature" embraces the "School of Emptiness," and by the gate of total inclusion it embraces the "School of Characteristics"; see *T*. 48, p. 405c.

Origination-by-Nature do we have total inclusion, a truth that Chinul says is very near to us but hard to apprehend.[70] Nor does world denial mean simple rejection of the empirical world, because the mysterious Essence of True Mind gives rise to mysterious Function, by which all phenomena come alive again, as we have seen.

Chinul, like Tsung-mi, thinks that Sŏn tends to be closer to the gate of total exclusion, whereas Kyo is nearer to the gate of total inclusion—even though one is never without the other—in their modes of discourse on the *Dharma*.[71] Whichever path we may follow, however, we must not become trapped by the method; one should be completely free as to exclusion and inclusion, and there should be no obstruction between Nature and Characteristics. To this end, Chinul says that we must not "succumb to the understanding of meaning" (*ŭihae* 意解) according to mere words; rather, by the act of inwardly illuminating the mind, we must have the experience of "the sudden enlightenment of One Mind."[72] How this should be done is the topic of our next section, which concerns the act of Sŏn and is entitled "the beginning of Sŏn." And with this we now move from the discussion of the world as seen by enlightened eyes, that is, True Mind (the "source of Sŏn") to the discussion of the religious problems faced by ordinary unenlightened beings—what their problems are and how the act of Sŏn can overcome them and enter into the world of truth.

2. *The Beginning of Sŏn: Sudden Enlightenment or the Path of Complete-sudden Faith and Understanding*

The foregoing verbal discussion of the ultimate reality, "the origin of Sŏn," is not meant to replace or to substitute for the dynamic "act of Sŏn" whereby we are to have the direct experience of that reality by ourselves. It is only a "mirror for the act of contemplation," not the act itself. To claim to know True Mind without the act of con-

---

[70] *Chŏryo*, p. 782.
[71] *Ibid.*, pp. 783–84.
[72] *Ibid.*, p. 781.

templation is foolish, like counting the wealth of other people.[73] "If one knows the potency [of the Mind]," says Chinul, "without having well illuminated inwardly one's own mind, one is a *Dharma* master of letters seeking fame and gain."[74]

Particularly, after the "exotericization" of Sŏn tradition by Shen-hui's enunciation of the word "knowing" as the key to the understanding of True Mind, Chinul thinks that we may be tempted to substitute word for experience. Thus an imaginary questioner asks Chinul whether the enlightenment after Shen-hui's exotericization can still be regarded as genuine. Chinul replies:

> Did I not tell you already? If one, without the personal effort of inward illumination, merely nods his head and says, "The present knowing thing [in me] is the mind of the Buddha," such a person is really far off the point. ... What I mean by those who realize Mind does not refer to those who merely remove doubt by words; it rather means those who directly get hold of this word of empty quiescence and spiritual knowing and make the effort of inward illumination and who, based upon that illumination, attain the Essence of Mind free from thoughts (*C.* 803–804).

The essential thing here is "inward illumination," Chinul's favorite word for the act of contemplation. More fully, it is called *hoegwang panjo*, which means "turning the light back and illuminating inwardly."[75] The "light" refers to the light of our eyesight, and hence figuratively the direction of our attention and concern. Turn the direction of your concern inward: this was Chinul's cry to Koryŏ Buddhism, the attention of which was occupied by the external world and its quest for fame and gain. It was the call to leave the world of superficialities in search of the inner realm where the mystery of the ultimate reality is to be met.

Inward illumination means not to be enchanted with external Characteristics and Phenomena, not to "follow the mere Character-

---

[73] *Chŏryo*, p. 747.
[74] *Hwaŏmnon chŏryo*, p. 451.
[75] *Pŏbŏ*, p. 19.

istics" nor to "run seeking in the outside [world]." From the viewpoint of inward illumination, not merely secular activities but also various religious acts could become no more than superficial, secondary affairs:

> The recitation of the name of the Buddha, reading the *sūtras*, and myriad [good] acts are the regular things monks should follow; what harm could there be in them? Yet if one does not penetrate to the root but, being attached to Characteristics, seeks externally, I am afraid that such a person will be laughed at by the man of wisdom (*Po*. 3).

Any realistic conceptions of Pure Land Buddhist practices is excluded, for to seek the Pure Land outside one's own Mind is to seek externally:

> Recently many monks devoted to doctrinal studies seek the *Tao* even forsaking their lives; but they are all attached to external Characteristics. They face towards the west, raise their voices, and call upon the Buddha, thinking it to be the act of *Tao*. They regard the secret of the ground of the mind that has been studied and elucidated by the Buddha and the patriarchs of old as the learning of fame and gain; they also consider it as no area for them and would never put their hearts into it, giving it up in an instant. Having already abandoned the secret of the cultivation of mind, they are ignorant of the potency of inward illumination. They adhere in vain to their clever minds and waste their lifetime efforts; they turn their backs on their minds and cling to the Characteristics, deeming it to be relying upon the sacred teaching. How would the man of wisdom be not pained by this (*Po*. 28.)?

Inward illumination, for Chinul, is not even to be identified with the contemplation of the *Dharmadhātu*, so far as the latter is understood as external truth. The contemplation of truth, however profound it may be, should be brought to bear upon one's own mind by inward illumination. Thus Chinul says:

> Even though people versed only in verbal explanation may talk about the nonobstructed Origination-by-condition of the *Dharmadhātu*, from the very beginning they do not inwardly reflect upon the

power and function of their own minds. Since they no longer contemplate [and understand] the Nature and Characteristics of the *Dharmadhātu* as the Essence and Function of their own minds, when will they be able to open up the dust of passion in their own minds and take out the fascicles of the *sūtra* as large as billions of worlds?[76]

In short, inward illumination has to be a searching of one's own mind above all; mind, nothing else, is the *locus* of the encounter with truth.

But for what purpose are we supposed to turn the light back and illumine inwardly? What concrete benefit is to follow this act of inward illumination? According to Chinul, the goal of inward illumination is to be enlightened in Mind (*osim* 悟心), that is, to have the experience of sudden enlightenment, or to realize that one's own mind, not something external, is none other than Buddhahood. This sudden enlightenment constitutes, according to Chinul, the very *beginning* of the act of Sŏn, whereby we are initiated into the realm of True Mind, or whereby we return to "the source of Sŏn." Here, of course, lies the radical nature of the message common to all Sŏn masters, not merely Chinul. But what is sudden enlightenement? Can it be discussed or explained at all?

Chinul does not avoid discussing sudden enlightenment. On the contrary, the discussion is necessary precisely because of the radical message of Sŏn—that Buddhahood is something that one begins with in Sŏn, not something one ends up with after a long process of self-cultivation. Chinul is concerned that some students of Sŏn might spend their whole lives in vain simply looking for sudden enlightenment, but gain no result at all—something Chinul thought as foolish as the "crazy wisdom that merely delves into texts" without the act of inward illumination. This is why Chinul warns against "those who simply regard the place of mutual esoteric transmission [of the *Dharma*] as the *Tao* [enlightenment]." And this is why clear and firm intellectual guidance is needed to prevent such a danger. But we must pay a price for this guidance. We must admit *two* kinds of sudden

---

[76] *Pŏbŏ*, p. 21. About this huge *sūtra*, see pp. 27–29 of this book. "Billions of worlds" is a translation of the word *taech'ŏn segye*, a technical term in Indian cosmology; see 'sanzen daisen sekai," *Bukkyōgo daijiten*.

enlightenment: understanding-enlightenment (*haeo* 解悟) and real-ization-enlightenment (*chŭngo* 證悟). One is exoteric enlightenment, so to speak, based upon clear "genuine teaching in words," and the other is esoteric enlightenment, "separate transmission outside of Kyo," accessible only through *hwadu* Sŏn.[77] Quoting from Ch'eng-kuan, Chinul puts the difference as follows:

> If we elucidate the forms of enlightenment, there are no more than two. One is understanding-enlightenment which clearly understands Nature and Characteristics, and the other is realization-enlighten-ment, which refers to the mind having profound subtlety (*C.* 724–725).

According to Chinul, understanding-enlightenment is the enlighten-ment that is given before, or even without, the process of cultivation.[78] Thus when Chinul talks about sudden enlightenment as the beginning of Sŏn, he means understanding-enlightenment that has yet to be followed by the process of gradual cultivation. This is why Chinul regards sudden enlightenment, understood as understanding-enlight-enment, as only the beginning of the act of Sŏn. Then the question arises why Chinul does not take gradual cultivation as the beginning, rather than such an understanding-enlightenment. Chinul's reason for not doing this will be considered in the next section when we dis-cuss Chinul's conception of cultivation in Sŏn. That sudden enlighten-ment should be the beginning of Sŏn is immutable in Chinul's ap-proach to Sŏn. It is only that this sudden enlightenment is exoteric understanding-enlightenment. It is time now to examine Chinul's view of sudden enlightenment.

---

[77] The meaning of this distinction, an important aspect of Chinul's approach to Sŏn, will be made clearer later. It needs our special attention here because in ordinary discussions of Zen, no such distinction has been made. Usually "satori" refers to realization-enlightenment rather than to understanding-enlightenment (which is a less decisive form of enlightenment, as we shall see). Suzuki's characterization of the nature of enlightenment, for instance, as "irrationality," "intuitive insight," "authoritative-ness," and others would seem to be more suitable for realization-enlightenment than for understanding-enlightenment though Suzuki does not make such a distinction; see his *Second Series*, pp. 31–39.

[78] *Pŏbŏ*, p. 119, or *Chŏryo*, pp. 726, 742, 755.

The content of sudden enlightenment is the Essence and Function of True Mind that we have already examined. But as an act constituting the beginning of the act of Sŏn, by which we are to recover our lost "original face," it necessarily means an enlightenment that deeply touches our own state of being, not simply intellectual insight into the ultimate reality conceived of as objective reality. In other words, the understanding in "understanding-enlightenment" is basically a self-understanding. Thus Chinul explains sudden enlightenment as follows by Tsung-mi's words:

> When a person who, erring and fallen from eternity, takes the four elements for body and the deluded thought for mind and calls them "I," meets a good friend who explains to him the meaning of Unchanging and Changing, Nature and Characteristics, and Essence and Function, he suddenly realizes that this spiritual clear knowing is his True Mind, and that the Mind is originally always quiescent, devoid of Nature and Characteristics, and is none other than the *Dharmakāya*; that body and mind are not different, it [Mind] being his true self that does not have the slightest difference from Buddhahood. Thus this is called "sudden." It is as if a high official, in a dream, is in a prison; his body is chained and he is harassed and troubled; he tries to escape in a hundred ways. When, however, a man calls to him, he suddenly awakes and sees that his body is in his house, and that his comfort, pleasure, wealth, and position are not different from other colleagues in the court at all.[79]

Sudden enlightenment thus means the sudden discovery of one's true self, that is, True Mind, which has remained unrecognized because of a dreamlike delusion. It is sudden, because the change from delusion to enlightenment, or the awakening from dream, is instantaneous; it is a mental revolution happening all of a sudden, not an evolution gradually emerging. And this discovery of one's own Nature is, according to Chinul, "seeing into Nature and becoming a Buddha."[80] Chinul says that "Nature" here does not mean Nature as

---

[79] *Chŏryo*, pp. 708–09.
[80] *Chŏryo*, pp. 711, 787.

opposed to Characteristics, but Nature which transcends such contrast ("devoid of Nature and Characteristics" in the above quotation), the Absolute that is neither Nature (Emptiness, quiescence) nor Characteristics (Form, Function) but at the same time both Nature and Characteristics.[81]

To know more clearly what enlightenment means, it is necessary to examine what constitutes delusion or ignorance:

> True Mind is identical in both ordinary beings and saints; yet ordinary beings view things with deluded mind and lose their own pure nature, and thus become distant [from saints]. For this reason True Mind does not appear before them, just as they do not recognize the shadow of a tree in darkness or the stream flowing under the ground, even though they exist. Thus a *sutra* says: "O men of good birth, it is as if a precious *mani* jewel, pure and clear, were shined upon by five colors and appeared in each way; the foolish ones would think that the *mani* really had the five colors. O men of good birth, the pure nature of complete enlightenment appears in body and mind, responding to each kind; those foolish ones say likewise that pure, complete enlightenment really has such a self-nature of body and mind (*Po.* 70).

According to this metaphor, the heart of delusion consists in mistaking the nature of the reflections or the Functions of True Mind. The deluded mind thinks foolishly that the jewel really has five colors, and it would not even believe someone who said that the jewel is clear.

According to Tsung-mi, various sects in Sŏn agree that the clear jewel exists, but the ways in which they see the relationship between the jewel and the reflections on it, and hence their conceptions of sudden enlightenment, differ from sect to sect.[82] First, the Northern Sect would acknowledge the hidden existence of the clear jewel, but it still thinks that the black color on it, for instance, really covers up the clarity of the jewel. Hence it should be wiped away, so that the clarity may reappear. This sect is ignorant of the nature of reflection,

---

[81] *Chŏryo*, p. 787. See the note 68 on pp. 88–89 of this book.
[82] The following description of the positions of the four representative sects of Sŏn is from Chinul's *Chŏryo*, pp. 694–707.

the Function of True Mind, and so it is ignorant of what sudden enlightenment is; it does not know that the reflection does not cover, and thus there is nothing to be wiped away. The Hung-chou Sect, on the other hand, is the opposite of this Northern Sect. Since the black jewel is the clear jewel, every mental defilement (*kleśa*) and every false thought is regarded as true, no distinction being made between the true and the false. Acts of discrimination in our daily life are nothing but Suchness. And for fear that people might get attached to the clear jewel, this sect deliberately emphasizes the identity of the clear jewel with the colored one, and regards the Essence of the clear jewel (its clarity) unobtainable forever. Tsung-mi believes that this sect places too much weight upon the reflections or the Functions at the expense of the Essence of True Mind. Hence it is apt to make the stupid mistake of not being able to recognize the clear jewel when it exists divested of the various colors, for "it does not see the colors [wherewith] to recognize [the jewel]." Also, it often mistakes other jewels for the clear *maṇi* jewel. From yet another perspective, the Niu-t'ou Sect says that everything is empty hallucination, not merely the reflections but even the clear jewel itself. Not merely are the various Characteristics and Functions empty, but the Essence and Nature of True Mind are also empty. Tsung-mi thinks that this sect merely removes the wrong but does not positively reveal the right; it is correct, so far as it does not admit the existence of defilements to be removed, but wrong, so far as it does not admit the nonempty Essence of True Mind to be revealed.[83] Thus it has only half a sudden enlightenment. Lastly, we come to the Sect of Ho-tse (Shen-hui), which Tsung-mi endorses. We have examined Shen-hui's view in our last section. Now let us compare it with the views of the other sects:

> When we are not deluded about the jewel, the black is no-black; it is none other than the [transparent] jewel itself. Likewise are all the other colors. Thus we are free with regard to being and non-being; since the clarity and the black interfuse, what obstruction can there be (*C.* 702)?

---

[83] Again, see our previous discussions on pp. 74–75.

Commenting on this, Tsung-mi says:

> To say that the black is no-black is the same as in the Niu-t'ou Sect [nonbeing]; to say that the black is none other than the jewel is the same as in the Hung-chou Sect [being]. If one personally sees the clear jewel, the deep [Shen-hui's view] necessarily covers the shallow [Niu-t'ou and Hung-chou] (C. 702).

Then Tsung-mi concludes:

> If one does not recognize that the clarity [of the jewel] is the Essence capable of reflection, and that it has no change forever, but merely says that the black and other [colors] are the jewel [Hung-chou], or thinks of seeking the jewel apart from the black [Northern Sect], or regards both the clarity and the black as nonexistent [empty; Niu-t'ou], all of these mean not yet seeing the jewel (C. 703).

What does Chinul think about this exposition of the views of the various sects? Impressed by the clarity of thought of both Shen-hui and Tsung-mi, Chinul confesses that this is why he once said that Shen-hui's enlightened understanding is high and bright and his decisions clear-cut (C. 703). Chinul agrees with Tsung-mi's judgment that the Northern Sect misses the essence of sudden enlightenment. He specifically points out that it is ignorant of Origination-by-Nature 性起, that is, the Function of True Mind, so that it falls into the dualistic view of the true and the false (C. 698).

As for Tsung-mi's evaluation of the other two sects, however, Chinul shows reservations. According to Tsung-mi, the Hung-chou Sect is close to sudden enlightenment, but not quite there; and the Niu-t'ou Sect half understands sudden enlightenment. Chinul apologizes for the sectarian view of Tsung-mi by complementing it with what is said in Tsung-mi's other work, the Ch'an-yüan.[84] Thus with

---

[84] See Chŏryo, pp. 691–708, passim for Chinul's apologetic remarks. The Ch'an-yüan was composed by Tsung-mi in a harmonizing spirit, with the aim of showing the unity between Sŏn and Kyo as well as between the various sects of Sŏn, whereas the Pŏpchip pyŏrhaengnok (on which our discussion of Tsung-mi's view has been based), like his Ch'an-men shih-tzu ch'eng-hsi-t'u, was not. But even in the latter, Tsung-mi leaves us the following intriguing remark, which is worth pondering for the student of comparative religion:

regard to the Niu-t'ou Sect, Chinul asserts that Tsung-mi is not really ignorant of the other aspect present in its teaching; Tsung-mi declares it to be only "half-understanding" of sudden enlightenment lest the followers of this sect should be preoccupied with "empty quiescence," neglecting "spiritual knowing." Likewise, Chinul draws our attention to Tsung-mi's statement (in his *Ch'an-yüan*) that Shen-hui and Hung-chou agree in their basic position, which is defined as "gathering Characteristics and attributing [them] to Nature" (*hoesang kwisŏng* 會相歸性). But Chinul says that Tsung-mi makes such a judgment about the Hung-chou Sect (that it is only "close" to sudden enlightenment) lest the followers of the sect should be trapped by Functions according to changing conditions, not doing justice to the quiescent knowing, that is, the unchanging Essence of True Mind.[85] Defending Tsung-mi in this manner, Chinul concludes:

> Today's cultivators of mind in this period of degenerate-*dharma* should first of all decide and discern, according to the words and teaching shown by Shen-hui, the Nature and Characteristics and the Essence and Function of their own minds, neither falling into empty quiescence nor being trapped by Function. If, after this

---

The difference between the above three views is: The first teaches that everything is false [Northern Sect], the second teaches that everything is true [Hung-chou Sect], and the last teaches that everything is empty [Niu-t'ou]. ... I, Tsung-mi, am by nature fond of verification, so I personally studied each of them and found out such to be their views. Should one take my words, however, and ask the scholars of those sects, they [my words] would all be rejected; if one asks [whether they teach] "being," they would answer "emptiness"; if one asks "emptiness," they would answer "being." Some might say that both are wrong or both unobtainable; likewise, "cultivation," "no cultivation," and so on and so forth. Their intention is that they are always afraid of falling [victim] to letters, and always concerned lest they should be trapped by what they had [already] obtained. Thus they repudiate whatever is said [about them]. Only when they meet students with serious mind would they instruct in detail and make them contemplate and illuminate [their minds] for long so that their act and understanding may ripen. [Yet, each sect again has many kinds of *upāya* with which they reject the blame of others and lure followers. All of this cannot be written here in detail. I have only displayed their chief views and the main outlines.]

The last portion in brackets is my addition from Kamata's text and translation, *Zen no goroku* 9, pp. 315–17, to the text in *Chŏryo*, p. 689. There is some difference between my translation and that by Jan Yün-hua, "Tsung-mi," p. 35.
[85] *Chŏryo*, pp. 691–93.

cultivation of authentic understanding, they review the teachings of the two sects, Hung-chou and Niu-t'ou, [the three teachings] would perfectly fit with each other; how can one generate the vain thought of adoption and rejection (*C.* 693)?

The above discussion of sudden enlightenment may suggest that it is an intellectual enterprise. Indeed, sudden enlightenment is for Chinul an intellectual accomplishment to some extent, because it is understanding-enlightenment. It is not a carefully guarded esoteric tradition accessible only to a small group of people, but is available to anybody, so long as one is possessed of the "sudden capacity" (the capacity for sudden teaching)[86] and so long as one is willing to venture. Nevertheless, as we have emphasized at the beginning of this section, even this exotericized sudden enlightenment is genuinely possible only at the price of a personal effort of inward illumination; it does not mean a purely verbal intellectual understanding. For there is a vast difference between theory and practice, and between word and experience. To put the matter more accurately, sudden enlightenment is for Chinul an experience of enlightenment *by the act of inward illumination based upon a "genuine teaching in words"*, such as we have considered thus far. Thus Chinul warns:

> If one does not generate timidity upon this [hearing the truth about the clear jewel] but has faith in one's mind, reflects the light even a little, and personally tastes the flavor of the *Dharma*, it is called the place of understanding-enlightenment for the cultivators of mind. If one, without the personal effort of inward illumination, merely nods his head and says that the present clear knowing (in me] is none other than the Buddha-mind, such a person is very far from getting at the point (*C.* 697).

So stated, Chinul's view of sudden enlightenment does not diverge

---

[86] By "sudden teaching" Chinul does not mean the fourth teaching in the five categories of teaching in the Hua-yen doctrinal classification system. According to Tsung-mi and Chinul, there are two kinds of sudden teaching: one according to the Buddha's mode of teaching (*hwaŭidon* 化儀頓) and the other according to man's capacity (*ch'uk-kidon* 逐機頓). The former is represented by the *Hua-yen Sūtra*, and the latter by the *Yüan-chüeh-ching* (*Sūtra of Complete Enlightenment*). In the present context, Chinul has in mind the latter type of sudden teaching; see *Chŏryo*, pp. 732–35. On Tsung-mi's view, see Araki Kengo, *Bukkyō to jukyō* (Kyoto: 1963), pp. 91–109.

much from that of Tsung-mi. But there is another feature in Chinul's theory of sudden enlightenment that adds to it an entirely new and unique aspect. We recall that Chinul twice had the experience of what was tantamount to his own sudden enlightenment. One experience occurred through his encounter with the *Platform Sūtra,* and the other came at his discovery of the *Treatise on Hua-yen.* This latter experience forms the background for a new version of sudden enlightenment by Chinul, the Hwaŏm version, so to speak. Though a Sŏn master, Chinul clearly says that sudden enlightenment is not a monopoly of the so-called Southern Sect.[87] If for Tsung-mi Sŏn and Kyo agree in their basic teachings, Chinul pushed this position even further and found such unity in the experience of sudden enlightenment itself, the hallmark *par excellence* of Sŏn Buddhism. Chinul not merely confirmed this unity in his own religious experience, but also elucidated it explicitly, calling it "the path of complete-sudden faith and understanding" 圓頓信解門 in at least two of his works, *Hwaŏm-non chŏryo* and *Wŏndon sŏngbullon* [*Treatise on the Complete-sudden Attainment of Buddhahood*]. By his systematic exposition of this path, Chinul not only articulated the meaning of sudden enlightenment more clearly, thus further helping the cause of exotericization, but at the same time tried to embrace Kyo in the act of Sŏn by interpreting Hwaŏm thought in terms of Sŏn, and—to no lesser degree— by interpreting Sŏn in terms of Hwaŏm inevitably. In short, by identifying the path of complete-sudden faith and understanding with the sudden enlightenment in Sŏn, Chinul "Sŏnized" Hwaŏm as well as "Hwaŏmized" Sŏn. This was Chinul's solution to the problem of the conflict between Sŏn and Kyo that was plaguing Koryŏ Buddhism. Let us now examine this solution.

First, before examining the meaning of "faith" and "understanding," we should clarify to what the term "complete-sudden" refers. Originally it was a term applied by the T'ien-t'ai School to its own teaching as the most perfect one. The *Lotus Sūtra,* for instance, was called the "complete-sudden *sūtra,*" the T'ien-t'ai system of medi-

---

[87] *Pŏbŏ,* p. 18; Chinul uses the word "sudden gate" which virtually means sudden enlightenment.

tation was called "complete-sudden *chih-kuan*," and so on.[88] In the Hua-yen doctrinal classification system, "sudden" refers to the fourth category of teaching, which transcends every word and thought, such as is taught in the *Vimalakīrti-sūtra* and by Ch'an. "Complete" refers to the Hua-yen teaching, meaning the most perfect teaching. Chinul uses the term "complete-sudden" to refer to the teaching of "one vehicle" or the "Buddha-vehicle" as contrasted with the teaching of the "three vehicles."[89] But more specifically, he means the Hua-yen teaching as interpreted by Li T'ung-hsüan. This is most evident in his *Wŏndon sŏngbullon*, which is an exposition of Li T'ung-hsüan's Hua-yen thought. The actual meaning of "complete-sudden," however, can only be known when we examine what Chinul means by "faith" and "understanding," the two concepts modified by it. Particularly, the meaning of "sudden," on which Chinul as a Sŏn master puts more emphasis, will be known clearly as we go on to study Chinul's conception of "faith."

"Faith," says Chinul, "is the origin of the *Tao* [enlightenment] and the mother of merits; it nourishes the root of all the good [*kuśala-mūla*]."[90] But the conception of faith, according to Chinul, is generally different in Sŏn and Kyo. He says:

> The gate of Kyo makes men and gods believe in cause and effect. Those who love blessing and happiness believe in the ten good deeds as the mysterious cause and in [the rebirth as] men and gods as the good effect; those who take delight in quiescence [*śrāvakas* and *pratyekabuddhas*] believe in the conditions [*hetu-pratyaya*] of birth-and-destruction as the right cause and in the four noble truths as the sacred effect; those who desire the fruit of Buddhahood [Bodhisattvas] believe in the six *pāramitās* during the three incalculable *kalpas* as the great cause and in *bodhi* and *nirvāṇa* as the right effect. The right faith in the gate of the patriarchs is different from the above. It does not believe in any cause and effect of conditioned [*saṁskṛta*] nature. It simply believes that one's own self is originally nothing other than Buddha; that everybody is possessed of the

---

[88] Taken from Nakamura's *Bukkyōgo daijiten*, "endon."
[89] *Pŏbŏ*, pp. 112–13, 18.
[90] *Pŏbŏ*, p. 61.

heavenly true Self-Nature; and that the mysterious Essence of *nirvāṇa* is perfectly provided in each person so that we do not have to seek it from others, it being furnished in ourselves from of old (*Po.* 61–62).

The difference between Sŏn and Kyo with regard to the understanding of faith is that Kyo takes faith as belief in the karmic law of cause and effect, whereas Sŏn believes in the direct identity of sentient beings with Buddha. In other words, Sŏn believes in the identity or simultaneity of cause and effect (in the process of cultivation), so that Buddhahood is not something to be achieved in the remote future after a long process (as the cause), but is already present in ordinary sentient beings.

But Kyo as defined above covers only the "three vehicles"; it does not include the teaching of the "one vehicle" (*ekayāna*) or the "complete-sudden" teaching, where the conception of faith does not differ from that in Sŏn. Chinul first learned of this radical understanding of faith in Kyo, we may recall, from Li T'ung-hsüan's interpretation of the "ten faiths" (ten pious thoughts of faith) that constitute the first ten of the fifty-two positions of cultivation. Here is the passage that moved him so profoundly:

> It [the treatise] said: "Kaksu Posal [Enlightenment-Head Bodhisattva] realizes three things. First, he realizes that his own body and mind are originally none other than the *Dharmadhātu*, being white and pure without defilement … Second … Third …. [Right] at the beginning of the mind of faith, he realizes these three things, and [thus] is called Enlightenment-Head Bodhisattva. It further said that the reason why it is difficult for ordinary beings to enter into the ten faiths is because one recognizes oneself as an ordinary being and does not recognize one's own mind as none other than the Buddha of Immutable Wisdom.[91]

According to this passage, one has to realize the three things—which all mean the identity of oneself with Buddhahood—at the beginning of the ten faiths. So faith involves understanding. This is why Chinul does not sharply distinguish between faith and "understanding,"

---

[91] See pp. 29–31 of this book.

another concept modified by "complete-sudden." But we defer discussion of the latter for the moment. More important, however, is to know that faith has for Chinul a clearly volitional element. This element is evident in the word "recognize" (*in* 認), which not merely means cognitive recognition but also has the connotation of "admit" and "affirm" volitionally. Faith means self-understanding, that is, to understand oneself as a Buddha, but in order to do that one needs to overcome timidity and have courage. For an undeniable gulf exists between one's own state of being and Buddhahood, and this gulf should not merely be demolished by the act of understanding but also transcended by the act of courage in making the leap and affirming the identity. Thus Chinul says:

> It is only that sentient beings, deceived by their own karma, distinguish between ordinary beings and the saints, self and others, cause and effect, the pure and the impure, and Nature and Characteristics; they themselves practice self-debasement, but not the Wisdom of Universal Light. If they could arouse a courageous mind and realize that their ignorance is originally divine and true, and that it is the unchanging *Dharma* with great effortless Function, then suddenly this [ignorance] is nothing else than the Immutable Widsom of all the Buddhas (*Po.* 101).

It is clear that faith means first of all not to debase oneself but to have the courage to affirm one's identity with the Buddha, and then to "realize" that identity.

Faith, for Chinul, should be directed to one's own being. Faith directed to external things, be it Buddhas, Bodhisattvas, or any set of propositional truths, cannot be properly called faith; only when it is directed to one's own mind, only when it is understood in relation to one's state of being, is it worthy of the name of faith:

> [The treatise] says "To be equal to the effect-virtue 果德 of all the Buddhas in the cause of faith [as the beginning of the process] without the slightest difference is [the mark of] the faithful mind; the existence of Buddhahood outside of the mind [so that we may adore or aspire after it] is not called faith; it is called a greatly distorted view (*Po.* 116).

104

It is for this reason that Chinul, like Li T'ung-hsüan, does not take the various names appearing in the "Chapter on Tathāgatas' Names" 如來名號品 of the *Hua-yen Sūtra* (it is in the interpretation of this chapter that Li discusses the ten faiths) as proper nouns but as abstract nouns that denote universal principles to be understood in relation to oneself. Thus, for instance, the Golden World in the East is nothing other than "the Principle [Nature] of one's own white, pure, and immaculate *Dharmakāya*," and the Buddha of Immutable Wisdom is nothing other than "one's own seed of ignorance making distinctions."[92] For the same reason Chinul is critical of Fa-tsang's interpretation concerning the mysterious nature of the ten worlds revealed by the miraculous power of the Buddha in the same chapter of the *sūtra*:

> According to this interpretation of master Fa-tsang, we can see that in the stage of the ten faiths the effect [Buddhas and their worlds] relied on by the cause [faith] is not separated from sentient beings; the distinctions of various rewards of karma, of worlds and their inhabitants, are, along with the *Dharmadhātu*, extremely profound and hard to imagine. Yet, simply to look up to and believe the lands and seas of the Tathāgatas to be mysterious and hard to imagine is to be ignorant of the fact that the effect-virtue of the original wisdom of one's own mind [i.e., one's own Buddhahood] is extremely hard to imagine; it means that there exists Buddhahood outside of mind, and how could this constitute faith?[93]

What Chinul says here is that Fa-tsang's conception of faith is directed to the realms of Buddhas external (i.e., unrelated) to us, however mysterious a reality these may be. But for Chinul, not merely do the cause and effect coincide—Fa-tsang also knows this in the above interpretation, Chinul says—so that the wonderful effect of Buddhahood is subjectively appropriated (becomes one's own reality) already in the stage of faith as the cause (beginning of the process), but the subject and object of faith coincide as well. For faith is directed to the mystery of one's own mind.

---

[92] *Pŏbŏ*, p. 93.
[93] *Hwaŏmnon chŏryo*, p. 257.

Since faith means the affirmation within oneself of timeless reality, the Fundamental Wisdom of Universal Light,[94] in faith every phenomenal distinction is canceled. Quoting from Li's treatise, Chinul says:

> If in this realm of the Wisdom of Universal Light, the Buddha-effect [mentioned] in this *Mahāvaipulya-Buddha-avataṁsaka-sūtra*, one admits olden times and establishes today, and makes time divisions such as remote and recent, before and after, and the past, present, and future; if one distinguishes between the place with a Buddha and one without, or between the right-*dharma*, counterfeit-*dharma*, and degenerate-*dharma*; or if one differentiates between old Buddha and new Buddha among the various Buddhas in the ten directions and three times or between pure land and impure land, it is to be known that such a one cannot yet form faith (*Po.* 116).

Here is a passage showing the practical significance of this transcending of time in faith:

> As we may go on from this faith [ten faiths] to cultivate *samādhi* and *prajñā* and go through the process—ten dwellings, ten acts, ten transferences of merit, ten grounds, and the eleventh ground [the position of subtle enlightenment (妙覺)]—time of day, month, year, and *kalpa* does not move. The *Dharmadhātu* is ever like the original, and the Buddha of Immutable Wisdom is the same as before, forming the sea of wisdom containing all the seeds [of the good] and edifying sentient beings. ... If innumerable *kalpas* really exist, if this body is an ordinary being, if there exist two separate paths, that of the ordinary being and the saint, if time and *kalpa* change, and if there exists Buddha outside of mind, it cannot constitute the mind of faith.[95]

Once one enters into this faith, therefore, every moment is eternity, every position is the final position, and every place is the *Dharma*-

---

[94] "Universal Light" is the name of the hall in Magadha where the Buddha is said to have preached at the second, seventh, and eighth assemblies mentioned in the *Hua-yen Sūtra*. But Chinul and Li T'ung-hsüan take it as an abstract noun signifying the *Dharmadhātu* or True Mind, hence "Fundamental Wisdom." It is identical with "the Buddha of Immutable Wisdom."

[95] *Hwaŏmnon chŏryo*, pp. 268.

dhātu[96]—hence "sudden" and yet "complete" (or perfect).[97]

Thus far, we have considered Chinul's conception of faith in "the path of complete-sudden faith and understanding." Faith basically means the courage to affirm one's own existence as the eternal Buddha. This act of faith, however, is not a mere self-assertion, because it is accompanied by "understanding." Faith and understanding should go hand in hand:

> Once right faith is born, it should be accompanied by understanding. Yung-ming [Yen-shou] says, "Faith without understanding enhances ignorance, and understanding without faith enhances distortion of view." Only when faith and understanding are combined can one enter fast (*Po.* 62).

In fact, Chinul does not even sharply differentiate between faith and understanding. He says that when faith reaches its utmost degree it naturally produces the opening of understanding.[98] We could say that for Chinul faith itself includes understanding, not the understanding of objective fact and truth but a self-understanding.

Just as faith means ultimately faith in one's own true self, understanding is likewise self-understanding. Particularly important for our self-understanding is to understand the "interfusion of sentient beings and Buddhas" (*saengbul hoyung* 生佛互融), because this has direct bearing on our true self-understanding, that is, understanding ourselves as Buddha. According to Chinul, the logic of the interfusion of sentient beings and Buddhas is based on the truth of Origination-by-Nature in Hwaŏm doctrine. Thus Chinul says:

> In accordance with the meaning of the above words of the treatise, I have given deep thought three times. The significance of the interfusion, shown by the author of the treatise, between sentient beings and Buddhas is to let those who enter enlightenment by the contem-

---

[96] *Pŏbŏ*, pp. 20, 100.

[97] It should be clear by now that "sudden" and "complete" modify the *content* of faith rather than the *act* of faith; in other words, by "complete-sudden faith" Chinul refers to the faith as understood in the "complete-sudden teaching" (best exemplified by the Hua-yen teaching as interpreted by Li T'ung-hsüan). The same observation holds true for "understanding" as well in the following discussion.

[98] *Chŏryo*, p. 762.

plation of their mind believe that their body, word, and thought, and the Characteristics of the external world, are all born out of the Tathāgata's body, word, thought, and world; all of these are devoid of substance and nature [*svabhāva*] and hence are not originally two different things, there being no difference in their Essence. Since they are born out of the condition of the uncreated Self-Nature of the *Dharmadhātu*, the Characteristic of condition after condition arises entirely out of Nature. Nature is itself the *Dharmadhātu* and has no inside, outside, or middle. The treatise lets people know and observe in this manner. That is, since sentient beings and Buddhas appear originally like hallucinations on the sea of Nature [called] the Fundamental Wisdom of Universal Light, although the Characteristics and Functions of sentient beings and Buddhas may look different, they are entirely the Characteristics and Functions of the Fundamental Wisdom of Universal Light. Therefore, they are originally one Essence and yet the arising of Function is manifold; this corresponds to the path of Origination-by-Nature (*Po.* 97).

"Every single Buddha," says Chinul, "originates from Fundamental Wisdom" (*Po.* 99). There may be differences in the names of Buddhas and in their worlds, but all of them are Characteristics and Functions of the Fundamental Wisdom of Universal Light of one's own mind (*Po.* 99). When sentient beings and Buddhas are all understood in this way as "originations" out of Nature or as the Functions of True Mind, their differences lose ultimate significance, for in the "Nature-sea" all the diverse Characteristics are dissolved; all the empirical differentiations are simply Origination-by-Nature, and hence no origination after all.

Chinul thinks that this truth of the interfusion of sentient beings and Buddhas can also be understood by way of the Hwaŏm doctrine of "nonobstruction between Phenomena and Phenomena" 事事無礙, which is based on the "gate of Origination-by-condition" (distinguished from Origination-by-Nature).[99] Although both Origination-by-Nature and Origination-by-condition, or both the "nonobstruction between Principle and Phenomena" 事理無礙 and the "nonobstruc-

---

[99] Pŏbŏ, p. 98; Chinul understands the truth of *shih-shih wu-ai* by the logic of *shih-li wu-ai* here. On the significance of this, see the following note.

tion between Phenomena and Phenomena," lead us to the identical conclusion of interfusion, Chinul is definitely in favor of the former way of thinking, which he believes is well illustrated in Li T'ung-hsüan's Hua-yen thought. In fact, this inclination toward the truth of *shih-li wu-ai* in preference to *shih-shih wu-ai* was already apparent in the Hua-yen thought of Ch'eng-kuan who was under the influence of Ch'an.[100] Chinul seems to have thought that the contemplation of *shih-shih wu-ai* tends to give rise to mental impediments and hence is not as effective as *shih-li wu-ai*—"gathering Characteristics and attributing to Nature," or the "gate of Origination-by-Nature."[101] It is after all in the timeless Nature and Essence of True Mind that time and history are overcome.

In conclusion, to understand by the act of inward illumination the identity of one's own self and Buddha is what is meant by "understanding" in the path of complete-sudden faith and understanding. And this understanding is nothing other than the sudden enlightenment, or the understanding-enlightenment, that constitutes the beginning of the act of Sŏn. Chinul says:

> If you achieve faith and doubt ceases suddenly; if you express the ambition of man and produce the authentic view and understanding so that you, personally tasting the flavor, arrive at the position where you can affirm [the truth, i.e. your Buddhahood], this is the place of understanding-enlightenment for the cultivators of mind. There being no further grade and order, it is sudden, just as it is said that only when one fits in with the effect-virtue of Buddhas in faith as the cause without the slightest difference does one have faith (*Po.* 47).

---

[100] Concerning this tendency in Hua-yen thought in relation to Ch'eng-kuan, see Kamekawa Kyōshin, *Kegongaku*, pp. 51–59; Kamata, *Kegon shisōshi no kenkyū*, pp. 501–74, particularly 547–55. Fa-tsang himself showed this tendency in his *Wang-chin huan-yüan-kuan*, a work written near the end of his life; see Kamata, *Chūgoku Bukkyō shisōshi kenkyū* (Tokyo: 1968), pp. 357–79. There is some doubt whether it is really the work of Fa-tsang; see *ibid.*, pp. 359, 376–79. This tendency became even more marked in Tsung-mi's thought as set forth in his exposition of the *Yüan-chüeh-ching*. He really retrogressed from the position of *shih-shih wu-ai* to that of *shih-li wu-ai*, represented by the *Ch'i-hsin-lun*; see Araki, *op. cit.*, pp. 91–108. Anyway, the optimistic philosophy of *shih-shih wu-ai* must not have appealed to Chinul who had to wrestle with the gloomy social and religious situation of his time.
[101] *Pŏbŏ*, p. 98; *Hwaŏmnon chŏryo*, p. 1 of the preface.

Thus far we have examined Chinul's theory of sudden elightenment and its Hwaŏm version, i.e., the path of complete-sudden faith and understanding. In other words, we have examined Chinul's theory of "seeing into Nature and becoming a Buddha," of which, as we have mentioned, there are two kinds according to Chinul: one is understanding-enlightenment and the other realization-enlightenment. We have considered only the first, the enlightenment based on "genuine teaching in words." Although it is *understanding*-enlightenment, we have also pointed out that it is genuinely possible only on the basis of the act of inward illumination, because it is *self-understanding* where the subject and object of understanding coincide. Chinul compares "seeing into Nature" to seeing one's own eyes. Strictly speaking, it is impossible. The best way to see one's own eyes is to know that one already has them and not to seek them at all; likewise, the best way to see one's own "spiritual knowing" is to realize that it is unknowable and not to seek it, for it is one's own mind (*Po.* 44). If we need more help than this paradoxical statement by the *already* enlightened mind, then Chinul tells us to go to the act of inward illumination and to the words of genuine teaching—such as we have discussed thus far.

3. The Process of Sŏn: Gradual Cultivation or the Path of Parallel Keeping of Quiescence and Wakefulness

According to the famous story about the competition in "mind-verse" between Shen-hsiu and Hui-neng, two disciples of the Fifth Patriarch, Shen-hsiu is said to have offered the following verse:

> The body is the Bodhi tree,
>   the mind is like a clear mirror.
> At all times we must strive to polish it,
>   and must not let the dust collect.[102]

In response to this, Hui-neng is said to have composed the following one:

---

[102] Quoted from Yampolsky, p. 130.

110

Bodhi originally has no tree,
the mirror also has no stand.
Buddha nature is always clean and pure.
Where is there room for dust?[103]

Scholars of Ch'an Buddhism now discredit this story of the competition as a later fabrication with no factual basis.[104] But whoever may have invented the story, the two verses certainly have the virtue of sharply focusing our attention on one of the most subtle and fundamental issues in the history of Chinese Buddhist thought, especially with regard to Ch'an Buddhism. The story concerns the problem of sudden enlightenment versus gradual cultivation. The issue that can be raised is this: If what Hui-neng says is true and better expresses the experience of enlightenment, does it mean that no act of cultivation and no process of "polishing" is necessary?

Chinul begins his discussion of gradual cultivation by facing similar questions: Why should sudden enlightenment be followed by the process of gradual cultivation? Does not enlightenment tell us that all *dharmas*, good and evil or pure and impure, are empty, being no more than the reflections or the Function of True Mind? Does there still exist for the enlightened eye any dirt that is so real as to require diligence to remove it? Are we not enlightened already and and so no different from Buddhas after all? These are the questions raised by Chinul's imaginary questioners in the dialogues throughout his works. There is a further question: Granted that sudden enlightenment is to be followed by gradual cultivation, why in this order? Why not *vice versa*, namely gradual cultivation and then sudden enlightenment, which would seem to be an even more natural way? After we have considered Chinul's response to these basic problems, we will examine his conception of gradual cultivation itself, its content and method. Let us first take up the former issue.

---

[103] Yampolsky, p. 132. There are several versions of this verse. The more famous one changes the third line to "From the beginning not a thing is." See p. 94 and the footnotes on p. 132 of Yampolsky; see also K. Ch'en, *Buddhism in China*, p. 355 for another translation of the verses.

[104] For a critical examination of the story, see Ui Hakuju, *Zenshūshi kenkyū*, pp. 345–50.

In replying to this question, Chinul is fond of Tsung-mi's metaphorical way of answering. For example, we know that ice is actually water, but it takes time for ice to melt into water under the warm sunlight.[105] Or, we know that the baby, as soon as it is born, is man; but it needs time and care for the baby to grow into an adult.[106] What these metaphors suggest to us is that there exists a split between knowing[107] and being. Chinul attributes this split to the gap between Principle (*li* 理) and Phenomena (*shih* 事):

> As the *sūtra* [Nŭngŏmgyŏng] says, Principle is suddenly realized; upon enlightenment it [ignorance] melts away at the same time. Phenomena, however, cannot be removed suddenly; they are exhausted gradually (*Po.* 42).

From at least as early as the time of Tao-sheng (d. A.D. 430) in Chinese Buddhism, it was asserted that Principle is to be understood suddenly, because it is without Characteristics or grades, and so is indivisible. Thus our understanding of it is either all or nothing; we understand it all at once or not at all. Chinul agrees with this. But the particulars or Phenomena, says he, cannot be removed suddenly. Yet the question remains for us: Are there any Phenomena apart from Principle, Phenomena that do not partake of Principle? Just as Principle is always the Principle of Phenomena, are not Phenomena always the Phenomena of Principle for the enlightened mind?

Here is a shift of position in Chinul's way of thinking. When he talks about sudden enlightenment, he does not admit of a discrepancy or "obstruction" between Principle and Phenomena. The nonobstruction between Principle and Phenomena was the cornerstone of his theory of sudden enlightenment, where every Phenomenon is understood as empty and as given rise to by Nature (Origination-by-Nature), and hence is ultimately attributable to Nature. But now, as he comes to discuss gradual cultivation, he talks as if Phenomena were independent of Principle, and argues for the necessity

---

[105] *Pŏbŏ*, pp. 8, 42.

[106] *Ibid.*, p. 44.

[107] That is, enlightenment, which, though not a purely intellectual thing, is still a form of knowing, particularly in the case of Chinul's *understanding*-enlightenment.

of gradual cultivation. How should we understand this shift?

There seems to be no clear theoretical solution to this problem in Chinul's thought, because the very experience of the gap between theory and practice or between knowing and doing[108] underlies his view of cultivation. As we shall see, for Chinul the gap between knowing and doing is not absolute. Knowing has significance for doing and deeply affects it; that is, the enlightenment alters the quality of the cultivation that follows it. Nonetheless, like Tsung-mi, Chinul was not a naive idealist lacking realistic insight into human nature and the situation of ordinary beings in actual life. In reality, an undeniable gulf exists between saints and common people, who are constantly under the power of concrete evils and passions in spite of their enlightenment. Thus, following Tsung-mi, Chinul says, "One is enlightened from delusion suddenly, but one is transformed from ordinary being to saint gradually."[109] It is for this reason that Chinul distinguishes between "the purity of Self-Nature" 自性清淨 (to be realized by sudden enlightenment) and "the purity by removal of dirt" 離垢清淨 (to be gradually cultivated) and talks not only about "liberation of Self-Nature" 自性解脫 but also about "liberation by the removal of impediments" 離障解脫.[110] It is also for this reason that in his *Kye ch'osim hagin mun* Chinul urges students of Sŏn to practice not only *ich'am* (repentance according to Principle, i.e., by the contemplation of the emptiness of defilements) but also *sach'am* (repentance through Phenomena, i.e., through concrete acts and rituals).[111] The *Ch'i-hsin-lun* is also aware of this problem when it distinguishes, according to Wŏnhyo's interpretation, between "the fundamental ignorance," which can be removed suddenly, and "the secondary ignorance," which cannot.[112] Likewise, the *Yüan-chüeh-*

---

[108] The fundamental problem is the gap between knowing and being; but this gap is known by the discrepancy between knowing and doing (the removal of phenomena, which cannot be done suddenly). We *know* that we are Buddhas, but we do not *act* like Buddhas and hence *are* not Buddhas in reality.

[109] *Chŏryo*, p. 708.

[110] *Ibid.*, p. 754.

[111] *T.* 48, No. 2019B, p. 1004b.

[112] *Kisillon-so*, T. 44, No. 1844, p. 212a. "The secondary ignorance" refers to the "three subtle" defilements and the "six gross" ones; see Hakeda, pp. 43–45. See also Araki, pp.

ching or *Sūtra of Complete Enlightenment* mentions two kinds of impediment; one is the "impediment of Principle" and the other the "impediment of Phenomena."[112] To use the famous Mahāyāna mode of discourse, according to the higher level of truth *saṁsāra* is *nirvāṇa* and *nirvāṇa* is *saṁsāra*; but according to the lower level of truth, *saṁsāra* is still *saṁsāra* and *nirvāṇa* is *nirvāṇa*. We may even say that *de jure* (from the viewpoing of *li*) we are already saved, being none other than Buddhas, but *de facto* (from the viewpoint of *shih*) we are not yet saved, being no more than sentient beings still tormented in *saṁsāra*. Tsung-mi gives to this antinomical reality a vivid expression:

> The Question: If greed, anger, and the like are empty, this could be called the nonexistence of every thought; why do we need to control them?
> The Answer: If so, suppose you suddenly have a serious illness and pain; if the pain is empty, it could be called the nonexistence of illness; why should you cure it by medicine? You should know that though greed and anger are empty, they can generate karma; though the karma is empty, it can bring pain; and empty as the pain may be, it is hard to endure. Therefore, the previous diagram says that the Essence is empty and yet it produces Phenomena.[113]

Perhaps Chinul came to acquire his deep insight into the painful reality of the discrepancy between Principle and Phenomena through his own religious experiences. We should be reminded of the long process of self-cultivation he had to go through despite his experience of sudden enlightenment through the encounter with the *Platform Sūtra* and the *Treatise on Hua-yen*. What then is the reason behind this gap between knowing and doing? Chinul attributes it to the fact that we, enlightened or not, have for a long time been subject to the habitual forces of ignorance and defilements (*kleśas*):

116–17 for a discussion of this problem.
   [112] *T.* 17, No. 842, p. 916b.
   [113] *T.* 48, p. 411c; the "diagram" refers to the one made by Tsung-mi himself on the essentials of Buddhist truth.

Ordinary beings have transmigrated from the beginningless great *kalpas* until today through the five destinies of sentient beings. They have, coming at birth and going at death, been stubbornly attached to the Characteristic of ego, forming their nature out of deluded thoughts and perversion and out of the habitual force of the seed of ignorance; although they may in the present life suddenly realize that Self-Nature is originally empty and quiescent and not different from the Buddha, their old habits are difficult to get rid of suddenly. Therefore whenever they face desirable or undesirable situations, anger and joy and right and wrong rise and disappear like burning fire, and so their defilements, like the external dust, remain ever as before. If they do not apply exertion and effort with wisdom, how will they be able to govern ignorance and arrive at the land of great rest and repose? Thus it is said that though sudden enlightenment is same as with the Buddha, the habitual forces [formed] throughout many lifetimes are deep. The wind ceases and yet the waves still roar; the Principle appears and yet thoughts still invade.

Chinul continues:

Sŏn master Ko [Ta-hui] says: "Often persons with sharp capacity do not spend much effort and hit upon this thing [sudden enlightenment]; this gives rise to "easy mind" and they do not cultivate further. As days and months pass, however, they wander as before and cannot avoid transmigration. How could they quickly put aside later cultivation at the instant of enlightenment?" Therefore one should illumine and examine [one's mind] long after the enlightenment; if deluded thoughts suddenly arise, one should not follow them but reduce them until one reaches nonaction [*wu-wei*, Suchness]. Only then will one have reached the final realm. It is precisely this that is called the act of "cow-tending" by all men of good learning in the world (*Po.* 48).

"The wind ceases but the waves roar still": this was Chinul's apprehension of the concrete human situation. This is why he had to talk about "the act of cow-tending" and why he used to call himself *Moguja*, one who tends cows.[114] It is this act of cow-tending that is

---

[114] Suzuki tells us the following beautiful Zen story: Tai-an studied the Vinaya texts at Huang-po Shan, which, however, failed to satisfy him, for he had as yet no

designed to demolish the gap between knowing and doing; hence it is an indispensable part of the act of Sŏn for Chinul. Not everything is finished in a single moment.

Previously we have seen how much Chinul stressed courage and faith, which are needed to overcome unnecessary self-debasement and to cross the bridge of sudden enlightenment. However, because of his realistic assessment of human predicament, Chinul now cautions us against the danger of self-elevation, which takes sudden enlightenment as the end of the journey. Thus "neither self-debasement nor self-elevation" is the constant advice Chinul gives to the students of Sŏn:

> I ask the men of high aim, the cultivators of mind, to reflect very carefully. The reason why I have over and again explicated the meaning of prior enlightenment and later cultivation, the root and branch, is to let the beginning student of mind be neither self-debased nor self-elevated, but to see clearly the rationale behind it without confusion. The text says that to be suddenly enlightened to the fact that the original mind constantly knows is like recognizing the unchanging nature of water; that the mind already without delusion and ignorance is like the sudden cessation of the wind; and that the natural gradual release of attachment to conditions after enlightenment is like the gradual calming down of the waves. When one helps and perfumes one's body and mind with *śīla, samādhi,* and *prajñā,* and becomes gradually free and without obstruction in the miraculous powers, and can benefit sentient beings, such a one is called a Buddha (*C.* 799–800).

If self-debasement is the particular danger among the students of

---

approach to the ultimate meaning of Buddhist truth. He went about on his disciplinary pilgrimage and came to Pai-chang. Tai-an remarked, "I have been seeking for the Buddha, but do not yet know how to go on with my research." Said the master, "It is very much like looking for an ox when riding on one." "What shall a man do after knowing him?" "It is like going home on the back of an ox." "May I be further enlightened as to the care I shall have to bestow on the whole matter?" Pai-chang said, "It is like a cowherd looking after his cattle, who using his staff keeps them from wandering into another's pasture." *Second Series,* p. 83.

See also pp. 369–76 of the *First Series* on the act of cow-tending compared to the process of Buddhist spiritual cultivation; and "jūgyūzu" in Mochizuki's *Bukkyō daijiten* should also be consulted.

Kyo, self-elevation is the particular temptation for the students of Sŏn, according to Chinul. Thus he says:

> As I see the man of Kyo, they are trapped by the teaching of expedient doctrines; so they separate and cling to the true and false and debase themselves. Some talk about the nonobstruction between Phenomena and Phenomena but do not cultivate the act of contemplation, nor do they believe in the existence of the secret by which they might realize their own minds. When they have heard of the Sŏn peoples' "seeing into Nature and becoming a Buddha," they call it no more than the Principle transcending words as taught by the sudden teaching [the fourth teaching in the Hua-yen doctrinal classification]. They do not know what is meant here by the original mind of complete enlightenment, of which the Unchanging and Changing, Nature and Characteristics, Essence and Function, and wealth and comfortableness are said to be same as the Buddhas. How can they be men of wisdom?

Then Chinul goes on to criticize the rash self-elevation prevalent among the followers of Sŏn:

> As I see the men of Sŏn, on the other hand, they only know about the aspect of the direct transcending to Buddhahood without going through the process by men of supercapacity; they do not believe that this record [*Pŏpchip pyŏrhaengnok* of Tsung-mi] teaches that one merely enters into the position of the ten faiths after the enlightenment-understanding. For this reason, scarcely have they experienced an opening of the mind, they are not aware of the depth and shallowness in the understanding and act [cultivation] nor of the rise and disappearance of defiled habits. Often they have arrogance with regard to the *Dharma*, uttering what is beyond their lot and capacity (*C.* 710–711).

Here, we notice Chinul's underlying intention, namely, the harmonization or combination of Sŏn and Kyo, at work also in his theory of gradual cultivation. Just as he incorporated the Hwaŏm path of complete-sudden faith and understanding into his theory of sudden enlightenment, so now he tries to accomodate the gradual path of Kyo into Sŏn. But he does all this not in a purely theoretical way but with an eye to the actual problems that students of Sŏn often face. Thus Chinul's conception of Sŏn requires "the path of cultivation" as much as "the path of Nature". They are like the two wings of a bird:

> For this reason, the cultivators of mind should neither debase themselves nor trust themselves. If they trust themselves, the mind does not preserve the Self-Nature but becomes engaged in momentary creations, now an ordinary being now a saint, and hence they fall back to the changes of floating and sinking. They should day and night practice sincerely, wakeful without delusion and quiescent and [yet] bright, and not deviate from the *path of cultivation*. If they debase themselves they lose the virtue of this Mind which, spiritually permeating and responding to things, is ever present before their eyes and yet unchanging all day long, though responding to conditions all day long. Therefore, they should form out of stupidity and attachment the true source of liberation, and handle avarice and anger and reveal the great Function of Englihtenment [*bodhi*]. Free in the face of the desirable and undesirable, and not bound by either bondage or liberation, they should follow the *path of Nature*. These two paths are like the two wings of a bird; neither is dispensable.[115]

We have examined why Chinul thinks that sudden enlightenment has to be followed by gradual cultivation. In short, the "revolution" of sudden enlightenment has to be complemented by the "evolution" of gradual cultivation in order for the gap between knowing and doing to be filled. And in this world of evolution (as we can already anticipate) the law of cause and effect matters, time counts, and gradations and positions according to the degree of cultivation reappear.

But does this suggest that we are reverting to the world of common sense before the mental revolution, and that sudden enlightenment has no bearing upon the gradual cultivation that follows it? No. Here we need to examine why Chinul insists on the temporal priority of sudden enlightenment to gradual cultivation, rather than the other way around. This was the second question we raised at the outset of the present section on the process of Sŏn.

---

[115] *Pŏbŏ*, p. 22; italics supplied. Chinul also compares the two paths to the two wheels of a cart, p. 49.

We have previously mentioned in our study of the nature of True Mind and of sudden enlightenment that the Northern Sect (represented by Shen-hsiu), according to Chinul, does not know what sudden enlightenment is. Since it does not know the emptiness of defilements (the reflections on the jewel), it sees the process of cultivation as comparable to the process of removing dirt from a bright mirror. It is caught by the dualistic view of the true and false, being ignorant of the basic Mahāyāna teaching of the identity of *nirvāṇa* and *saṁsāra*. In particular, it does not realize the truth of Origination-by-Nature, the mysterious Function of True Mind. So it tries to "seek the true apart from the false" (C. 698). Chinul concludes: "Since its enlightenment is not thorough, how could its cultivation be true."[116] According to Chinul, cultivation without enlightenment is like pressing the grass with stones without cutting the root out; however harshly you may press down upon it, it will grow even more fiercely. Thus Chinul says:

> Some not knowing the empty nature of good and evil sit firmly without moving, suppressing and controlling the body and mind just as stones press down the grass, thinking it to be the cultivation of mind. This is a great delusion. Thus it is said that *śrāvakas* [Hīnayāna disciples] cut off delusions one by one, but this idea of cutting is itself the enemy. If you contemplate that murder, theft, fornication, and lies originate out of Nature, the origination is no origination; right at that moment they are suddenly quiescent, so why should we further cut them? It is said that we should not be afraid of thoughts arising but only be afraid of the slowness in realizing [the empty nature of them]. Again it is said that if thoughts arise, we should immediately realize; if we realize, they are nonexistent (*Po.* 50).

Accordingly, the gradual cultivation that has not been baptized by sudden enlightenment is for Chinul not the proper from of cultiva-

---

[116] *Chŏryo*, p. 685. We have already noted that this view of the Northern Sect is not accepted by modern critical scholars of Ch'an Buddhism; we have referred to Ui Hakuju's study. For an even more radical view which completely denies any "gradualistic" position in the Northern Sect, see Sekiguchi Shindai, *Daruma Daishi no kenkyū*, pp. 213–45, and *Zenshū shisōshi*, pp. 102–08.

tion; it is mere "supression" (*pongnal*),[117] and from the beginning it is a lost fight. This supressionist view of cultivation is held not merely by the Northern Sect of Sŏn but also by all expedient vehicles. Chinul urges students of Sŏn not to follow this form of cultivation but the true cultivation that "cultivates without cultivating and cuts without cutting":

> Some people are attached to the expedient teaching concerning the Characteristics of *dharmas* in the sacred teachings; they debase themselves and take pains to cultivate gradual acts, digressing from the school of Nature. They do not believe that the Tathāgata had opened up, for the sake of sentient beings in the degenerate age, the door to the secret, but they remain attached to what they have heard previously, abandoning the gold to carry the hemp. I have come across this kind of person very often. Though I explain it to them, they do not believe and accept but only add doubt and slander. How can they be equal to those who first believe and understand the Mind-Nature to be originally pure and the defilements originally empty, and yet who do not [let this faith and understanding] obstruct the perfuming [*vāsanā*] cultivation based upon that understanding. Externally, these latter embrace precepts and rituals and yet they are free from binding and attachment; internally, they cultivate quiet thought [another name for Ch'an or *dhyāna*] and yet they do not suppress. It could well be said that in cutting evils they cut without cutting, and in cultivating good they cultivate without cultivating; hence it is true cultivation and cutting (*Po.* 10).

We could call the true cultivation that comes after the sudden enlightenment a paradoxical cultivation. Grounded upon insight into Nature, it is a carefree and effortless cultivation. This is why the sudden enlightenment must precede gradual cultivation, and this is why, despite the gradual cultivation, we are not reverting to the world of common sense—the world of effort and suppression *before* the revolution of sudden enlightenment. Chinul clearly states:

> Although there exists the later cultivation, due to the prior sudden enlightenment that deluded thoughts are originally empty and the

---

[117] *Pŏbŏ*, pp. 10, 50.

Mind-Nature originally pure, we cut off evil without cutting and cultivate good without cultivating; this is the true cultivation and true cutting. Therefore it is said that though we widely cultivate the myriad [good] acts, we take no-thought as the chief (*Po.* 49).

Here, the idea of no-thought is important as characterizing the kind of cultivation made possible by sudden enlightenment. No-thought (*munyŏm* or *wu-nien* 無念) is often contrasted with leaving-thought (*inyŏm* or *li-nien* 離念), which presupposes the existence of thoughts to leave, whereas the former does not. Based upon the wisdom of Emptiness, it does not admit the existence of any defilement to cut off or leave. No-thought, however, does not simply mean nonexistence of thoughts; it is even present where all of our ordinary thoughts are present—just as True Mind has both the aspect of Emptiness and the aspect of fullness (Function). The idea of no-thought is prominent in the *Platform Sūtra*[118] and in Shen-hui's thought. It was particularly from the latter that Chinul learned of this idea, but by way of Tsung-mi. Concerning Shen-hui's view, Chinul says:

> If you meet a good friend who opens and shows [the truth to you] and are suddenly enlightened as to the empty quiescent knowing, knowing has no thought and form; who will have the notions of self and other? If one realizes various Characteristics as empty, the mind is of itself no-thought. If thought arises, one realizes [its emptiness], and if one realizes this, it does not exist. The subtle gate of cultivation exists here only. This is exactly what is meant by the cultivation of no-thought after enlightenment (*C.* 730).

It is clear, then, that no-thought is identical with True Mind, the empty quiescent knowing.[119] But at the same time it is the key to the "subtle cultivation" 妙修 called "the cultivation of no-thought"

---

[118] It is said in the *sūtra*: "Good friends, in this teaching of mine, from ancient times up to the present, all have set up no-thought as the main doctrine, non-form as the substance, and non-abiding as the basis. Non-form is to be separated from form even when associated with form. *No-thought is not to think even when involved in thought.* Non-abiding is the original nature of man." Yampolsky, pp. 137–38, my italics.

[119] For a fine study of the concept of no-thought in Shen-hui, see Gernet, pp. iv–ix of the introduction. Suzuki's *No Mind* as a whole is devoted to this topic.

無念修 after enlightenment. In fact, to have the enlightenment of no-thought is itself true cultivation, the cultivation which is therefore no cultivation. We might even say that cultivation is here subsumed under or absorbed into enlightenment.[120] This is the radical effect produced by enlightenment upon cultivation, and this is why the order of "sudden enlightenment and gradual cultivation" (*tono chŏmsu* 頓悟漸修) must not be reversed for Chinul. Let us finally adduce one more passage from Chinul that demonstrates the difference enlightenment makes with regard to cultivation:

> The National Preceptor Ch'ung said: "To cut off defilements is the business belonging to the two vehicles; the nonarising of defilements is named the Mahāyāna *nirvāṇa*." What this means is that one does not attain enlightenment by cutting off defilements but that this very freedom from defilements is enlightenment; this is the true cultivation and the true cutting. Thus a former sage said that when deluded, Bodhisattvas take enlightenment for defilement; but when enlightened, they take defilement for enlightenment. This is exactly what is meant by this [Ch'ung's word] (*C*. 796).

The reason why Chinul adheres to the scheme of "sudden enlightenment and gradual cultivation" as the "footprint of all the sages and saints" is now clear.[121] Gradual cultivation overcomes the gap between knowing and doing, between Principle and Phenomena; and sudden enlightenment transforms gradual cultivation into the true cultivation that "acts with nonaction and does not act with action,[122] the Sŏn Buddhist's version of the Taoist ideal of life. It is now time to look into the content and method of gradual cultivation according to Chinul's explanation.

---

[120] This is ultimately what made Hu Shih characterize the Ch'an Buddhism initiated by Shen-hui as "no ch'an at all" ("ch'an" being understood as the cultivation of *samādhi* through *dhyāna*). See his "Ch'an (Zen) Buddhism in China: Its History and Method," *Philosophy East and West*, III, 1 (1953), pp. 7, 17. We will discuss this problem further later on.

[121] For this reason, all other alternatives such as "gradual cultivation and sudden enlightenment," "gradual cultivation and gradual enlightenment," "sudden enlightenment and sudden cultivation," and others are not recommended by Chinul. We will not discuss them here; see *Chŏryo*, pp. 738–45 for this. Also, for an excellent discussion of Tsung-mi's view on this matter, see Araki, pp. 109–29.

[122] *Chŏryo*, p. 794.

"Since all sentient beings," says Chinul, "are born out of the Fundamental Wisdom of all the Buddhas, one takes for that reason the Fundamental Wisdom of Universal Light as the beginning of the generation of the thought [or desire] of enlightenment."[123] This, according to Chinul, happens at the beginning of the Buddhist process of cultivation (which has fifty-one positions: ten faiths 十信, ten dwellings 十住, ten acts 十行, ten transferences of merit 十廻向, ten grounds 十地, and the subtle enlightenment),[124] that is, in the first position of faith. Right away in the position of an ordinary being, one appropriates Buddl.ahood through the act of faith and understanding. This is, we have seen, sudden enlightenment. But this sudden enlightenment, since it precedes the act of cultivation, is only an understanding-enlightenment. And as such, it is bound to result in creating the gap between knowing and doing, necessitating the process of gradual cultivation for us. This is what Chinul calls "the trouble of the understanding[-enlightenment] 解礙 of the ordinary beings in [the position] of the ten faiths." Thus, in spite of the cancelation of time and the consequent "simultaneity of cause and effect" in the act of faith and understanding, one still has to go through the rest of the process, namely the fifty (or fifty-one) positions—even though this process is now not understood as a purely gradualistic act of cultivation, but as "the cultivation of no-thought," as we have seen. Thus Chinul says:

> Since one realizes that one's own ignorance is originally divine and true and is the constant *Dharma* with great Function without effort, one cultivates cessation [*śamatha*] and contemplation [*vipaśyanā*]

---

[123] *Pŏbŏ*, p. 96. In the *Hua-yen Sūtra* this "initial generation of the thought of enlightenment and sudden attaintment of perfect enlightenment" 初發心時便成正覺 is said to occur at the beginning of the ten dwellings, not of the ten faiths as with Chinul and Li T'ung-hsüan. As we shall see, for Chinul the enlightenment that takes place at the beginning of the ten dwellings is a different kind of enlightenment, not understanding-enlightenment.

[124] This Mahāyāna conception of the process of cultivation is taught in the *Inwang-gyŏng* (*Jen-wang-ching*), and there are some variations concerning the process in other *sūtras*. For details, see "gojūnii," *Bukkyō daijiten*; another theory puts another position, "equal [to Buddha] enlightenment," before "subtle enlightenment." thus making the total number of positions fifty-two instead of fifty-one.

123

as an expedient means in the ten faiths. When the effort is freely accomplished, *samādhi* and *prajñā* become perfect and clear. This is suddenly called the dwelling of the generation of the thought [of enlightenment]. It is in this dwelling [the first of the ten dwellings] that according to the "Chapter on the Act of Purity" one attains supreme enlightenment at the moment of the initial generation of the thought (*Po.* 113).

According to this passage, one has to cultivate cessation and contemplation or *samādhi* and *prajñā* to enter into the first position of the ten dwellings. And then, right at this position, another enlightenment happens, this time a different enlightenment from the understanding-enlightenment that occurs *before* the cultivation of *samādhi* and *prajñā*. According to Chinul, this is the realization-enlightenment (*chŭngo* 證悟) where the gap between knowing and doing no longer exists. Once one enters into this position of the ten dwellings, one's own spiritual training is more or less concluded and one begins an active Bodhisattvaic practice and cultivation. Thus Chinul goes on:

> After one enters into the ten dwellings, one constantly situates oneself in the world with the Wisdom of Universal Light and edifies sentient beings, widely responding to their capacities (*Po.* 113).

With this, we now have the framework of Chinul's conception of the process of Sŏn: It basically consists of two parts, one the cultivation of *samādhi* and *prajñā* before one enters into the first position of the ten dwellings or the realization-enlightenment,[125] and the other the life of Bodhisattva practice and cultivation beginning at that position. Let us now examine these two parts more closely. First, the cultivation of *samādhi* and *prajñā*, or cessation and contemplation.

---

[125] It is only from this position of the ten dwellings that a person is counted as having entered into the position of spiritual accomplishment, the so-called five positions; see "goi," *Bukkyō daijiten*. One who has entered into the first of the ten dwellings is called *hyŏn* 賢, and one who has entered into the first of the ten grounds (*bhūmi*) is called *sŏng* 聖.

We have already seen through our biographical study of Chinul that *samādhi* and *prajñā* were his life-time concern and preoccupation. Chinul says: Formerly I had reviewed the Mahāyāna literature and extensively examined what is taught by the *sūtras* and treatises pertaining to the ultimate [*nītārtha*] vehicle; not a single *dharma* does not return to the path of the three learnings and not a single Buddha has attained enlightenment without relying upon the three learnings" (*Po.* 35). Chinul explains the three learnings as follows:

The two words *samādhi* and *prajñā* are abbreviation for the three learnings: *śīla, samādhi,* and *prajñā.* The meaning of *śīla* is to prevent wrong and to stop evil, so that we may avoid falling into the three [evil] destinies of sentient being; the meaning of *samādhi* is to control distraction on the basis of truth, so that we may transcend the six kinds of desire [arising from the six organs]; and *prajñā* has its meaning in choosing *dharmas* and in contemplating their emptiness, so that we may be mysteriously liberated from *saṁsāra.* All the perfect saints learn these in their acts of cultivation as the cause [for their sainthood]; thus they are called the three learnings. And in these three learnings there is the distinction of the *Characteristic-oriented* and the *Nature-oriented.* The Characteristic-oriented is as has been explained above. The Nature-oriented means that *śīla* is the absence of ego in the Principle [Nature]; *samādhi* is the original absence of distraction in the Principle; and *prajñā* the original absence of delusion in the Principle. *Once you realize this truth, this is the true three learnings.* When a former sage asserts that his gate of *Dharma* has been transmitted by the former Buddhas and does not discuss meditation [*dhyāna*] and effort [*vīrya*] but only attains Buddha's view, he intends to negate the names of [the three] Characteristic-oriented governing [control or cultivation]; he does not mean to abolish the Nature-oriented three learnings. The words of Ts'ao-ch'i [Hui-neng] that the ground of the mind without the wrong is the *śīla* of Self-Nature, without distraction is the *samādhi* of Self-Nature, and without stupidity is the *prajñā* of Self-Nature, refer to this. Also in what is called Sŏn, some are shallow and some deep; hence the Sŏn of non-Buddhists, the Sŏn of ordinary beings, the Sŏn of the two vehicles, the Sŏn of Mahāyāna, and the Sŏn of the supreme vehicle, as have been extensively covered in the *Ch'an-yüan chu-ch'üan-chi.* What is now being discussed, namely that Mind-Nature is originally pure and defilements originally empty, corresponds to the Sŏn of the supreme vehicle.[126]

What Chinul means by the Characteristic-oriented *samādhi* and *prajñā* 隨相定慧 is plain. *Samādhi* is understood as mental concentration achieved with "effort" and "governing" (of *kleśas*) in the face of manifold Characteristics or Phenomena; *prajñā* is likewise understood as contemplation of the emptiness of particular *dharmas* case by case without delusion about them. According to Chinul, this Characteristic-oriented cultivation is the form of cultivation followed by the expedient vehicles as well as the Northern Sect; it is at best the "Sŏn of Mahāyāna," but not the "Sŏn of the supreme vehicle." Hence it is not recommended to the students of Sŏn. The Nature-oriented *samādhi* and *prajñā* 自性定慧, on the other hand, simply refer to the two aspects of the Nature of True Mind, quiescence and knowing, as we have seen. These two aspects, we recall, were identified by Chinul with *samādhi* and *prajñā* (*t'i* and *yung*) of the Essence of True Mind. The cultivation of Nature-oriented *samādhi* and *prajñā*, accordingly, means the cultivation of these two aspects already inherent in our Mind-Nature, hence a cultivation that is not a cultivation—the true cultivation or the paradoxical cultivation of no-thought. Nature-oriented *samādhi* and *prajñā* are not even something to cultivate at all but something simply to realize or to understand by sudden enlightenment. This is what is meant by Chinul when he says, "Once you realize this truth [that Principle originally has no ego, distraction, and delusion], this is the true three learnings." The consequence is that cultivation is subsumed under enlightenment—a radical development that, as Hu Shih puts it, made

---

[126] *Pŏbŏ*, pp. 11–12; italics mine. The words of Hui-neng are found in the *Platform Sūtra*; see Yampolsky, p. 164. Also see his note on "mind ground" on the same page; mind is compared to a field where seeds have been planted. Another thing to note in the above passage is Chinul's reference to Tsung-mi's *Ch'an-yüan chu-ch'üan-chi*, which seems to confirm Jan Yün-hua's view that it was actually written by Tsung-mi; see his "Two Problems concerning Tsung-mi's Compilation of *Ch'an-tsang*," *Transactions of the International Conference of Orientalists in Japan*, 19 (1974), 37–47. But Chinul may be referring only to the preface of it (extant).

Chinese Ch'an no ch'an (understood as *dhyāna*, meditation) at all.[127] For one does not have to make any special effort to achieve *prajñā* and *samādhi*; they are already there in our Mind-Nature only to be discovered or to be enlightened about. In this free and effortless paradoxical cultivation of Nature-oriented *samādhi* and *prajñā*, bodily posture, breath control, effort to attain mental concentration, and the wakefulness or mindfulness to overcome mental blankness are all made superfluous.[128] And in this Nature-oriented cultivation of *samādhi* and *prajñā*, there is no distinction of priority between the two. That is, as the two aspects of the Essence of True Mind, they form an inseparable unity; we cannot and should not try to develop one of them first in order to have the other.[129] Nor is there in this Nature-oriented cultivation of *samādhi* and *prajñā* any dichotomy of subject and object (i.e., the cultivator and the cultivated), because *samādhi* and *prajñā* are the Nature of our mind as well as the goal of cultivation.[130]

This carefree cultivation of Nature-oriented *samādhi* and *prajñā*—which is no cultivation at all—is the most desirable form of cultivation after sudden enlightenment. Yet, since even among people with the capacity for sudden enlightenment there are some with

---

[127] Hu Shih, *op. cit.*, pp. 7, 17. There seems to be currently in the West some discussion (and confusion) going on with regard to the importance of *dhyāna* in Zen Buddhism. Both Hu-shih and Suzuki, emphasizing the idea of the unity of *prajñā* and *dhyāna* in Hui-neng and Shen-hui, tend to regard it as entirely nonessential in Zen. Yampolsky understands the doctrine of the unity as not so much the abolition of *dhyāna* as a new version of it (*op. cit.*, pp. 115–17). On the other hand, P. Kapleau, in *The Three Pillars of Zen* (Boston, 1967; pp. 3–24), emphasizes the importance of traditional *dhyāna* practice in Zen, introducing to the West the Sōtō approach to Zen. Chinul's attitude is dual, as we shall see. In Nature-oriented cultivation, it is made superfluous; but he recommends it to some groups of people as a provisional means.

[128] Shen-hui even goes so far as to say that to cultivate concentration (*samādhi*) is the spirit of error; see Gernet, pp. 34–35.

[129] *Chŏryo*, pp. 720–22; see also Gernet, pp. 50, 63–65 for the same idea in Shen-hui. Suzuki emphasizes the idea of the unity of *prajñā* and *dhyāna* in Hui-neng as "revolutionary in the history of Buddhist thought in China"; see his "Zen: A Reply to Hu Shih," p. 28. See also his *No Mind* where he discusses the idea throughout the book. According to Chinul, Hui-neng identifies *prajñā* with *samādhi* as the two aspects of Self-Nature, but not *prajñā* with *dhyāna*; *dhyāna* may be unnecessary because of the *samādhi* of Self-Nature, but it is not identified with *prajñā* by Hui-neng. The fact is that we do not know exactly what Hui-neng's view of *dhyāna* practice was.

[130] *Chŏryo*, p. 720.

particularly heavy defilements, Chinul recommends to such people provisional borrowing of the Characteristic-oriented cultivation of *samādhi* and *prajñā*, which originally belongs to those of inferior vehicles who have only the capacity for gradual cultivation. But this borrowing, Chinul emphasizes, does not mean a total endorsement of "the act of gradual-capacity." Chinul says:

> If we judge the act of the two paths, those who are engaged in the cultivation of *samādhi* and *prajñā* of the Self-Nature use the effortless effort of the sudden path, mobilize both [*samādhi* and *prajñā*] as well as empty them, cultivate their Self-Nature, and attain the Buddhist enlightenment; whereas those engaged in the Characteristic-oriented cultivation of *samādhi* and *prajñā* use the effort of governing that belongs to the inferior capacity of the gradual path without enlightenment, cut off illusory thoughts one by one, and seek quietude as the act [of cultivation]. The acts of these two paths, one sudden and the other gradual, are different; they should not be confused. Yet when I at the same time talk about the Characteristic-oriented governing [even] in the path of cultivation after the enlightenment, it does not mean completely following the acts of the people of gradual capacity; it rather means to take their expedient means [*upāya*] and merely to use the road for a short stay. For what reason? Even in the sudden path some have excellent capacity and some inferior; thus one should not make a sweeping judgment about their acts on the basis of one instance. In the case of those whose defilements are light and not thick and whose body and mind are light and easy; who are free from the good in the act of good and free from the evil in the act of evil; those who are not moved by the eight kinds of wind [gain and loss, honor and dishonor, etc.], and who take the three feelings [pleasure, pain, and the neutral] in calm manner, such persons can indulge in the free combined cultivation based upon the *samādhi* and *prajñā* of the Self-Nature. Being naturally true without doing anything, their movement and rest are always Sŏn itself. They achieve the natural truth, so what reason would there be for them to borrow the Characteristic-oriented governing? Being without the illness, they do not seek medicine.

Chinul continues:

In the case of those, however, whose defilements are, despite the sudden enlightenment in advance, dark and thick, whose habitual force is solid and heavy; those who give rise to passion thought after thought in the face of [external] objects, whose mind responds to every condition encountered, and who are overcome by obscurance and distraction and are blind to the constant Suchness of quiescence and knowing, these people have to use the Characteristic-oriented *samādhi* and *prajñā*; they should not forget governing but must control obscurance and distraction and enter into nonaction [Suchness]. Although they may borrow the study of governing and temporarily control the habitual forces, due to the prior sudden enlightenment that the Mind-Nature is originally pure and defilements originally empty, they do not fall into the defiled cultivation of the inferior capacity of the gradual path. ... For the enlightened ones, though they may use the *upāya* of governing, every thought has no doubt, so that they do not fall into defiled [cultivation]. When days and months pass, they will naturally fit in with the naturally true subtle Nature; they will be free in quiescence and knowing, and in thought after thought they may respond to all kinds of external objects, but in mind after mind they cut off all defilements forever. Without leaving Self-Nature they will keep *samādhi* and *prajñā* in balance and will achieve supreme enlightenment, being equal to the previously mentioned people of excellent capacity. For those already enlightened, even though the Characteristic-oriented *samādhi* and *prajñā* may be the acts of those with gradual capacity, they could well be the iron made into gold.[131]

The gist of this long quotation from Chinul is that ideally one should be able to fit in with the *Tao* without effort (Nature-oriented cultivation) after "seeing into Nature," but that in reality some people still have to rely temporarily on the Characteristic-oriented cultivation of *samādhi* and *prajñā* even after their sudden enlightenment. This provisional reliance, however, is still qualitatively different from the pure gradual path followed by those who are ignorant of sudden enlightenment. Chinul calls the former "perfect-gradual" 圓漸 in distinction

[131] *Pŏbŏ*, pp. 54–56. "Defiled cultivation" means Characteristic-oriented (hence, defiled) cultivation, whereas undefiled cultivation means Nature-oriented cultivation which does not admit from the beginning any defilements to be cut off or removed.

to the latter's "gradual-perfect" 漸圓.[132] The idea is that one already has the perfection in oneself—or has clinched the victory already, so to speak—but still needs some light work of spiritual adjustment and control case by case ("gradual"), and this is different from the laborious effort to reach perfection step by step. Using different terms, Chinul says that such provisional reliance means "Phenomena-accomplishing cultivation not far removed from the cultivation of no-thought."[133] In short, as the term "perfect-gradual" indicates, it is still a form of paradoxical cultivation made possible by the power of sudden enlightenment, an "evolution" after the "revolution."

Thus, whether one follows the Nature-oriented cultivation of *samādhi* and *prajñā* or provisionally relies on the Characteristic-oriented cultivation, the quality of cultivation no longer remains the same as it was before the complete turn in one's mental outlook resulting from sudden enlightenment, and one may take one form of cultivation or the other according to one's spiritual capacity. But Chinul's theory of Sŏn is generally oriented to people with less than the highest capacity. Thus what Chinul ordinarily means by the gradual cultivation that has to follow sudden enlightenment is the practice of having provisional recourse to the Characteristic-oriented cultivation of *samādhi* and *prajñā* rather than that of the straight carefree Nature-oriented cultivation that Chinul considers to be essentially the *sudden* cultivation that Ch'eng-kuan talks about.[134] The former is the most appropriate form of cultivation for those possessed of a capacity that is neither too high nor too low: high enough to have sudden enlightenment but at the same time low enough to have affinity with those who find in themselves a gap between knowing and doing.

Through our discussion of the two kinds of *samādhi* and *prajñā*

---

132 *Chŏryo*, p. 730.
133 *Chŏryo*, p. 730.
134 *Ibid.*, p. 729. Ch'eng-kuan's conception of sudden cultivation is described as "free cultivation, which fits in with the *Tao* in an empty manner, with no [act of] watching and purifying."

thus far, we have become acquainted to some extent with the meaning of *samādhi* and *prajñā* for Chinul. Let us examine the two from a somewhat different angle, so that we may be able to determine more exactly their concrete significance in Chinul's conception of the process of Sŏn. The following passage, which Chinul quotes from Tsung-mi, is revealing:

> As it is said in the *Pŏpchip pyŏrhaengnok*: "From the generation of the thought [of enlightenment] to the attainment of Buddhahood, there is only quiescence and knowing. Changeless and ceaseless as they are, their names vary slightly according to the positions [of cultivation]. With regard to the moment of clear enlightenment, they are called Principle [quiescence] and wisdom [knowing]; with regard to the moment of the generation of the thought [of enlightenment] and cultivation, they are called cessation [*chih, śamatha*] and contemplation [*kuan, vipaśyanā*]; with regard to the free accomplishment of the act [of cultivation], they are called *samādhi* and *prajñā*; and with regard to the moment when defilements are completely exhausted and the Buddhahood realized with merits perfectly fulfilled they are named *bodhi* and *nirvāṇa*. From the beginning of the generation of the thought to the final state there is only quiescence and knowing (*Po. 19*).

The main point in this statement is that the pairs of concepts, each denoting the different levels of spiritual attainment in the process of cultivation, are all based on the two aspects, quiescence and knowing, of the Essence of True Mind. Thus, as in *samādhi* and *prajñā*, with regard to each of these pairs of concepts we can distinguish between the Nature-oriented and the Characteristic-oriented meanings. As far as the Nature-oriented meaning of them is concerned, they are identical, namely quiescence and knowing of the True Mind, in which no empirical or verbal distinction, such as the above pairs of concepts, has ultimate significance. It is only when we leave this world of the Essence (Nature, Principle) and talk about its various manifestations or Functions (Characteristics, Phenomena) at the various levels of cultivation that a difference begins to emerge. It is on this level that we now take a close look at these pairs of concepts.

Since "the moment of clear enlightenment" refers to sudden enlightenment, we exclude it from consideration here, which is concerned with the problem of cultivation. Nor do *bodhi* and *nirvāṇa* come into our discussion, for they are the final effect of the process of cultivation. Thus we are only concerned with the two interim pairs of concepts, namely *śamatha-vipaśyanā* and *samādhi-prajñā*. We have already mentioned that the cultivation of these two constitutes the process of cultivation from the first position of the ten faiths to the first position of the ten dwellings, where a different kind of enlightenment, called realization-enlightenment, is said to be attained.[135] Thus what we are discussing here is the process of cultivation that leads us from the understanding-enlightenment as the very beginning of the act of Sŏn to the realization-enlightenment where the gap between knowing and doing becomes no longer a serious problem.

It seems clear from the passage quoted above that Chinul understands the cultivation of *chih-kuan* to be the means for attaining *samādhi-prajñā* (which, in turn, lead to *nirvāṇa* and *bodhi* ultimately). But Chinul seldom gives us concrete explanations of *chih-kuan*, nor does he use the term often. Instead, he is very fond of another equivalent pair of concepts, "quiescence" and "wakefulness" of "the path of parallel keeping of quiescence and wakefulness" 惺寂等 持門. Chinul seems to use the expressions "combined cultivation of *samādhi* and *prajñā*" and "parallel keeping of quiescence and wakefulness" interchangeably. But in terms of the nuance of the expression, quiescence-wakefulness, like *chih-kuan*, represents the concrete means for attaining *samādhi-prajñā*. Concerning quiescence and wakefulness, Chinul gives us the following explanation:

> Namely, in the early, middle, and late night, one should forget all conditions quietly and sit firm and straight; one does not grasp external Characteristics but embraces one's mind to illumine internally. First one governs thoughts following conditions by quiescence, and then governs obscurance by wakefulness. One controls obscurance and distraction in balance, and yet without the thought of grasping or rejecting, letting the mind be clear, bright, and not

---

135 See pp. 123–24.

dark, knowing without thoughts .... I-hsiu-chüeh [Yung-chia Hsüan-chiao] says, "Quiescence means not to think about external circumstances, good or evil and the like; wakefulness means not to produce obscurance and mental blankness and the like. If quiescent and not wakeful, there is obscurance; if wakeful and not quiescent, there are thoughts following conditions; if neither quiescent nor wakeful, there are not only thoughts following conditions but there is also falling into the dwelling of obscurance. If both quiescent and wakeful, one is not merely clear but also quiescent, and this is nothing other than to return back to the origin of the mysterious Nature (*Po.* 14).

The passage describes the act of cultivation that makes us "return back to the origin of the mysterious Nature."[136] What obstructs the movement of return is not merely the mental distraction caused by our involvement in manifold external phenomena. Even when the mental distraction is overcome, the danger of mental blankness may remain, and if so the clarity of the "jewel" will not appear. Thus one should govern the mental blankness by means of wakefulness until the luminous state comes into being where one "knows without knowing." The parallel keeping of quiescence and wakefulness, then, is the act of retrieving or revealing the ultimate reality of the True Mind, its quiescence and knowing. But just as there is the distinction of the Nature-oriented and Characteristic-oriented *samādhi* and *prajñā*, we have the same kind of distinction in the meaning of quiescence and wakefulness.[137] The above description concerns the Characteristic-oriented cultivation of quiescence and wakefulness, but only on a provisional basis, as we have seen.

We have mentioned previously that the Nature-oriented cultivation of *samādhi* and *prajñā*, as the most desirable form of cultivation after sudden enlightenment, corresponds to the "cultivation of no-thought." Both are effortless and free "cultivation without cultiva-

---

[136] Gramatically, "the mysterious Nature" is modified by "return back to the origin"; but in terms of meaning, the way I have translated them seems to be correct.
[137] See *Pŏbŏ*, p. 17.

tion" made possible by the power of sudden enlightenment. In his *Chinsim chiksŏl* Chinul uses the word "no-mind" (*musim, wu-hsin* 無心) instead of no-thought, but the meanings are identical.[138] Concerning no-mind Chinul says:

> Now what is called no-mind does not mean the nonexistence of the Essence of Mind; it simply means the existence of nothing in the mind. It is just as when we say "empty bottle"; we mean the existence of nothing in the bottle, and not the nonexistence of the body of the bottle. Therefore a patriarch said, "If you simply have no things in your mind and no-mind in things, you become naturally empty, spiritually quiescent, and subtle." This refers to the meaning of this mind [no-mind]. Seen from this [perspective], there may be no deluded mind but not no mysterious Function of True Mind (*Po.* 72).

Chinul suggests to us ten practical methods of "studying no-mind" or "cessation of falsity." They are:[139]

1) Observation by realizing: if a thought arises, one destroys it by realizing (its emptiness); then even realizing is forgotten as well, leading to no-mind.

2) Resting: one does not think of either good or evil; when thought arises, one rests suddenly like a foolish person or like the incense burner in an old shrine.

3) Existence of objects with the extinction of mind: disregarding external objects, one concentrates on the cessation of one's own deluded mind; if the deluded mind ceases, no object can harm one.

4) Existence of mind with the extinction of objects: contemplate every object, internal as well as external, as empty and quiescent. Let One Mind exist alone.

5) Extinction of both mind and object: first empty external objects and then destroy the internal mind.

6) Existence of both mind and object: let mind stay in the position

---

[138] See Suzuki, *No Mind*, p. 29, and his analysis of the two words, *wu-hsin* and *wu-nien*, in his *Third Series*, p. 30.

[139] The following are excerpts from *Pŏbŏ*, pp. 72–76. Each of the ten methods could be discussed at length, but this must be saved for a later study.

of mind, and object stay in the position of object, so that they do not engage with each other.

7) Everything, external and internal, as Essence: let one regard the entire world, subject and object, as the Essence of the True Mind, so that nowhere may the deluded mind be found.

8) Everything, internal and external, as Function: let one contemplate the entire world, body and mind, and all activities as the Function of the True Mind.

9) Freedom with regard to Essence and Function: let one quietly fit in with the True Essence of empty quiescence, and yet let there be spiritual clarity, so that one may be not merely quiescent but also wakeful at the same time.[140]

10) Transcendence of Essence and Function: here one makes no distinction between internal and external, or between Essence and Function; everywhere One Gate of Great Liberation is formed.

As Chinul himself indicates, numbers three, four, five, and six are identical with the "fourfold. *liao-chien*" of Lin-chi.[141] Chinul says we do not have to study all these ten methods; we only need to follow whatever is suitable for us according to our capacity and habit. The most important thing to remember, according to Chinul, is that the study of these ten methods is "effort without effort" 無功之功, not "effort with mind" (*Po.* 76). That is, it is a paradoxical cultivation.

---

[140] Here Chinul seems to be identifying the unchanging function, knowing, with the changing Function of the True Mind. It is indeed this unchanging function that is the very source of the live world of changing Function.

[141] *Liao-chien* means, according to Suzuki, "to consider," "to estimate"; see *Third Series*, p. 19. n. 5. About the fourfold *liao-chien*, H. Dumoulin says the following in his *History of Zen Buddhism* (New York: 1963), p. 120:

> Lin-chi's sharp mind delighted in dialectics. In his collected sayings there is a text frequently commented upon by teachers of the sect in later periods. The ascent to the grasp of reality by the enlightened one is explained by four attitudes toward subject and object:
>
> > Sometimes take away [i.e. negate] the subject and not the object; another time take away the object and not the subject; yet another time take away both subject and object; and finally take away neither subject nor object [therefore affirm both at the same time].
>
> In form, the text depends upon the well-known "Four Propositions" of Indian Buddhist logic (*catushkotika*); as to meaning, it corresponds to the four aspects of reality in the Hua-yen doctrine.

Chinul's conception of cultivation after enlightenment is not exhausted by the cultivation of *samādhi* and *prajñā* or by the ten methods of studying no-mind. Gradual cultivation is used also for the benefit of other sentient beings. We have said earlier that for Chinul the cultivation after sudden enlightenment consists of two main parts. One is the cultivation of *samādhi* and *prajñā* to demolish the gap between knowing and doing, so that we may experience realization-enlightenment, not merely understanding-enlightenment. The other is the practice and cultivation of Bodhisattva activities. According to Chinul, the Bodhisattva's positive virtues are not automatically provided at the moment of "seeing into Nature." Wisdom and compassion, no less than knowing and doing, do not necessarily go together. Thus Chinul states:

> The path of cultivation after enlightenment is not just undefiled [cultivation]. It includes cultivation of myriad [good] acts, so that both self and others may be saved. Today's men of Sŏn all assert that when one clearly sees the Buddha-Nature the act and vow for the benefit of others is naturally fulfilled. I, Moguja, do not agree with this view. When one clearly sees the Buddha-Nature, it only means that Buddhas and sentient beings are equal and that there is no distinction of self and others. If, however, one does not generate the vow of compassion, I am afraid that one may be trapped by quiescent tranquility. This is what is meant by the *Treatise on Hua-yen* when it says that the nature of wisdom is quiescent tranquility, and that it should be protected by the vow. In the state of delusion before enlightenment, though there may be the will of the vow, the ability of the mind is dark and weak so that the vow cannot be fulfilled. After enlightenment, however when one contemplates with distinguishing wisdom the suffering of sentient beings, generates the mind of the compassionate vow, and practices the path of Bodhisattvahood according to one's capacity and lot, the act of enlightenment will be gradually perfected. What a delight it will be (*C.* 760)!

Here it is pronounced that the enlightenment that sees the identity of sentient beings with the Buddha is one thing, the vow of compassion is another. The latter is based on the distinguishing wisdom (or differentiating wisdom 差別智, contrasted with the wisdom of

136

equality), in which all empirical distinctions, such as Buddha and sentient being or saint and ordinary being, reappear in spite of the enlightenment through which they have been dissolved in the "sea of Nature."

The Bodhisattva path also requires various miraculous powers. According to Chunul, these are only developed by gradual cultivation after enlightenment. Chinul says critically:

> These days some who read the biographical records [of eminent masters] notice the miraculous things accompanying the obtainment of the *Dharma*, and assert that right at the moment of seeing into Nature there always appear the miraculous wisdom and the talent of fluent speech. When they see persons lacking the mysterious functions of wisdom and speech, they straightway call them fakes and have no trust in them. These people failed to meet a good friend and did not learn well. They do not know that even after enlightenment the wisdom to discern illusions [of other people, sentient beings] and the myriad acts of Bodhisattvas are only gradually acquired (*C*. 760–61).

Chinul says that seeking miraculous powers without gradual cultivation is just like blaming the crookedness of the river while one does not know how to handle the boat (p. 9), and even if we have those powers, Chinul says they are only "secondary affairs of the saint" (*Po*. 42).

In addition to the "myriad acts" 萬行 of Bodhisattvas Chinul also mentions "numerous good things" 衆善 or "various good *dharmas*" 諸善法, and regards the cultivation of all these acts as "the auxiliary" 助 of the True Mind in distinction to "the primary" 正 of the True Mind, which is the study of no-mind or the cultivation of *samādhi* and *prajñā* for one's own spiritual perfection (*Po*. 81–82). Concerning the specifics of the myriad acts of Bodhisattvahood, Chinul does not talk much.[142] But he points out the basic spirit governing the cultivation of the myriad good acts:

> Although there are such *upāya* assisting the *Tao* as giving, precepts,

---

[142] He mentions, for instance, the "giving without dwelling upon Characteristics" of

perseverance, and others, and the practice of myriad acts; due to the prior enlightenment of the empty nature of defilements, the habitual forces to be governed are born without being born and the act of enlightenment that governs [defilements] acts without action. Free from the subject [one who governs] and the object [the governed, i.e., defilements], doing nothing [artificial] while following conditions, this is called true cultivation (*C.* 776).

Thus far, we have studied Chinul's concept of the cultivation that has to follow sudden enlightenment. Before we conclude this study of what we call the process of Sŏn, we have to discuss Chinul's view of Pure Land practices. We have seen that as a Sŏn master who is firmly convinced of the truth that Mind is Buddha, Chinul naturally discredits any realistic conception of Amit'a Buddha and the Western Paradise, conceived of as external objects. He criticizes such notions with words from the *Treatise on Hua-yen*:

This path of the teaching of the one vehicle is established by the Fundamental Wisdom and is called the vehicle of complete wisdom. Since the worlds of the ten directions, as broad as empty space, become the realms of Buddhas, the minds and worlds belonging to all the Buddhas and sentient beings interpenetrate each other like the multiple reflections [of mirrors]. It does not teach whether a world has a Buddha or not, nor does it discuss the existence of the counterfeit-*dharma* or degenerate-*dharma*. Every moment is the time when Buddhas arise and every moment is the right-*dharma*. This is the [teaching] of the ultimate [*nītārtha*] *sūtras*, whereas the expedient *sūtras* talk about this world as an impure land, a separate world as the Pure Land, the places with a Buddha or without a Buddha, and the counterfeit-*dharma* and degenerate-*dharma* (*Po.* 3).

According to Chinul, the understanding of the Mahāyāna doctrine of Mind-only is crucial for the proper attitude toward Pure Land Buddhism.[143] One who knows it, although he may desire rebirth in

---

the *Diamond Sūtra*, but without much discussion (*Pŏbŏ*, p. 82). In *Chŏryo*, he mentions worship of the Buddha, recitation of *sūtras*, precepts, perseverance, and so on (pp. 774–75).

[143] *Pŏbŏ*, pp. 30, 32.

the Pure Land and be engaged in the recitation of the Buddha's name, realizes that "all the glorious things in the Buddha's world have no coming or going, being solely manifestations of Mind and not separate from Suchness.[144] Chinul even says that if one clearly understands Mind-only and practices contemplation following it, one will surely be born in the Pure Land, even though one may not seek rebirth by means of recitation.[145] He supports his view on many authorities:

> The *Chŏngmyŏnggyŏng* [*Vimalakīrti-sūtra*] says: "If one desires to purify the Buddha-land, one should duly purify one's mind; following the purification of the mind, the Buddha-land is also purified." The *Platform Sūtra* says: "If the ground of the mind is without impurity, the West is not far from here; but if one's nature produces impure thoughts, what Buddha would come to welcome and invite [at the time of his death]?" The Sŏn master Yen-shou says, "If one knows Mind, one is born in the Pure Land of Mind-only; to be attached to external circumstances means merely to fall into the circumstances with which one happens to be associated." The meaning of seeking rebirth in the Pure Land, as expounded by the Buddha and the patriarchs above, is in every case not separate from one's own mind. I do not know from where, if not from the source of one's own mind, one is to enter [the Pure Land] (*Po.* 28).

Yet despite this spiritualized and internalized conception of the Pure Land, Chinul endorses the practice of recitation and longing for rebirth in the Pure Land in at least two cases. First, he prescribes it for those for whom the cultivation of *samādhi* and *prajñā* alone is not enough and who thus need the help of "other-power" (*t'aryŏk, tariki* 他力) in addition to one's own power (*charyŏk, jiriki* 自力). Chinul says:

> Some cultivators, although they hear about the pure and mysterious power of their own minds, and so have faith and joy and are engaged in cultivation and practice, are unable to forget passions due to the strong attachment, from the beginningless past, to the Character-

[144] *Pŏbŏ*, p. 29.
[145] *Ibid.*, p. 28.

istics of ego and the formation of various obstacles of illusion out of the extremely heavy habitual forces. They should destroy [the defilements] by the inference that the body and mind of oneself and others, and the four elements and five groups [*skandhas* composing man] come into being like hallucinations out of the [various] conditions; that they are empty and temporary and not real, just like a bubble the inside of which is empty; hence, what can we take for self and what for others? If they deeply contemplate thus and adroitly wash away the dust of passions; if their minds become humble and pious, far away from arrogance; if they cut and suppress the appearance [of defilements]; and if they take recourse to *samādhi* and *prajñā*, they will gradually enter into the clear and quiet Nature.

Chinul continues:

Yet if these people lack the myriad good things to help open their own power, I am afraid that they will be stuck. So they must directly serve the Three Jewels with diligence, read and recite Mahāyāna [sūtras], practice *Tao*, worship, repenting and generating the vow ceaselessly from beginning to end. Due to the magnanimous heart that loves and honors the Three Jewels, they acquire the divine protecting power of the Buddhas, annihilate the karmic obstacles and their root of the good does not retrogress. If they in this manner seek the supreme enlightenment with the mutual support of own power and other-power, and of internal and external, would it not be beautiful (*Po.* 26)?

According to Chinul there are two types of those who "seek the mutual support of the internal and the external," and their vows are different:

There are some whose vow of compassion is strong, and who do not feel averse to the birth-and-death [*saṁsāra*] of this world. They seek the benefit of self and others, grow in compassion and wisdom, and seek the great enlightnment. Wherever they may be born, their vow is to meet the Buddha and hear the *Dharma*. These people do not particularly seek the Pure Land, nor do they worry about backsliding in difficult situations (*Po.* 27).

Contrasted with this first type of person are those who have to seek the Pure Land:

140

There are, on the other hand, some who strongly feel aversion and attraction of the impure and the pure and of pain and pleasure. Their vow is to transfer [the merit of] whatever *samādhi* and *prajñā* they may have cultivated, and the root of the good [good acts understood as the root producing good reward], towards rebirth in the other land. They want to meet the Buddha, hear the *Dharma* and quickly attain the nonbacksliding position, in order to return to this world to deliver sentient beings. Though these people have the intention of solely concentrating on internal illumination, their perseverance is not enough, so that they are afraid that if they stay in this world and encounter difficult situations they might backslide (*Po.* 27).

Unfortunately, Chinul does not elaborate on this apparently "realistic" concept of Pure-Land faith. How this concept squares with his more prominent Mind-only view of the Pure Land, Chinul leaves unanswered. But this dual approach is consistent with his scheme of "sudden enlightenment and gradual cultivation," and with his insight into the reality of the gap between knowing and doing and between Principle and Phenomena; we *know* that our Mind is Amit'a Buddha and the Pure Land, but it is a different problem whether we *are* (in action) really Amit'a Buddha and the Pure Land. It is also not very clear what Chinul has in mind when he mentions "other-power." Still, a few points need to be noted in his concept of Pure Land faith. The Pure Land itself is not the goal, but merely a means, in the sense that it provides more favorable circumstances for cultivation—perhaps it is in this sense that Chinul talks about other-power. The idea of returning back to this world for Bodhisattva's activity draws our attention as well. But the most important aspect is the idea of the transference of the merit acquired by one's own power accumulated through the cultivation of *samādhi* and *prajñā* and other "roots of the good" (*kuśala-mūla*). Whatever other-power may have meant for Chinul, he never intended it to mean total abandoning of one's own spiritual effort. Thus Chinul says:

The aim of these two types of person who rely on the mutual support of the internal and the external agrees with the sacred teaching, and each type has its rationale. Those who seek the Pure Land have the

141

effort of *samādhi* and *prajñā* in the midst of the quiet and clear Nature, and so already fit in with the realm internally realized by the Buddha [Amit'a]. Thus when compared with those who hope for rebirth by mere recitation of the name and by the imagination of the revered face [of the Buddha], the inferior and the superior can be readily known (*Po.* 27).

Another legitimate way of practicing the recitation is to do it as a means of attaining *samādhi* (*yŏmbul sammae, samādhi* by *nien-fo* 念佛三昧), by which one achieves mental concentration even if one's passions are deep and one does not know "upon hearing the truth about Mind ... where to put one's thought."[146] Thus *yŏmbul* is conceived of as a form of cultivation. Chinul recommends ten kinds of *yŏmbul* for the purpose of attaining *samādhi*:[147] *yŏmbul* by precepts for body, precepts for mouth, precepts for mind, by thinking (of the Buddha) while moving, by thinking in quietude, while in talking, while in silence, by contemplation of the Characteristics, by contemplation of no-mind, and by contemplation of Suchness. The first three emphasize the observance of precepts before the recitation. Chinul is critical of those who are engaged in recitation without cultivation of precepts:

> These days, [some] lay people and perverted ones do not cut off the ten evils [murder, theft, lying, and so on] or the eight vicious errors [the opposites of the eight right paths]. They do not cultivate the five precepts [for lay people] or the ten goods [the opposite of the ten evils], but with distorted understanding and private desires erroneously seek the invocation of the Buddha, giving vent to wrong wishes and seeking rebirth in the West. This is like trying to fit a square peg into a round hole. Even though these people think they are observing the recitation of the [name of the] Buddha, how would the intention of the Buddha fit with it?[148]

Chinul says that all ten kinds of *yŏmbul* arise from the "true

---

146 *Pŏbŏ*, p. 32.

147 We give here only their names, from the part of the *Yŏmbul yomun* contained in *Chōsen zenkyōshi*, pp. 191–192.

148 Translated from the *Sammun chikchi*, ed. by Chinhŏ P'algae (Unjŏk Monastery: 1769), "*yŏmbulmun.*"

enlightenment of one thought." And he explains that *yom* (*nien*) means to keep and nourish the True Nature and not to forget it, while *bul* (*fo*) means to reflect and illuminate the True Mind and to be constantly enlightened and not obscured.[149] As Nukariya Kaiten rightly points out, the "true enlightenment of one thought" refers to sudden enlightenment, while the ten kinds of *yŏmbul* are meant to be gradual cultivation from shallow to deep.[150]

Chinul's theory of Sŏn is from the outset not meant for those of the highest capacity, for whom no theory or "genuine teaching in words" is necessary. Thus in the theory of sudden enlightenment, the exoteric path of understanding-enlightenment is established by Chinul to bring more people into the Sŏn experience of sudden enlightenment. He even opened the door to students of Kyo by establishing "the path of complete-sudden faith and understanding." Then in his theory of gradual cultivation Chinul again demonstrated the spirit of accommodation to the people endowed with a not very high spiritual capacity. Hence the distinction of Nature-oriented cultivation of *samādhi* and *prajñā* (or simply the cultivation of no-thought) and the provisional cultivation of the Characteristic-oriented *samādhi* and *prajñā*. Then also, for the sake of those who find even the latter path difficult to follow, Chinul allows Pure Land faith and practice, as we have just seen. Even though this tendency to make the Buddhist path easier and more accessible to people did not go as far as it did with his contemporaries, the Buddhist leaders in Kamakura Japan, still it forms one of the prominent features of Chinul's approach to Sŏn.

Chinul does not stop with gradual cultivation. There should be the final moment of perfection, a decisive experience of spiritual consummation. Chinul's own religious quest came to its end through such an experience when he encountered the *hwadu* Sŏn of Ta-hui. Hence our discussion of his theory of Sŏn cannot conclude without treating his concept of *kanhwa* Sŏn.

---

[149] "Yŏmbul yomun," *Sammun chikchi*.
[150] *Chōsen zenkyōshi*, p. 192.

4. The Perfection of Sŏn: The Path of Direct Cutting

Considering what we have discussed thus far, we may get the superficial impression that Chinul's Sŏn is a very intellectual Sŏn—or, more accurately, Sŏn based upon Kyo and upon "genuine teaching in words"—and that there is no element that really fits in with the popularly known characteristics of Ch'an Buddhism such as "nonestablishment of letters," "transmission from mind to mind," or "separate transmission outside of Kyo." Chinul himself would have been the last one to deny this, for he knew what he was doing and why he was doing it. For Chinul, Sŏn should not be solely an esoteric tradition accessible only to a small number of people whom we might call "spiritual aristocrats." Yet this is only half of Chinul's approach to Sŏn. One may enter into Sŏn through Kyo, or "genuine teaching in words", but one should not end up only with Kyo. To borrow the famous simile of the raft, when one reaches the other shore of the river one should immediately leave the raft. According to Chinul, this leaving, however, is as difficult as using the raft, if not more difficult. Thus one needs a special method for it, namely the *kanhwa* Sŏn. Furthermore, according to Chinul, there are some persons endowed with "supercapacity" who are able to enter directly into the truth, or fit in with the True Mind, without having recourse to the "genuine teaching in words" at all—hence "the path of direct cutting" (*kyŏngjŏlmun* 徑截門). This again is possible through *kanhwa* Sŏn 看話禪.

Had Chinul's approach to Sŏn merely stopped with gradual cultivation (and the sudden enlightenment that precedes it) and not established this path of direct cutting, he himself would not have been able to escape the epithet of "a master of intellectual understanding" that he assigns to Shen-hui. Had he not encountered the *kanhwa* Sŏn of Ta-hui, his Sŏn might have suffered from a lack of those distinct features pertaining to the world of Sŏn—the immutable sense of self-assurance, the sudden leap that utterly defies intellectual comprehension, the spontaneous expression of spiritual creativity, and the immediate and perfect unity with the *Tao*. But throughout his works Chinul also talks about a different approach to Sŏn from the two paths we have considered so far, and hence a different level of spiritual awareness and attainment. The following two examples adduced by Chinul may give some indication of the level of truth to which this third path of Chinul's Sŏn intends to lead us:

> The Sŏn Master Ta-hui says: "Kyubong [Tsung-mi] calls it the spiritual knowing, and Shen-hui refers to it saying that the one word "knowing" is the gate to myriad mysteries; and Hwangnyong Sasimsu [Huang-lung] says that "knowing" is the gate to myriad woes; it is easy to understand Tsung-mi and Shen-hui, but it is difficult to understand the mind of Sasim. At this point, one should be equipped with transcendental eyes, for it cannot be explained to others nor transmitted. Thus Unmun [Yüan-men] said that if one is going to utter a word, one should do it as if holding a sword in front of the gate; at one phrase, there must be a path for the body to escape, for otherwise only death will be there under the phrase" (C. 805).
>
> The Sixth Patriarch said: "There is one thing upholding the sky above and supporting the earth below. It exists always in the midst of [our] movements, and yet it cannot be grasped in them. What do you call it?" Shen-hui, moving forward from the gathering, said that it is the original source of all the Buddhas as well as my Buddha-Nature. "Even If I called it a thing," said the patriarch, "it would still not be fitting; how are you able to call it the Buddha-Nature of the original source? Even though you may later cover your head with hay, you will become no more than a disciple of intellectual understanding" (C. 805–806).

Here we see Chinul suddenly turning around and siding with Ta-hui in cutting down the two masters Shen-hui and Tsung-mi, with whom he had been so closely associated thus far. Though Shen-hui's famous phrase "one word 'knowing' is the gate to myriad mysteries" is the cornerstone of the doctrine of exoteric sudden enlightenment, as we have seen, it comes to be ridiculed, and Shen-hui is branded a "disciple of intellectual understanding." This is the world of *kanhwa* Sŏn that Chinul is going to talk about now.

We have already said that Chinul distinguishes between two kinds of enlightenment, understanding-enlightenment and realization-enlightenment. We have also seen that understanding-enlightenment, because of its intellectual character, ensues in the gap in us between knowing and doing—what Chinul calls "the obstacle arising from understanding [-enlightenment]"—and that we need the gradual cultivation of *samādhi* and *prajñā* to overcome this gap and achieve realization-enlightenment. But we did not refer to any specific step or moment clearly marking the attainment of realization-enlightenment. It was simply understood to be accomplished at some point when "*samādhi* and *prajñā* become perfect and clear" in us. No mention is found either in Tsung-mi or Li T'ung-hsüan concerning any particular way to attain that enlightenment. As for Tsung-mi, gradual cultivation is the process as well as the end; we simply continue it as far as we can, and there is no specific moment when we can have the assurance of realization-enlightenment. Li T'ung-hsüan, according to Chinul, thinks:

> Since today's people, engaged in the act of contemplation, are inclined toward hearing and understanding, only after they have gone through seeing, hearing, understanding, and acting [cultivation] will they enter into realization [enlightenment]; upon entering into realization, however, they should transcend what they had previously heard and understood, and fit in with [the Tao] by no-thinking [same as no-thought].[151]

This certainly talks about the realization-enlightenment that comes after "hearing, understanding, and cultivation." But it does not tell us *how* to "transcend what they had previously heard and understood and fit in with the *Tao* by no-thinking."

But now, according to Chinul, a special method exists, called the path of direct cutting, to achieve this realization-enlightenment, a direct way to enter into the enlightenment where no breach between knowing and doing is found—but without going through the scheme of sudden enlightenment and gradual cultivation. And for Chinul[152]

---

[151] *Pŏbo*, p. 131; Chinul is fond of this passage from Li and quotes it often, see pp. 124, 135.

[152] Cf. Dōgen, for whom realization (*satori*) is identified with—or subsumed under—cultivation. It is said that he was troubled in his young days with the question of why

this new enlightenment constitutes a distinct step, clearly marked off from the process of cultivation, not a vague point in that process. Just as the understanding-enlightenment suddenly occurs to a person as a distinct experience, so is the realization-enlightenment an independent religious experience. Chinul's *Kanhwa kyŏrŭiron* is a discussion of this really sudden path in Sŏn: what it is, how it is to be practiced, and how it is differentiated from other forms of enlightenment taught in Kyo. In that work, Chinul says:

> What is now being discussed, namely, the gate of entrance through the direct cutting, separately transmitted by the School of Sŏn outside of Kyo, is difficult to believe and enter not only for the students of Kyo; even in our School [i.e. Sŏn], those with lower capacity and shallow knowledge are vague [about it] and do not know. Now I will tell a few stories of how they entered it, in order to make those, who do not believe and do not know, realize that there exists in the gate of Sŏn an entrance by direct cutting that is different from the sudden teaching as well as from the entrance by the complete teaching [Hwaŏm]. This is with regard to the slowness and fastness [of entering into enlightenment], which depends upon "reliance on Kyo" or "leaving Kyo" (*Po.* 131).

A substantial part of the *Kanhwa kyŏrŭiron* addresses itself to this issue of how the enlightenment accessible through *kanhwa* Sŏn differs from the enlightenment in the sudden teaching (the fourth of the five categories of Buddhist teaching in Hwaŏm doctrinal classification) and in the complete teaching (Hwaŏm teaching, the fifth and the highest teaching). Before we examine this problem, let us first see what the *kanhwa* Sŏn Chinul has in mind is like.

---

one still needs cultivation at all if one is already endowed with the Buddha-Nature. The answer he came up with was the idea of the unity of cultivation and realization, *shu-shō ichinyo* 修證一如. He said:

> In Buddhism, practice and enlightenment are one and the same. Since practice has its basis in enlightenment, the practice even of the beginner contains the whole of original enlightenment. Thus while giving directions as to the exercise, [the Zen master] warns him not to await enlightenment apart from the exercise, because this [the exercise] points directly to the original enlightenment. Since enlightenment is already contained in the exercise, there is no end to enlightenment, and since it is the exercise of enlightenment, it has no beginning. Quoted from H. Dumoulin, *A History of Zen Buddhism* (Boston, 1963), p. 166.

Chinul definitely calls Shen-hui "a master of intellectual understanding" and says that he is not the proper heir of the Sixth Patriarch. The opposite of "master of intellectual understanding" (*chihae
chongsa* 知解宗師) is for Chinul "authentic master" (*ponbun chongsa*
本分宗師),[153] and he finds the true representative of such a master
in Ta-hui. Concerning him Chinul says:

> Ching-shan Ta-hui, the revered monk whom we follow, is an authen-
> tic master, the seventeenth in the orthodox line of transmission right
> from Ts'ao-ch'i [the Sixth Patriarch]. The way we enter [enlighten-
> ment] by studying the phrases [*hwadus*] belonging to the path of
> direct cutting established by him is far different from these [other
> theories about *hwadu* Sŏn]. Why? The *hwadu* suggested by him such
> as: "the cypress tree in front of the courtyard," "three *chin* of
> hemp," "nonexistence of Buddha-Nature in dogs" are entirely
> devoid of any direct disclosure of truth. He simply gives an uninter-
> esting and ungraspable *hwadu* and then warns us saying, "If illusory
> thoughts have not been destroyed, the fire in the mind will blaze
> up; in such a moment one should simply grasp [take and think hard
> about] the *hawdu* about which one had doubt.[154]

Then Chinul continues to quote Ta-hui's instructions about the way
to grasp the *hwadu*:

> It is like a monk asking Chao-chou whether dogs also have the
> Buddha-Nature; Chao-chou answered "no". Now when one simply
> grasps and thinks about this, neither the right nor the left is proper.
> [Here follow the ten prohibitions]: Do not have the thought of
> existence or nonexistence; do not try to figure out whether non-
> existence means true nothingness; do not try to understand its reason,
> nor cogitate and figure out with the mind; do not turn to where the
> eyebrows are lifted and the eyes are blinking [gestures of Sŏn mas-
> ters] in order to settle there, nor turn to the path of words to find
> the living device; do not be high in the state of no·concern, nor try
> to seek the understanding where [the *hwadu*] is being grasped;
> do not take letters for proof, nor wait for enlightenment out

---

[153] This means the master directly concerned with the authentic (or original, proper)
thing itself, i.e. True Mind.

[154] "The cypress tree in front of the courtyard" is a translation of Suzuki's: *chin* is a
little more than a pound.

148

of [your] ignorance. Let there be no use of mind, and when mind has no place do not be aftaid of falling into emptiness; in it is after all the good place. All of a sudden you will find that the old mouse will enter into the cow horn so that it dies immediately [a Chinese custom to catch a mouse by putting greasy things in a cow horn].[155]

Chinul then concludes:

Since Ta-hui presents *hwadu* with comments like this, students simply grasp it and think about it throughout the twelve divisions of a day and in the four modes of acting [walking, dwelling, sitting, and lying]. With respect to the Enlightenment Principle of Mind-Nature, they have neither the understanding [consciousness] of transcending words and Characteristics nor of the nonobstruction of Origination-by-condition [of the *Dharmadhātu*]. As soon as a single thought of intellectual understanding of the Buddhist truth arises, they will be trapped by the ten kinds of the disease of intellectual understanding. Thus they should let down each [thought] without at the same time calculating whether they are letting down or not, or whether they are trapped by the disease or not. Suddenly in that uninteresting and ungraspable *hwadu*, at one leap off the ground [sudden enlightenment] the *Dharmadhātu* of One Mind will be revealed clearly so that the hundreds of thousands of *samādhis* provided in Mind-Nature and the gate of infinite aspects [of Mind] will be completely obtained without seeking. For it is free from what had been previously obtained incompletely by reason, hearing, and understanding, and this is the secret of entering [enlightenment] by realization [enlightenment] through the study of *hwadu* in the path of direct cutting in Sŏn (*Po.* 129–30).

---

[155] *Pŏbŏ*, p. 129. This passage is Chinul's quotation from *Words of Ta-hui* (*T.* 47, No. 1998; it is found on p. 921c). Chinul does not quote exactly from Ta-hui, but inserts two more prohibitions; "Do not try to figure out whether nonexistence means true nothingness" and "Do not wait for enlightenment out of ignorance," to make ten prohibitions altogether. In his *Chŏryo*, however, he quotes exactly and thus gives only eight prohibitions. But then Chinul comments: "I, Moguja, say that this discourse on the *Dharma* only elucidates eight kinds of disease; but if we examine what is said before and after, there are two more" (*C.* 813). Suzuki gives a translation (somewhat different from mine) of the ten prohibitions in his *Second Series* (pp. 105–06) where he wrongly attributes them to T'ui-yin, a famous sixteenth-century Korean Sŏn master (better known as Sŏsan or Hyujŏng).

This lengthy quotation from Chinul's *Kanhwa kyŏrŭiron* tells us about his view of Ta-hui and *kanhwa* Sŏn. The predominant concern in Chinul's adoption of the *kanhwa* Sŏn of Ta-hui is how to overcome the "disease of intellectual understanding" (*chihae pyŏng* 知解病). There is no indication throughout his works that Chinul subscribed to—in fact, it is not even clear whether he was aware of—the strong polemical stance of Ta-hui's *kanhwa* Sŏn against the so-called silent-illumination Sŏn 默照禪. In many ways, indeed, his emphasis on the parallel keeping of *samādhi* and *prajñā*, or quiescence and wakefulness, seems to be close to the spirit of the silent-illumination Sŏn.[156] Thus it was purely on the basis of his personal experience of the power of *kanhwa* to destroy the disease of intellectual understanding that Chinul came to establish this third path.

The idea that understanding or consciousness prevents us from perfect unity with the truth, or that it spoils the purity of the immediate religious experience, is not confined to Sŏn Buddhism alone. The yearning for the pre-conscious or supra-conscious primordial world where there is no split of subject and object and no divided self underlies all mystical aspirations. The Taoist yearning for spontaneous unity with the way of nature and the Vedānta conceptions of *Ātman* and *Brahman* are classic illustrations of this aspiration. Nowhere in Buddhist literature is this yearning to overcome the barrier of intellect better expressed than in the *Prajñāpāramitā* literature, which propounds the philosophy of Emptiness (*śūnyatā*). Again and again in this literature, we come across self-canceling remarks designed to preclude conscious attachment arising from the remark itself, because this attachment betrays the very principle of Emptiness. Thus it is natural that Chinul's imaginary interlocutor questions him whether the removal of intellectual disease through the method of studying *hwadu* is after all not identical with the philosophy of "transcending words and thoughts" set forth in the *Prajñā-*

---

[156] Nor does Chinul share the close orientation to the Confucian literati and bureaucrats of Ta-hui's Sŏn; on this matter, see Araki Kengo's discussion of Ta-hui Sŏn in his *Bukkyō to jukyō*, pp. 194–234.

pāramitā-sūtras and in the "sudden teaching" (represented by the *Vimalakīrti-sūtra*, which emphasizes the ineffable nature of truth):

> The Question: If so, the so-called "no-wisdom" and "no-attainment" in the *Prajñāpāramitā sūtra*, and what is said in the sudden teaching that, when not a single thought arises, one becomes a Buddha, and so forth, that is, to transcend words and thoughts: is this what is meant by you (*Po. 124*)?

To this question Chinul replies:

> All five teachings [of the Hwaŏm doctrinal classification system] have the aspect of transcending words and thoughts, because each teaching has a way of cutting off words and thereby letting us forget the words and know the meaning. Hīnayāna realizes Suchness where man is empty, and Mahāyāna Bodhisattvas realize Suchness where *dharmas* are empty. Under the gate of realization [證] all teachings transcend words and thoughts; if words and thoughts are not transcended, how could it be called realization?[157]

And Chinul says:

> The men of supercapacity in Sŏn who study *hwadu* and are well acquainted with its subtleties, do not generate the ten kinds of disease of intellectual understanding, and thus they can also be said to transcend words and thoughts. Yet suddenly, at one leap off the ground, the *Dharmadhātu* becomes brightly clear and they become naturally provided with virtues in a perfect and comprehensive way (*Po. 125*).

Chinul is saying in these passages that the aspect of "transcending words and thoughts" is present in all levels of Buddhist teaching, not merely in the sudden teaching alone, and that it also characterizes the spiritual realm realized by the path of *hwadu* Sŏn. But there is a difference of depth between the realm of realization available

---

[157] The "five teachings" are: Hīnayāna, elementary Mahāyāna (San-lun and Fa-hsiang teaching), final or advanced Mahāyāna (*Ch'i-hsin-lun*, T'ien-t'ai), sudden teaching (*Vimalakīrti-sūtra*), and the complete teaching of Hua-yen, according to Fa-tsang.

through *hwadu* Sŏn and the one possible through the sudden teaching. Chinul calls the latter "attainment of Buddhahood by the realization of Principle [Emptiness]" in distinction to the former which is "the realization of the *Dharmadhātu* of nonobstruction" or "the realization of the One Mind of the *Dharmadhātu*" (*Po.* 126–27). The implication is that the *Dharmadhātu* is a richer world than the rarefied world of mere Principle; it is the realm of Principle as well as of Phenomena, of Nature as well as of Characteristics, of Essence as well as of Function. In fact, Chinul says that the sudden teaching was merely established by Fa-tsang as an expedient, as an *upāya* meant specifically for "some group of sentient beings" who are "attached to empty and illusory names and Characteristics and so have difficulty in attaining mysterious enlightenment."[158] If Sŏn accommodates the sudden teaching, Chinul says that it is for the sake of those with inferior capacity who cannot cope with the esoteric transmission. But such people are not free from intellectual disease and are unable to find complete freedom with regard to "the phenomenal *dharmas* arising before their eyes" (that is, they only know Principle).[159]

If this is the case, then the further question is how the spiritual realm accessible through *kanhwa* Sŏn is to be differentiated from the *Dharmadhātu* of nonobstructed Origination-by-condition taught by the Hwaŏm complete teaching, and why is this esoteric path necessary at all?[160]

The "genuine teaching in words" which belongs to the path of complete-sudden faith and understanding is now called by Chinul "dead phrases" 死句 in contrast with the "living phrases" 活句 of the path of direct cutting:

> In the gate of Sŏn, the kinds of genuine teaching in words pertaining to complete-sudden faith and understanding are as many as the sands of the Ganges. Yet they are called dead phrases because they

---

[158] *Pŏbŏ*, pp. 124, 126, 127.
[159] *Ibid.*, p. 135.
[160] *Ibid.*, p. 134.

let people generate the obstruction of understanding 解礙. At the same time, however, since the beginning students of Mind are unable to study the living phrases pertaining to the path of direct cutting, [the gate of Sŏn] shows them the complete words [words of complete teaching] on the basis of Nature and lets them have faith and understanding so that they may not backslide. If, however, the man of higher capacity, who is capable of coping with the esoteric transmission, can free himself from the trap; when he has heard the uninteresting talk pertaining to the path of direct cutting, he is not trapped by the disease of intellectual understanding but suddenly knows the "falling place" [disappearance of ignorance]. Such a person is called one who acquires the great *dhāraṇī* by realizing a thousand things upon hearing one (*Po.* 122).

Thus, the path of complete-sudden faith and understanding is merely an expedient teaching for those unable to cope with the esoteric path of direct cutting. In understanding-enlightenment, the understanding becomes an obstacle. "If a man cuts forever the mundane thoughts," says Chinul quoting from the *Wŏngakkyŏng* (*Yüan-chüeh-ching*), "and attains the purity of the *Dharmadhātu*, then he will fall victim to the understanding of purity and thus will never be free in the complete enlightenment" (P. 124). To be sure, in Sŏn, Chinul says, the genuine teaching in words is much more concise in comparison to that in Kyo; yet even it cannot but be called dead phrases in the face of *hwadus*:

> Seen from the *hwadus* of the path of direct cutting, the genuine words and phrases like this [the *Dharma* gate of nonobstruction] in the gate of Sŏn, concise as they may be in comparison with the gate of Kyo, still do not transcend the ten kinds of disease caused by the existence of the intellectual understanding of the Buddhist truth. Thus it is said that students should study living phrases, not dead phrases. If they are enlightened by living phrases they will never forget for an eternity, but if they are enlightened by the dead phrases they will not even be able to save themselves completely.[161]

Furthermore, Chinul is well aware that the so-called ten kinds of disease of intellectual understanding could be done away with even

---

[161] Suzuki says about these two kinds of phrases:

in the path of complete-sudden faith and understanding by the knowledge of Origination-by-Nature. Yet he thinks that this is still not free from the disease:

> Again, according to the path of complete-sudden faith and understanding, even these ten kinds of disease of intellectual understanding arise out of True Nature, and so we have nothing to choose or reject. Since it has the path of words, the path of meaning, hearing, understanding, and ideas, it may well be trusted, accepted, upheld, and carried by the beginning students of mind. With regard to personal realization and esoteric fitting [in with truth] in the path of direct cutting, however, there exists no path of words, no path of meaning, and no hearing, understanding, or thoughts. There, even the principle of the nonobstructed Origination-by-condition of the *Dharmadhātu* is rather turned into an obstruction of explanation and understanding. Thus if not a man of great wisdom with higher capacity, how could one obtain it clearly and how could one acquire it with penetration (*Po.* 123)?

Chinul concludes:

> Those who enter [enlightenment] by direct cutting in the gate of Sŏn, do not from the beginning set their minds upon hearing and understanding of the *Dharma* and [its] aspects [Essence and Function, or Unchanging and Changing], but directly grasp and think about an uninteresting *hwadu*. Therefore, there is no path of words and meaning and no place of thinking by the [discriminating] consciousness of the mind; nor is there any [distinction of] before and after at the time of hearing, understanding, and acting [cultivation]. Suddenly, when the *hwadu* leaps up off the ground, the *Dharmadhātu* of the One Mind becomes brightly clear and round. If we compare the one who experiences [such a] leap in the gate of Sŏn with those who are

---

The Zen masters generally distinguish two kinds of *chü* [phrase]; the live one and the dead one. By the 'live *chü*' are meant such statements as give no clues whatever to rational interpretations but put an end to the functioning of the empirical consciousness; whereas the 'dead *chü*' are those that lend themselves to logical or philosophical treatment and therefore that can be learned from others and committed to memory. This according to T'ui-yin. *Second Series*, p. 105.

Again, it is not Sōsan (T'ui-yin) but Chinul who is the source of the distinction, at least as far as the *Mirror for Sŏn Students* (*Sŏn'ga kwigam*) is concerned, from which, I believe, Suzuki derived this particular information. The above passage by Chinul is from *Pŏbŏ*, p. 137.

engaged in the act of contemplation in the complete teaching, there is a vast difference of "inside of Kyo" and "outside of Kyo," and the difference in the fastness and slowness [in attaining enlightenment] can be known. Therefore, the separate transmission outside of Kyo far surpasses the vehicles of Kyo; it is not something that can be coped with by men of shallow knowledge (*Po.* 135).

To sum up, Chinul distinguishes the path of direct cutting on the one hand from the sudden teaching, which aims at the mere negative goal of "transcending words and thoughts" by the realization of Emptiness, and on the other hand from the understanding-enlightenment available through the path of complete-sudden faith and understanding. And thereby he defends the uniqueness of the esoteric path, "the separate transmission outside of Kyo," against the challenge by the skeptical minds of the students of Kyo—a challenge which must have been prevalent in Chinul's time, at least strong enough to call for his composition of a separate work exclusively devoted to the problem, namely the *Kanhwa kyŏrŭiron* [*Treatise for the Settlement of Doubts on* Kanhwa].

According to Chinul, we can apply ourselves to this esoteric path of direct cutting in two ways. One may directly go to this path without going through the scheme of sudden enlightenment (i.e. understanding enlightenment) and gradual cultivation. But in order to do so, one has to possess "supercapacity" (*Po.* 125). "The one supranormal path," says Chinul, "is difficult to believe in and to enter not merely for the students of Kyo but also for the men of lower capacity in Sŏn" (*Po.* 131). The worst thing for Chinul is that some people with lower capacity pretent to have supercapacity and are engaged solely in *hwadu* Sŏn, with no result at all. Chinul warns against these people:

As I see today's people cultivating mind, they do not rely on what letters point to, but regard the place of mutual esoteric transmission as the *Tao* [enlightenment]. Thus in this deluded manner they work in vain and fall asleep while sitting in meditation. Some even lose their minds or get confused in the act of contemplation.[162]

---

[162] We have discussed the meaning of this passage already earlier in the chapter.

Chinul says that "the man with the wisdom of realization present in him," "one who directly realizes the One Mind" by "the study of phrases", not by "the study of meaning [of the phrases or *hwadus*]" is nowadays hard to see and hear about (*Po.* 138). Thus merely to produce the "right intellectual view" by "the study of the meaning of a *hwadu*—something that Chinul says is not much different from the act of contemplation in the path of complete-sudden faith and understanding—is to be valued also. In fact, warning against those who are exclusively concerned with the removal of the intellectual disease without even having the true intellectual understanding, Chinul says:

> Let it be known that today's cultivators of the *Tao* in this period of degenerate-*dharma* should clearly distinguish the true and the false of one's own mind and the root and branches of birth and death according to genuine intellectual understanding. Only then with the words that mutilate the nail and cut the iron [namely, with *hwadus*] should they examine in detail the esoteric realm, and if they find the place of escape for their body [liberation], it may be regarded as the four corners [of the table] having settled on the ground. Even when thrown aloft, they do not move but obtain great freedom in coming to birth and in going to death (*C.* 814).

Thus, according to Chinul, one could either directly grapple with *hwadus* without any preceding paths, or go to them after one has gone through the two paths of sudden enlightenment and gradual cultivation. Chinul's *Kanhwa kyŏrŭiron* is more concerned with the former alternative, whereas his *Chŏryo* favors the latter approach. But ultimately the decision rests upon the spiritual capacity of the individual. We are inclined to think that Chinul preferred the latter approach to the former, as it was the course he himself took in his own religious quest. It is in this sense that we call the path of direct cutting "the perfection of Sŏn." But we should keep in mind that "perfection" here is not necessarily intended to mean the perfection obtainable only *after* the process. For some people endowed with supercapacity may attempt directly to obtain that perfection without previous preparation.

If the realization-enlightenment accessible through this path of direct cutting perfects the understanding-enlightenment based upon the genuine teaching in words, it also perfects at the same time the cultivation that follows upon sudden enlightenment. Unlike understanding-enlightenment, which creates a gap between knowing and doing, realization-enlightenment entered through this esoteric path is no longer accompanied by such a split. Perfect enlightenment entails perfect cultivation, and knowing is naturally translated into doing without any discrepancy. Chinul calls this perfect form of cultivation—if it can still be called cultivation—"the path of unity with the *Tao* in no-mind" (*musim haptomun* 無心合道門).

We have already examined the concept of "the cultivation of no-thought," or the study of no-mind, as the ideal form of cultivation after sudden enlightenment. We have also considered their equivalent, namely, the Nature-oriented cultivation of *samādhi* and *prajñā*, in distinction to the Characteristic-oriented cultivation of *samādhi* and *prajñā*. Chinul seems to hold the view that "the path of unity with the *Tao* in no-mind" (not even called "cultivation") is even higher than the path of Nature-oriented cultivation of *samādhi* and *prajñā* or the cultivation of no-thought. Chinul says:

> In the gate of Sŏn, in addition to the cultivation of *samādhi* and *prajñā*, there is the path of unity with the *Tao* in no-mind. So I record it here [*Chŏryo*] briefly so that the students of Kyo may know this one irregular path and have faith (*C.* 722).

Then Chinul goes on to explain:

> These two gates of *samādhi* and *prajñā* are the essence of cultivation; they are the great purport of the Buddha as well as of the patriarchs, and they are taught in the *sūtras* and treatises alike. But there is another path based upon the teaching of the patriarchs that is most concise and essential; it is called no-mind. What is it? If there is mind there is anxiety, but if there is no-mind then there is self-pleasure. ... If one does not directly realize the meaning of no-mind, one may govern, conquer, and cut off [defilements], but the appearance of anxiety will always be present before him. But if one knows no-mind, wherever one may go one will not be trapped; since there will be not a single piece of dust to face, what effort would one spend to remove and clean it up? Free from even a

157

single thought giving rise to passion, one does not have to rely on effort to forget conditions. Thus one should know that the unity with the *Tao* in no-mind, taught in Sŏn, is not bound by *samādhi* and *prajñā*. Why? Since they control distraction in accordance with Principle [quiescence, Emptiness], the students of *samādhi* [must] make effort to forget conditions; and the students of *prajñā*, since they choose a *dharma* and contemplate its emptiness, have the work of removing and cleaning up. Now, if one directly knows no-mind and is not trapped anywhere not a single piece of dust or thought comes externally nor does it constitute any thing particular; how could there be distorted expenditure of toilsome effort? Even the *samādhi* and *prajñā* of the Self-Nature are still caught in the realm where meaning functions; how much less would the path of leaving the dirt [i.e. the Characteristic-oriented cultivation of *samādhi* and *prajñā*] be able to reach it [no-mind]? Therefore, this is what is meant by the venerable Shih-t'ou when he says, "My gate of *Dharma* has been transmitted prior to the Buddha; it does not discuss meditation [*dhyāna*] and effort [*vīrya*] but is only versed in the Buddha's view." This unity with the *Tao* in no-mind is also to be entered through the path of direct cutting. The means of studying *hwadu* in it [the path] and making comment on it is so mysterious and esoteric that it cannot be set forth in detail. One who understands it is hard to come by (*C.* 722–24).

Here it is clearly stated that the unity with the *Tao* in no-mind denotes an even higher spiritual realm than the cultivation of Nature-oriented *samādhi* and *prajñā*, which Chinul says is still not completely free from "the functioning of meaning [or reason]." Nor is it in this realm of no-mind necessary at all to talk about the ten ways of studying no-mind. It is merely indicated that this highest form of cultivation—which is after all no act of cultivation but rather a life of freedom—is also to be made possible by way of the study of *hwadu*. Thus we may conclude that for Chinul this esoteric path, the third in the act of Sŏn, represents the perfection of the path of sudden enlightenment (or the path of complete-sudden faith and understanding) as well as of the path of gradual cultivation (or the path of parallel keeping of quiescence and wakefulness). It is this esoteric path that opens up the final realm where enlightenment is devoid of the hindrance of intellect, where the hiatus between knowing and doing does not ensue, and where even a verbal distinction between *samādhi* and *prajñā* becomes meaningless, there being no cultivation worthy of the name but simply spontaneous unity with the *Tao* in no-mind.

The inscription on the memorial stele of Chinul tells us that he established three paths for the students of Sŏn: the path of complete-sudden faith and understanding, the path of parallel keeping of quiescence and wakefulness, and the path of direct cutting. On this information our study of Chinul's theory of Sŏn (more accurately his theory of the act of Sŏn) has been primarily based. "Path" literally means the gate through which we enter into something. Thus by the three paths we are to enter into—or return to—the True Mind, the source of Sŏn. By the path of complete-sudden faith and understanding Chinul urges us to discover our true selves (Self); through the path of parallel keeping of quiescence and wakefulness he teaches us how to bridge the gap between the ideal and the real; and through the path of direct cutting Chinul shows us the secret of perfecting ourselves, not merely knowing and culti-vating ourselves. Self-discovery, self-cultivation, and self-perfection constitute for Chinul the beginning, process, and perfection of Sŏn.

Is self-perfection the end of the journey for Chinul? Yes and no. Yes, in the sense that one is fully integrated and at peace with the ultimate reality, the *Dharmadhātu* of the True Mind. No, since for Chinul Sŏn is not meant only for individual spiritual freedom. Social aware-ness, no less than individual aspiration, always remained a motivating force throughout Chinul's life. In accordance with the basic principles of the Mahāyāna one must learn not merely to transcend the world but also to remain in the world, not merely to develop the wisdom of Manjuśrī but also to develop the act and vow of Samantabhadra. We only need to be reminded of Chinul's own Bodhisattva activities carried out during the last period of his life in the Susŏnsa. These activities transformed Chinul from an anonymous hermit into a historic figure, the founder of the Korean Sŏn tradition. In our last chapter, we turn to an assessment of the significance of Chinul's Sŏn in the stream of the history of Korean Buddhism.

159

CHAPTER III

THE LEGACY OF CHINUL

HAVING EXAMINED THE LIFE AND THOUGHT of Chinul, it is now proper for us to conclude our study with a chapter devoted to the position that Chinul occupies in the history of Korean Buddhism. This chapter will also explain the title of our book: "Chinul, the Founder of the Korean Sŏn Tradition"; even though the major weight of our study does not lie in this concluding part. What we will do is simply to trace what remains of Chinul's Sŏn thought in the Korean Buddhist tradition down to the present day. Obviously, this has to be done in a very limited way; full treatment of the matter would easily require a separate volume. Here we will investigate Chinul's legacy under the following two headings.

1. *Chinul, the Susŏnsa, and the Buddhism of the Yi Dynasty*

In order to examine the influence Chinul had upon subsequent Korean Buddhism, it is necessary first of all to make a brief historical review of the course Buddhism took in Korea after Chinul. Heedless of Chinul's denunciations of the excessive pursuit of "fame and gain," Koryŏ Buddhism continued to follow its secular course as before. Many who shared Chinul's assessment of reality and his vision of the ideal flocked into the Susŏnsa under him, but the Susŏnsa itself had no external means of controlling or affecting the Buddhist community at large—the community that was deeply embedded in the socio-political structure of Koryŏ society itself in close alliance with its ruling class. Even the new political force of the Ch'oe family did not fundamentally alter the existing socio-political structure,

161

nor did it create a radically new social setting conducive to a fresh religious development such as we see in the evolving feudal order of contemporary Kamakura Japan. Furthermore, the Mongol invasion of Koryŏ absorbed almost the entire energy of the Ch'oe family as well as of the whole country, so that any new religious movement that arose would have had little chance to unfold.

It is true that the Ch'oe family, particularly Ch'oe U, who succeeded Ch'oe Ch'ung-hŏn, had a strong interest in the new spiritual movement initiated by Chinul in the Susŏnsa, as we have mentioned earlier. That this interest became even more marked with Hyesim, the heir of Chinul in the Susŏnsa, can be discerned from the correspondence Hyesim had with Ch'oe U[1] and from the inscription written for him by Yi Kyu-bo,[2] a famous man of letters of the time, who maintained a close relationship with Ch'oe U.[3] Moreover, the successors of Hyesim in the Susŏnsa, such as Chinmyŏng, Wŏno, and Wŏn'gam, were closely related to the Sŏnwŏnsa, the celebrated monastery built by Ch'oe U on the island of Kanghwa, where he fled during the Mongol invasion.[4] So there can be little doubt that the Susŏnsa assumed the leadership of Koryŏ Buddhism during the latter part of the Koryŏ dynasty, particularly during the Mongol invasion.[5] According to the tradition of the Susŏnsa (now the Songgwang Monastery), since the time of Chinul sixteen national

---

[1] *Chin'gak Kuksa ŏrok*, ed. by Yi Chong-uk (Poje Monastery, Kaesŏng: 1940), pp. 38–41. See also Im Ch'ang-sun, "Songgwangsa ŭi Koryŏ munsŏ," *Paeksan hakpo* 11 (1971): 43–45, where Im discusses Ch'oe U's financial contributions to the Susŏnsa.

[2] *Chogyesan che ise ko Tansoksa chuji Susŏnsa-chu chŭngsi Chin'gak Kuksa pimyŏng pyŏngsŏ*, *CKC*, I, pp. 461–64.

[3] On this, see *Han'guksa* 7 (1974): 287–89.

[4] In this monastery the famous *Koryŏ Taejanggyŏng* (the second woodblock edition) was made in faith in the grace of the Buddha in this national crisis. It had been preserved there before it was moved to the Haeinsa Monastery, where it is today. Concerning the first woodblock edition, which was reduced to ashes during the Mongol invasion, and on this second edition, see Ikeuchi Hiroshi, "Kōraichō no daizōkyō," *Mansenshi kenkyū: Chūsei* II (1937): 483–636. See also Paik Nak Choon, "Tripitaka Koreana," *Transactions of the Korea Branch of the Royal Asiatic Society* 32 (1951): 62–78.

[5] A factor possibly contributing to its leadership during this turbulent period could be its location in the remote southern corner of the peninsula, which made it relatively immune to Mongol harassment when the Koryŏ court was holding out against the Mongols on Kanghwa Island.

preceptors consecutively have presided over it as abbots.[6] This leadership of the Susŏnsa, however, was by no means an institutional one; it only meant a recognition of its spiritual authority, particularly during this period of national crisis. There is no indication that the Susŏnsa itself, or Chinul, understood it to be a new independent religious institution or order. It was simply one of the influential monasteries, still a part of the traditional monastic system, however new and refreshing its high spirit and ideal may have been. As far as we can tell now, the financial basis of the Susŏnsa seems to have come mostly from the powerful and the wealthy, and this must have become even more marked by the time of Hyesim.[7] Thus the Susŏnsa did not depart from the traditional pattern of monastic maintenance in Koryŏ aristocratic Buddhism, and the supporter of the *sangha* (*siju* 施主, *dānapati*) was not the common people but primarily the court, the nobles, and the local magnates. Furthermore, with the political power back in the hands of the king and the civil ministers after the surrender to the Mongols, things seem to have gone back to where they stood before the military regime, but this time under the political dominion of the Mongol regime of Yüan China. This seems to have been the fundamental internal as well as external limitation to the new Buddhist movement launched by Chinul and the Susŏnsa.

When Koryŏ Buddhism was thus continuing to enjoy its secular privileges as usual, in particular its enormous economic power, there began to develop a new attitude toward Buddhism among the Confucian scholars and officials, especially among the younger lesser bureaucrats. They viewed with alarm the breakdown of the system of *kongjŏnje* (Public Field System), the basis of the Koryŏ economic order, and the ever-shrinking government revenues due to the sequestering of large land holdings, called *nongjang* (manor),

---

[6] Thus the present Songgwang Monastery has a building called Kuksajŏn (Hall of National Preceptors), where the portraits of the sixteen national preceptors are enshrined. For a study of this tradition, see Sugano Ginpachi, "Kōrai Sōkeisan shōkōji jūroku kokushi no keishō ni tsuite," *Seikyū gakusō* 9 (1932).

[7] This is evident from the inscription written by Yi Kyubo; see also the article by Im Ch'ang-sun.

by the powerful high officials in the capital and by the numerous influential Buddhist monasteries throughout the country. Contemporary with this was the introduction of Neo-Confucianism into Koryŏ. Thus the voice of anti-Buddhist accusations began to be raised openly. Such accusations were heeded already in the time of King Kongmin (1351–1374), but the decisive measures were not taken until Yi Sŏng-gye took power in 1389, representing a new social force that called for land reform, pro-Ming approaches (against the moribund Yüan), and the curbing of Buddhism. The anti-Buddhist accusations and measures were at first moderate, and mostly confined to economic aspects, but they grew harsher and were applied with dogmatic fervency as time went on.[8]

Yi Sŏng-gye, who founded the new Yi dynasty (1392–1910), was in some ways a pious Buddhist. But with the change of the social and economic structure and the shift of political power, it was inevitable that Buddhism, which had been so closely identified with the established system of the previous dynasty, should suffer losses. Thus Yi abolished the tax-exempt status of the Buddhist monasteries, banned construction of new monasteries, and initiated the monk-license system called *toch'ŏpche.* King T'aejong (1400–1418) officially recognized only about 250 monasteries, confiscating the land and slaves of the others and laicizing many monks. In the capital only one monastery representing each sect was allowed to exist, and in the provinces only two, each representing Sŏn and Kyo. Then King Sejong (1418–1450) took even more drastic steps, consolidating the existing Five Schools of Kyo and Two Orders of Sŏn, called *ogyo yangjong* 五教兩宗,[9] into the Two Orders of Sŏn and Kyo, *sŏn'gyo*

---

[8] For studies of this important subject, the ideological shift from Buddhism to Confucianism at the dynastic change, see Yi Sang-baek, "Yubul yanggyo kyodae ŭi kiyŏn e taehan il yŏn'gu," *Han'guk munhwasa yŏn'gu non'go* (Seoul; 1948), pp. 3–170; Han U-gŭn, "Yŏmal sŏnch'o ŭi Pulgyo chŏngch'aek," *Seoul Taehakkyo nonmunjip: Inmun sahoe kwahak,* 6 (1957): 1–80; and Takahashi Tōru, *Richō Bukkyō* (Tokyo: 1929), pp. 30–71. The following brief review of the anti-Buddhist policy in the beginning of the Yi Dynasty is mostly based upon Takahashi.

[9] The five Kyo schools at the time were: Hwaŏm, Chaŭn (Fa-hsiang), Chungsin (amalgamation of Chungdo which was Wŏnhyo's Pŏpsŏng School and Sinin, the Esoteric School), Ch'ongnam (amalgamation of Ch'ongji, the Dhāraṇī School, and Namsan,

yangjong 禪教兩宗, making Hŭngch'ŏn Monastery the headquarters of the Sŏn Order and Hŭngdŏk Monastery the headquarters of Kyo. Thus began an unprecedented phenomenon in the history of Buddhism in any country; namely, Sŏn and Kyo themselves became the names of Buddhist denominations. In China and Japan, Ch'an and Zen have never been used as names of Buddhist denominations or orders as Son was in Korea from this time. Instead, such names as "Northern Sect," "Lin-chi (Rinzai) Sect," and "Ts'ao-tung (Sōto)" were used. "Ch'an-tsung" was a generic name.

The number of state-supported monasteries now shrank to thirty-six, and many in the capital (Seoul) were converted into public buildings. Sejong even banned monks from the capital and mobilized them for various construction works. These drastic measures were calamitous for the Buddhist community, which had never known such persecution since Buddhism was brought to the land about a millennium previously. To be noted with particular attention is the fact that all the denominational monk examinations were abolished, except those for the two orders of Sŏn and Kyo, so that the doctrinal studies pertaining to those dead or absorbed denominations vanished. Toward the end of his life, Sejong's attitude toward Buddhism turned around, and he supported many Buddhist works, but the damage he had done was never to be repaired. King Sejo (1455–1468) was a devout Buddhist who lent support to the *saṅgha*, but after his death an even stronger reaction set in. Thus King Sŏng-jong (1469–1494), a dedicated Confucianist, forbade people to become monks. The notorious despot Yŏnsan'gun put an end to whatever official relationship the state still had with Buddhism: he abolished

---

the Vinaya School), and Sihŭng (lit. "Newly-arising School"; the identity of this school is unclear; see Takahashi, pp. 140–44 and Kim Yŏng-su, "Ogyo yangjong e taehaya," *Chindan hakpo* 8 [1937]: 74–101). The amalgamation took place in the time of T'aejong, generally following the pattern of the *ogyo yangjong* of Koryŏ. Now out of the seven denominations, Hwaŏm, Chungsin, Chaŭn, and Sihŭng were further contracted into simply one order of Kyojong, and the other three into the single order of Sŏnjong. One thing that is clear from this arrangement is that the contrast and conflict between Sŏn and Kyo must have been too marked to ignore and form simply one body of Buddhism, which is actually what happened later willy-nilly, as we shall see.

the monk examination altogether and destroyed the two headquarters in the capital.

For a brief period during the reign of Myŏngjong (1545–1567), when his mother Queen Munjŏng took charge of governmental affairs behind the scene, Buddhism seemed to revive under her lavish patronage and under the able leadership of the monk Pou. The monk examinations for Sŏn and Kyo were revived, and the various restrictions against Buddhist activities were removed. During this time Sŏsan, regarded as the greatest monk of the Yi dynasty, took the examination and began his religious career. Once again, a violent reaction against this temporary revival ensued; Pou was exiled to the Cheju Island and murdered there. Never again thereafter was Buddhism to see such a turn of fortune in Korean history.

Sŏsan Taesa (1520–1604), or the Great Master of Western Mountain, a sobriquet taken from the name of the mountain (Myohyangsan) where he used to dwell, was the central figure in the history of Yi-dynasty Buddhism.[10] Most of the eminent Korean monks from the seventeenth century on, whether in Sŏn or Kyo, trace their spiritual lineage to either Sŏsan or Puhyu (who was, like Sŏsan, a prominent disciple of Puyong Yŏnggwan). Sŏsan's position in particular is immutable. After him, the distinction between Sŏn and Kyo, which had already become blurred after the abolition of the monks' examination system, grew even more tenuous. He himself, although a Sŏn master, became the head of both the Sŏn and Kyo orders—an indication of the relative insignificance at this time of the distinction between Sŏn and Kyo and of the superior position of Sŏn.[11] Thus Sŏsan signified the emergence of a new type of Buddhist leader in the following generations of Korean monks: one who is versed in both Sŏn and Kyo, but with definite identity as a Sŏn master nevertheless— precisely the way Chinul was, as we have seen. Thus through a queer

---

[10] For a study of the life and thought of Sŏsan, see Kim Yŏng-t'ae, *Sŏsan Taesa ŭi saengae wa sasang* (Seoul; 1975).

[11] It is possible that Sŏn Buddhism survived the long period of persecution better than the Kyo Order.

166

turn of events, Chinul's understanding of Buddhism became the practice in Korea, at least from the seventeenth century on. In the next section we will examine the ideological connection between Chinul's approach to Sŏn and that of Sŏsan and others. But it would be naive to disregard the historical developments in Yi dynasty Buddhism and try to discuss the ultimate outcome only in doctrinal terms.

2. *Chinul, Sŏsan, and the Present Chogye Order*

Insofar as we can ascertain through Sŏsan's own writings, such as his biography of Pyŏksong Chiŏm, his grandfather in the *Dharma*, Sŏsan's *Dharma* lineage can only be traced back to as far as Pyŏkkye Chŏngsim, who was the master of Chiŏm.[12] Some Buddhist scholars in Korea have held that Sŏsan's *Dharma* line goes back to T'aego around the end of Koryŏ,[13] whereas others assert that it should be traced back to Chinul.[14] What is at stake for these scholars with

---

[12] See Sŏsan's *Pyŏksongdang haengjŏk, Ch'ŏnghŏdang chip*, fascicle 3, pp. 31–34; for Korean translation of this, see *HTHK*, 1; 593–601 (particularly p. 594).

[13] The foremost representative of this view is Kim Yŏng-su, who expressed it in many articles. See his "Chogye Sŏnjong e taehaya," *Chindan hakpo* 9 (1938); "Chogyejong kwa chŏndŭng t'onggyu," *Pulgyo sin* 43–45 (1943); and "Chosŏn Pulgyo chongji e ch'wihaya," *Pulgyo sin* 8–9 (1937–1938). This view is ultimately based upon the biography of Sŏsan composed by his immediate disciple P'yŏnyang, *Ch'ŏnghŏdang haengjang* (abridged title). It is contained in the *Ch'ŏnghŏdang chip*, fascicle 4, pp. 44–46; for Korean translation, see *HTHK* 1; 748–52. And this view was popularized by Saam Ch'aeyŏng's *Sŏyŏk Chunghwa Haedong Pulcho wŏllyu* [*The Original Stream of Buddhist Patriarchs in India, China, and Korea*] compiled in 1764. The underlying intention of this view is to attribute Sŏsan's *Dharma* line to the popular Lin-chi tradition of China by way of T'aego, who is supposed to have received the *Dharma* from Shih-wu, the eighteenth generation of the Chinese Lin-chi tradition. As we shall see, this view has many problems.

[14] This view is represented by Yi Chong-ik's *KFKK*, pp. 551–81, and by Yi Chae-yŏl, "Ogyo yangjong kwa Chogyejong pŏpt'ong," *Pulgyo sasang* 1–6 (1973–1974), or his "Koryŏ ogyo yangjong ŭi sachŏk koch'al," *Sahak yŏn'gu* 4 (1959). The underlying intention of this view is, of course, to establish Chinul—over against T'aego in the above view—as the founder of the present Chogye Order by linking him to Sŏsan whose position, as we have said, is unanimously accepted as immutable. But this view also has some problems, as we shall indicate later. We have already seen through our study that Chinul cannot be regarded as the founder of the Chogye Order *of Koryŏ*. His position in Yi-dynasty Buddhism is our concern here.

regard to this problem is the question of who ultimately is to be regarded as the founder of the present Chogye Order in Korea. This is a complicated issue, and the arguments put forward are too complex and often too confused to be discussed here in detail.[15] Yet the question itself is important and is worthy of consideration in our discussion of the influence Chinul had upon the subsequent Buddhist tradition in Korea. In addressing ourselves to this issue, we will simply point out several crucial facts which should clear away unnecessary complications and confusions.

First of all, the name Chogyejong (Chogye Order), which had been in use since the middle of the Koryŏ dynasty, was abolished when King Sejong (1418–1450) combined Chogye, Ch'ŏnt'ae, and Ch'ongnam into the single order of Sŏnjong. Furthermore, even the identity of this Sŏnjong became uncertain when the monk examination system was abolished by Yŏnsan'gun in the fifteenth century. Thus the problem for the Buddhist communities thereafter was whether Buddhism itself could survive, not the issue of any denominational identity. Whether the Buddhism of the Yi dynasty wanted to or not, it was forced to become one amorphous body without a definite direction to follow. If, after Sŏsan and Puhyu, any identifiable form emerged, it came to be close to Chinul's version of Buddhism. When the name "Chosŏn Pulgyo Chogyejong" 朝鮮佛教曹溪宗 came to be adopted by Korean Buddhist leaders in 1941, it was a name given to Korean Buddhism as it stood at that time (even without a name), and not a narrow denominational appellation as it had been before King Sejong. For this reason, it is meaningless to ask who the founder of the *present* Chogye Order is, as if it had been a continuously expanding single order that came to absorb all the other denominations in the course of becoming what it is today. To determine the founder of the present Chogye Order is therefore not to be taken as a strictly historical problem; it is rather a religious problem with direct bearing

---

[15] All works mentioned above deal with this issue; but the best article on it, in my judgement, is Eda Shunyū's "Zenshū toshite no Chōsen Bukkyō no dentō ni tsuite" [On the Tradition of Korean Buddhism as a Sŏn Order], *Bukkyōgaku no shomondai* (Tokyo: 1935), pp. 898–914.

upon the self-understanding of the present community of the Chogye Order.

The second thing to point out with regard to this issue is that at the present moment no satisfactory way exists of establishing the link of *Dharma* transmission either between Sŏsan and T'aego[16] or between Sŏsan and Chinul.[17] Until we obtain more historical evidence, we have no choice but to be content with the fact that Sŏsan's *Dharma* line goes back through three generations before him, i.e. to Puyong Yŏnggwan, Pyŏksong Chiŏm, and Pyŏkkye Chŏngsim.[18]

Thirdly, since Sŏsan's central position in Yi-dynasty Buddhism

---

[16] We have no way of knowing who the master of Pyŏkkye Chŏngsim was. The *Pulcho wŏllyu* gives it as Kwigok Kagun, but the time interval between the two is too long, as Takahashi points out (*Richō Bukkyō*, pp. 187–89); nor can we establish the link between Kagun and Hwanam Honsu. On the other hand, we find concrete evidence that Kagun was the heir of Choram Yŏnon, who in turn inherited the line of the Susŏnsa. Also difficult to establish is the link between Honsu and T'aego; Honsu is associated with both T'aego and Naong, another great Sŏn master around the end of Koryŏ, but he seems to have been actually the heir of the latter rather than the former. About all this, see Eda's article. It appears that the link between Sŏsan and T'aego was fabricated by his disciples with the ultimate intention of linking Sŏsan to the Lin-chi Ch'an of China by way of T'aego. This view is supported by another fact pointed out by Eda. Hŏ Kyun, a famous literary man of Sŏsan's time, attributes Sŏsan's line to Naong in his preface written for an edition of Sŏsan's literary works; or, somewhere else, he attributes it to Chinul. All this further complicates our problem. We surmise that right after the death of Sŏsan various attempts were made by his followers to determine the *Dharma* lineage of their master, which Sŏsan himself left unclear, either because he was not interested or because he himself did not know. Through the influence of the *Pulcho wŏllyu*, many Korean monks have traditionally held that Sŏsan inherited the Lin-chi tradition by way of T'aego. Eda's article is a critical examination of this popular view.

[17] The difficulty of linking Pyŏkkye Chŏngsim to Kagun poses the same problem for this view as well. Another problem is that Choram Yŏnon was not one of the so-called sixteen national preceptors to preside over the Susŏnsa; so we are not sure how much weight we should attach to the fact that he was Kagun's master. The problem of *Dharma* lineage is of course a serious matter for Sŏn monks. But for us, it seems better to look at the matter more practically, that is, from the viewpoint of who, T'aego or Chinul, was more influential for Sŏsan's approach to Sŏn and for the Korean Sŏn tradition after him down to the present.

[18] It is said that Chŏngsim encountered the great persecution of Buddhism during King Sŏngjong and Yŏnsan'gun. Thus he had to grow his hair and get married, and retire into a mountain. It is probably due to this confusion in the Buddhist community that the line of *Dharma* transmission became unclear during the early part of the Yi dynasty. Not much is known about the life of Chŏngsim, and in spite of Sŏsan's word, his relationship with Pyŏksong Chiŏm as a disciple does not seem to have been very solid. It is only with Chiŏm that we are actually out of the darkness surrounding this matter of *Dharma* transmission in the early part of the Yi dynasty.

is unquestionable, his style of Sŏn and his understanding of Buddhism have to be paid careful attention in any consideration of the tradition, teaching, and spirit that the present Chogye Order represents. In addition, Puhyu's line of Sŏn has to be considered, because his disciples flourished also.

With these three points in mind, let us now investigate the traces Chinul left on Korean Buddhism as far as they can be determined through concrete evidence. The following facts emerge:

1) When Hŭngch'ŏn Monastery was established by Yi T'aejo, the founder of the Yi dynasty, its abbot Sangch'ong memorialized the king saying that all Sŏn monasteries in the country should base their rules and practices on those of the Songgwang Monastery (namely the Susŏnsa), which were formulated by Chinul. The king agreed to this. Sangch'ong also said that in the previous dynasty both Sŏn and Kyo were busy fighting against each other to occupy good monasteries, and not many places were devoted to the cultivation of Sŏn and doctrinal studies; and that recently their rules and practices had been modeled much after the Chinese fashion, but it was like wanting to draw a tiger but finishing up with a picture of a dog.[19] This remark was a criticism of the tendency during the latter part of the Koryŏ period to import the Chinese Lin-chi Ch'an practices under the influence of the Yüan regime. With the establishment of the new independent dynasty, Sangch'ong now calls for a return to the rules and practices formulated by Chinul that had proved effective in the Susŏnsa.[20] Concerning this memorial, Takahashi comments:

> Thereupon, the Korean Sŏn Order, we can observe, ceased imitating the Chinese Lin-chi Order and returned to its own ordinances. Later, when Sŏn and Kyo came to be cultivated in combination and practiced in confusion, the ordinances based upon the teachings of Sŏn, Hwaŏm, Esoteric Buddhism, Yŏmbul [Pure Land], and Pŏpsang [Fa-hsiang] were all mixed in the rituals and practices

---

[19] *Richō Bukkyō*, pp. 52–53.
[20] Most probably, Sangch'ong is referring to Chinul's *Kye ch'osim hagin mun* [*Admonitions to beginning students*].

170

of the monasteries; and these became the rules and practices of present-day Korean Buddhism. Yet since among them Sŏn was the most prevalent, most of the practices of Hŭngch'ŏn Monastery formulated at that time can be said to have been transmitted until the present day.[21]

2) Chinul's characteristic approach to Sŏn—first a clear intellectual grasp of the *Dharma* on the basis of the "genuine teaching in words" and then the removal of the intellectual disease by *hwadu* Sŏn—is, significantly, observed by Pyŏksong Chiŏm, Sŏsan's grandfather in the *Dharma*, whose biography he composed. Thus when Chiŏm taught his students he urged them to have, first, the genuine intellectual understanding of the *Dharma* on the basis of Tsung-mi's *Ch'an-yüan* and Chinul's *Chŏryo*. Then, he would let them go on to cure the disease of intellectual understanding by the study of the *Taehye ŏrok* [*The Words of Ta-hui*] and the *Sŏnyo* [*Essence of Sŏn*] by Kobong (Kao-feng, 1238–1285).[22] This was exactly Chinul's approach, and the texts used confirm our view. These four texts constitute the curriculum of the *sajip* class of present monastic education in Korea, about which more will be said later. Chiŏm used to lecture on such *sūtras* as the *Hwaŏm*, *Pŏphwa* (*Lotus*), and *Nŭngŏm* (*Lengyen*). This combined study of Kyo and Sŏn dates back to Chinul; besides, the *Nŭngŏmgyŏng*, not to mention the *Hwaŏm*, is one of the texts from which Chinul most frequently quoted.

3) Chinul's thought is nowhere better reflected than in the thought of Sŏsan. In particular, his *Sŏn'ga kwigam* [*Mirror for the Students of Sŏn*], to which we have already referred and which has been one of the most popular texts among Korean Buddhists, unmistakably reveals Sŏsan's indebtedness to Chinul. Thus phrases like "ten kinds of disease 十種病 (of intellectual understanding)," "dead phrase 死句 and living phrase 活句," "study of phrase 參句 and study of meaning 參意," "neither self-debasement 不自屈 (the 'disease of the

---

[21] *Richō Bukkyō*, pp. 53–54.

[22] Chinul, of course, did not know this work of Kaofeng Yüan-miao, whose work was introduced into Koryŏ when it was under Yüan domination. About Kao-feng, see Suzuki, *First Series*, pp. 251–54.

students of Kyo') nor self-elevation 不自高 (the 'disease of the students of Sŏn')," and others, are used by Sŏsan. Also, the way he contrasts (in his *Sŏn'gyo sŏk* [*An Interpretation of Sŏn and Kyo*]) *hwadu* Sŏn with the path of "complete teaching" on the one hand and with the "sudden teaching" on the other is much the same as Chinul's *Kanhwa kyŏrŭiron*.[23] His view of Pure Land Buddhism is also similar to Chinul's. Both allow recitation of Amita's name as a way of cultivation after insight has been acquired into one's own Nature. Each of them sets forth the teaching of "the Amit'a of Self-Nature" and "the Pure Land of one's own Mind" as the ultimate level of truth, but recognizes the validity of a more realistic conception of them for people with lower capacity.[24] Each recognizes *yŏmbul nien-fo*) as a means to assist Sŏn. Takahashi makes the following observation:

> Ever since Sŏsan appeared and roared like a lion that the substance of Sŏn and Kyo are not two, that Kyo is the word of the Buddha and Sŏn the mind of the Buddha, and that Kyo is an introduction, so that true students of Buddhism with clear vision might ultimately move over to get hold of the mind of the Buddha, his words gradually assumed a position of authority in the world of monks, and the conflict between Kyo and Sŏn was nearly settled. Thus a unique Korean sect, which takes sitting in meditation and the insight into Nature [*kyŏnsŏng* 見性] as the final important thing while cultivating Kyo and Sŏn in combination, came into being. Sŏsan's view of Buddhism emphasizes the combined cultivation of Sŏn and Kyo, and when we examine its origin, there is no doubt that it dates far back to the three paths established by the National Preceptor Pojo [Chinul],

---

[23] See his *Sŏn'gyo sŏk, HTHK*, 1; it is a very short work. On Sŏsan's view of Sŏn and Kyo, see U Chŏng-sang, "Sŏsan Taesa ŭi Sŏn'gyogwan e taehayŏ," *CKPN*, pp. 473–504; see also Kim Yŏng-t'ae, *Sŏsan Taesa*, pp. 121–54.

[24] Just like Chinul, Sŏsan regarded *yŏmbul* as belonging to the path of gradual cultivation after sudden enlightenment; one knows that one's own Mind is the Pure Land and one's own Nature the Amit'a Buddha, but one still sees a gap between the two, and so one needs the gradual cultivation of *yŏmbul*. Thus the gap between knowing and practice, Nature and Characteristics, and between Principle and Phenomena, underlies Sŏsan's view of Pure Land practices as it did for Chinul. For a presentation of the fascinating view of Sŏsan in this matter, see Kim Yŏng-t'ae, *Sŏsan Taesa*, pp. 199–213. In general, we have the impression that Sŏsan placed more emphasis on Pure Land practices than Chinul.

172

who revived the Chogye Order in Koryŏ; and that more recently it succeeds to the teaching of his grandfather in the *Dharma* Pyŏksong and of his father in the *Dharma* Puyong.[25]

The following words from Sŏsan's *Sŏn'ga kwigam* are sufficient to show what Takahashi means:

> Therefore students should first of all discern in detail, on the basis of the genuine teaching in words, that the two aspects of Unchanging and Changing are none other than the Nature and Characteristics of one's own mind, and that the two paths of sudden enlightenment and gradual cultivation are none other than the beginning and end of one's own acts. Then should they let go of the doctrinal meaning and study the heart of Sŏn, getting hold of the one thought present in one's own mind; they will surely obtain the fruit, what is called the living path of liberation.[26]

4) P'yŏnyang Ŏn'gi was one of the most prominent disciples of Sŏsan. Here is a statement of his that expresses his approach to Sŏn in a nutshell:

> The gate of Sŏn clearly shows [the truth] for the sake of those with the lowest capacity by borrowing Kyo, the so-called three schools of Nature, Characteristics, and Emptiness. But since it has the path of reason and word, and involves hearing, understanding, and thought, it becomes the dead phrase of the complete-sudden path, and it is called *ŭirisŏn* [Sŏn of meaning and reason 義理禪]. It is different from the previous *kyŏgoesŏn* [supranormal Sŏn 格外禪]. Nevertheless, there is no fixed meaning in the two terms; it depends upon the varying capacity of each person. If one loses it [the truth] through the mouth, even "holding up the flower and smiling" [the story of the Buddha's transmission of the *Dharma* to Mahākāśyapa] would completely fall into [mere] display of words; if, however, one acquires it through the mind, even the gross sayings and minute words would become a discussion of the true reality.[27]

---

[25] *Richō Bukkyō*, pp. 389–90.
[26] *Z.* 2, 17, V, p. 457.
[27] Translated from *Richō Bukkyō*, p. 458.

Once again, Takahashi correctly points out the origin of P'yŏnyang's Sŏn:

> Since the master attributes the three gates of Sŏn, Kyo, and *Yŏmbul* to the gate of One Mind and decides that the true gate to cultivate mind is Sŏn, we could observe that he integrated Kyo and *Yŏmbul* into Sŏn. This dates back precisely to the three paths of the National Preceptor Pojo of Koryŏ, and this is the reason why he surely is a successor to Sŏsan's *Dharma*.[28]

Thus it is no mere coincidence that in P'yŏnyang's *Dharma* line there also appeared many great lecturers of Kyo, such as Sangbong Chŏngwŏn (1627–1709), Wŏltam Sŏlche (1632–1704), Wŏlchŏ Toan (1638–1715), Inak Ŭijŏm (1746–1796), and Yŏndam Yuil (1720–1799).

5) Parallel to this line of P'yŏnyang was that of Pyŏgam Kaksŏng (1575–1660), who was the disciple of Puhyu Sŏnsu; he in turn, together with Sŏsan, was one of the two greatest disciples of Puyong Yŏnggwan. Many of Pyŏgam's disciples had a close relationship with the Songgwang Monastery, which seemed by this time to have regained some of its old prominence. Particularly noteworthy was Paegam Sŏngch'ong, who in 1678 reconstructed the memorial stele of Chinul with the inscription on it, calling Chinul "the great saint of the Eastern Land [Korea]."[29] In the same year, the memorial pillar of Songgwang Monastery was also erected. It referred to the monastery as "the greatest place of *Tao* in the Eastern Land,"[30] and adduced many salient past events and figures. Paegam contributed greatly to the publication and circulation of new Buddhist literature.[31] From his line other prominent masters of both Sŏn and Kyo

---

[28] *Richō Bukkyō*, p. 460.

[29] *CKC*, II, p. 952.

[30] *CSS*, I, p. 277.

[31] In the year 1671 an anonymous ship carrying much Buddhist literature drifted to an island by the name of Imjado on the Western Sea. It was some of this literature that Sŏngch'ong tried to circulate. In particular, he is credited with the recirculation of Ch'eng-kuan's commentaries on the *Hua-yen Sūtra*. The upsurge of study of this *sūtra* in the subsequent period seems to have owed not little to his effort. About Sŏngch'ong see *CPT*, I, pp. 518–21, and *Richō Bukkyō*, pp. 688–95.

appeared, such as Muyong Suyŏn (1651–1719) and Mugam Ch'oenul (1717–1790).

6) All these persons from the line of P'yŏnyang and Pyŏgam were masters versed in both Sŏn and Kyo, much like Sŏsan and Chinul. Nonetheless, their ultimate identity lay in Sŏn. Most of them were thoroughly acquainted with the *Hwaŏmgyŏng*, and many composed works on it. Other favorite texts included the *Kisillon* (*Ch'i-hsin-lun*), the *Sŏnwŏn chejŏnjip tosŏ* (Tsung-mi's *Ch'an-yüan*), the *Wŏngakkyŏng* (*Yüan-chüeh-ching*), and Chinul's *Chŏryo*. It was in this tradition of the combined study of Sŏn and Kyo that the curriculum of the present monastic school, called the *kangwŏn* 講院, was established.[32] We have mentioned that an early form of this can already be found in Pyŏksong Chiŏm (1464–1534), who established the *sajip* curriculum. But in the seventeenth and eighteenth centuries the curriculum became expanded and more systematized. Thus today, a novice or *sami* (*śrāmaṇera*) begins with the study of Chinul's *Kye ch'osim hagin mun*, Wŏnhyo's *Palsim suhaengjang*, and Yaun's *Chagyŏng mun*[33] and *Ch'imun kyŏnghun*,[34] which together constitute the curriculum of the *samikwa* 沙彌科 class. Then one moves over to the curriculum of the *sajipkwa* 四集科 class, which includes *Sŏchang* (Ta-hui's letters in *Ta-hui yü-lu*), *Tosŏ* (*Ch'an-yüan*), *Sŏnyo* (*Kao-feng ho-shang Ch'an-yao*), and Chinul's *Chŏryo*, as they call them in abbreviated forms. Then one studies the *Nŭngŏmgyŏng* (*Leng-yen-ching*), *Kisillon*, *Kŭmganggyŏng* (*Diamond Sūtra*), and the *Wŏngakkyŏng* (*Yüan-chüeh-ching* or the *Sūtra of Complete Englighten-*

---

[32] For a general survey of the curriculum, see Yi Chi-gwan, *Han'guk Pulgyo soŭi kyŏngjŏn yŏn'gu* (Seoul: 1969).

[33] Yaun's biography is not known well, but he was a disciple of Naong (1320–1376). "Chagyŏng mun" literally means "the text for self-warning."

[34] Literally means "warnings and exhortations to monks." It is an extensive collection of words by prominent Chinese masters made by Hwanju Yŏngjung (Huan-chu Yung-chung) in 1313. It is based upon a similar work called *Ch'imun pohun* (author unknown). See Kuroda Akira, *Chōsen kyūsho ko* (Tokyo, 1940), pp. 128–41. Kuroda also points out that Yung-chung was the man responsible for the publication of Kao-feng's *Sŏnyo*; see *ibid.*, pp. 142–44. The introduction of *Ch'imun kyŏnghun* into Korea is attributed to T'aego (1301–1382); see Yi Chi-gwan, *op. cit.*, p. 39. The text currently used in monastic schools is a selection of only sixty-seven items from it by An Chin-ho in 1936 with the commentary from Sŏngch'ŏng's *Ch'imun chipchu* (composed in 1695).

ment), which together form the curriculum of the *sagyokwa* 四教科. Then one advances to the study of the *Hwaŏmgyŏng*, which is called *taegyokwa* 大教科. Finally one may go further and study such texts as the *Pŏphwagyŏng* (*Lotus Sūtra*), *Kyŏngdŏk chŏndŭngnok* (*Ching-te ch'uan-teng-lu*), and *Sŏnmun yŏmsong*, which is a collection made by Hyesim, Chinul's disciple, of more than one thousand *kōan*, stories, and verses of Sŏn masters.[35] This optional study is called *suikwa* 隨意科. In this enumeration of the monastic curriculum, we can notice that except for the last category (*suikwa*) most texts are the ones closely related to Chinul's thought and most often quoted by him; we also notice that two of Chinul's own works are incorporated into the curriculum, *Kye ch'osim hagin mun* and *Chŏryo*.

Several points need to be made with regard to this monastic education system: Not all Korean monks go through this curriculum of the *kangwŏn* (monastic school). Some go straight to the *sŏnwŏn* (Sŏn hall or meditation hall) to study Sŏn without much background in doctrinal study, and many others are not interested either in study or in meditation and just spend their time and life in the monastery. But the more usual course for any serious-minded monk is to go through this *kangwŏn* education at least partly, though not necessarily in the order mentioned above. After this he moves over to the more rigorous study of Sŏn in the *sŏnwŏn*. In the present Korean monasteries, the prestige of the *sŏnwŏn* is higher than that of the *kangwŏn*, and the authority of the Sŏn master is greater than that of the lecturer of the *kangwŏn*. Yet both exist in peaceful union (only big monasteries have both of them), and most of the Sŏn masters do not discourage students from going to the *kangwŏn*; they only point out its limitations. The same thing can be said about the Pure Land practices in the monasteries, even though they are becoming increasingly less popular among the monks. All these

---

[35] When the monks' examination system was still alive in the Yi dynasty, the subjects of the examination for Kyo were the *Hwaŏmgyŏng* and the *Sipchigyŏng-non* (commonly called *Ti-lun* in China; *Daśabhūmika-sūtra-śāstra*) by Vasubandhu, and for Sŏn the *Chŏndŭngnok* (*Ching-te ch'uan-teng-lu*) and Hyesim's *Sŏnmun yŏmsong*. For more detailed information on the system in the Yi dynasty, see *Richō Bukkyō*, pp. 256–70.

phenomena, at least in their doctrinal and ideological connection, can be attributed to Sŏsan and his followers, and ultimately to Chinul.

7) Even a cursory survey of any catalogue of old books extant in Korea[36] shows that the works of Chinul, particularly his *Chŏryo*, have been the single most widely published and circulated category of Buddhist literature throughout the Yi dynasty.[37] In more recent days, the *Sŏnmun ch'waryo* [*Essentials of Sŏn*], one of the most popular texts among Korean monks today, contains five works of Chinul.[38] It was compiled by Kyŏnghŏ (1849–1912), who is generally credited with the revitalization of Sŏn in modern times; it was under him that such prominent masters as Song Man'gong, Pang Hanam (who, incidentally, published his edition of *Pojo Sŏnsa ŏrok*, a compilation of Chinul's works, in 1937), and Sin Hyewŏl appeared to lead the Korean Buddhist community until recently. His religious life, which began with a thorough mastery of a wide range of Buddhist literature (he was a famous lecturer in the *kangwŏn* of Tonghak Monastery) and ended with the discovery of the power of *hwadu* Sŏn, was a perfect exemplification of the spirit of Korean Buddhism as typified by Sŏsan and Chinul.[39]

Our examination should be sufficient to demonstrate that Chinul's Sŏn has constituted the mainstream of the Korean Sŏn tradition. Sŏn Buddhism in Korea is not one of the many sects or denominations of Buddhism; it represents rather the totality of Buddhism in its East Asian form of development. Already by the time of the new Sŏn Buddhist movement launched by Chinul in twelfth-century

---

[36] For instance, *Han'guk kosŏ chonghap mongnok* (Seoul: 1968) or *Kosŏ mongnok* (Seoul: 1970) I.

[37] Except perhaps the *Diamond Sūtra*, which, obviously due to its small size, was easy to publish and circulate. Buddhist books were published mostly by woodblock printing in the Yi dynasty, even though metal printing had been available in Korea from as early as 1234 A.D., some two hundred years earlier than Gutenberg's of Germany. Besides the mentioned texts of the curriculum of the *kangwŏn*, some other *sūtras* such as the *Lotus Sūtra*, *Platform Sūtra*, and the *Pumo ŭnjunggyŏng* [*Sūtra on the Deep Grace of Parents*] were popular.

[38] This is based upon the 1968 edition of Pŏmŏ Monastery. The original edition, which was published in 1908 by Pŏmŏ Monastery, contains four works, not five, of Chinul.

[39] On the life and thought of Kyŏnghŏ, see Sŏngt'a, "Kyŏnghŏ ŭi Sŏn sasang," *PHPS*, pp. 1103–1120.

Koryŏ, the form and direction taken by Korean Buddhism today had been prefigured. Partly due to the religious and ideological continuity of Chinul's approach to Sŏn, and partly as a result of the odd turns of secular history, this prefiguration became reality in the history of Korean Buddhism after him. The present Chogye Order is an embodiment of this historical process, and there can be little doubt that it faithfully and unmistakably reflects the tradition of Sŏn Buddhism initiated by Chinul about eight hundred years ago.[40]

---

[40] Eda Shunyū's article, "Zenshū toshite no Chōsen Bukkyō no dentō ni tsuite," concludes as follows after a cricital examination of the view that regards Korean Sŏn as Lin-chi tradition:

> "Then it is proper, from the standpoint of both history and reality, to take the National Preceptor Pojo of Koryŏ, who can be called the Korean Bodhidharma, as the patriarch of Korean Buddhism as a Sŏn order; and its denomination should be called Chogyejong, which was the unique Korean Sŏn Order unifying Sŏn and Kyo, with five hundred years of history from the middle of Koryŏ to the middle of the Yi dynasty."

I heartily agree with this view which suggests that if the present Chogye Order (what Eda calls "Korean Buddhism as a Sŏn Order") is going to have any patriarch, it should claim Chinul rather than any other figure. Ironically, even those who attribute Sŏsan's *Dharma* line to T'aego agree that in terms of the fundamental doctrinal principle of the present Chogye Order, it is the teaching of "sudden enlightenment and gradual cultivation" established by Chinul that the order espouses and represents. The most conspicuous example is Kim Yŏng-su who is ironically the most ardent supporter of the view which regards Sŏsan as the heir of T'aego and the latter as the patriarch of the Chogyejong. See his "Chogye Sŏnjong e taehaya," *Chindan hakpo*, No. 9 (1938), pp. 148–52, and "Chosŏn Pulgyo chongji e ch'wihaya," *Pulgyo sin*, No. 9 (1938), pp. 5–11.

GLOSSARY

Chagyŏngmun 自警文

Ch'an 禪

Chan-jan 湛然

Ch'angp'yŏng 昌平

Chaŭn 慈恩

Ch'egwan 諦觀

Cheju 濟州

Ch'eng-kuan 澄觀

Chiao 教

chidŏk 地德

Chien-t'ang 錢塘

Chih-i 智顗

chih-kuan 止觀

Chih-yen 智嚴

Ch'imun chipchu 緇門集註

Ch'imun kyŏnghun 緇門警訓

Ch'imun pohun 緇門寶訓

Chin 金

Chin'gak Kuksa 眞覺國師

Ching-te ch'uan-teng-lu
景德傳燈錄

Ching-yüan 淨源

Ch'ing-yüan 靑原

Chinmyŏng 眞明

Chinul 知訥

Ch'oe Ch'ung-hŏn 崔忠獻

Ch'oe Sŏn 崔詵

Ch'oe Sŭng-no 崔承老

Ch'oe U 崔瑀

Chogyejong 曹溪宗

Chŏlla 全羅

Chŏng Kwang-u 鄭光遇

Chonghwi 宗暉

Chŏnghyesa 定慧寺

Ch'ongji 總持

chŏng kup'um 正九品

Ch'ongnam 總南

chŏngsa 正史

Ch'ŏngwŏnsa 清源寺

Ch'ŏnt'aejong 天台宗

Ch'ŏnt'ae sagyoŭi 天台四教儀

ch'ulga 出家

Chungdojong 中道宗

chŭngo 證悟

Chungsin 中神

Dōgen 道元

Fa-hsiang 法相

Fa-tsang 法藏

Haeinsa 海印寺

haeo 解悟

Hagasan 下柯山

hakchŏng 學正

hangnok 學錄

hoegwang panjo 廻光返照

Ho-tse 荷澤

Hsin Hua-yen-ching-lun
新華嚴經論

*Hsiu-hua-yen ao-chih wang-chin
huan-yüan-kuan*
修華嚴奧旨妄盡還元觀

179

Hui-ch'ang　會昌
Hŭngch'ŏnsa　興天寺
Hŭngdŏksa　興德寺
Hŭngwangsa　興王寺
hwadu　話頭
Hwanju Yŏngjung　幻住永中
Hwaŏmgyŏng　華嚴經
Hyesim　慧諶
Hyujŏng　休靜
ich'am　理懺
Injong　仁宗
Inwanggyŏng　仁王經
Kaesŏng　開城
Kaksu Posal　覺首菩薩
Kamno　甘露
Kanghwa　江華
kangwŏn　講院
kanhwa　看話
Kao-feng ho-shang Ch'an-yao
　高峰和尚禪要
Kasong　歌頌
Kilsangsa　吉祥寺
Kim Pu-sik　金富軾
Kisillon　起信論
Kŏjosa　居祖寺
kongan, kōan　公案
kongjŏnje　公田制
Kongmin　恭愍
Kongsan　公山
Koryŏ　高麗
Koryŏ taejanggyŏng
　高麗大藏經
kugye　具戒
kujokkye　具足戒
kuksa　國師
kusan　九山

Kwangjong　光宗
Kyeyuljong　戒律宗
Kyo　教
kyogwan kyŏmsu　教觀兼修
Kyŏnghŏ　鏡虛
Kyŏngsang　慶尙
Leng-chia-tsung　楞伽宗
liao-chien　料簡
Li T'ung-hsüan　李通玄
Lin-chi　臨濟
malpŏp　末法
Ma-tsu Tao-i　馬祖道一
Moguja　牧牛者
Mo-ho chih-kuan　摩訶止觀
Mugam Ch'oenul　默庵最訥
Munjong　文宗
Munjŏng　文定
munsin　文臣
musin　武臣
Muyong Suyŏn　無用秀演
Myoch'ŏng　妙淸
Myohyangsan　妙香山
Myŏngjong　明宗
Nan-tsung　南宗
Nan-yüeh　南嶽
Naong　懶翁
nien-fo　念佛
Niu-t'ou　牛頭
nongjang　農場
Nŭngŏmgyŏng　楞嚴經
ogyo yangjong　五教兩宗
Paegam Sŏngch'ong　柏庵性聰
Pai-chang Huai-hai　百丈懷海
Palsim suhaengjang
　發心修行章
p'an-chiao　判教

180

Pang Hanam　方漢岩
Poje　普濟
Pomunsa　普門寺
pigu　比丘
pongnal　伏捺
Pŏphwagyŏng　法華經
Pŏpsangjong　法相宗
Pŏpsŏngjong　法性宗
Pou　普雨
pulpŏp　佛法
Puyong Yŏnggwan　芙蓉靈觀
Pyŏgam Kaksŏng　碧巖覺性
Pyŏkkye Chŏngsim　碧溪正心
Pyŏksong Chiŏm　碧松智儼
P'yŏnyang Ŏn'gi　鞭羊彦機
sach'am　事懺
Sagulsan　闍崛山
sajipkwa　四集科
Samguk sagi　三國史記
sami　沙彌
San-sheng yüan-jung-kuan-men
　三聖圓融觀門
Sangbong Chŏngwŏn
　霜峰淨源
Sangdangnok　上堂錄
Sangmujuam　上無住庵
sari　舍利
Sejo　世祖
Sejong　世宗
Shen-hsiu　神秀
Shen-hui　神會
shih-li wu-ai　事理無礙
shih-shih wu-ai　事事無礙
Shih-t'ou　石頭
Sihŭngjong　始興宗
Silla　新羅

Sin Hyewŏl　申慧月
Sinin　神印
Sipchigyŏng-non　十地經論
Sŏchang　書狀
Sŏhŭng　瑞興
Sŏn　禪
Song Man'gong　宋滿空
Sŏn'ga kwigam　禪家龜鑑
Songgwangsa　松廣寺
Songgwangsa sago, Inmulp'yŏn
　松廣寺史庫, 人物編
Sŏngjong　成宗
Sŏn'gyosŏk　禪敎釋
Sŏnjŏkchong　禪寂宗
Sŏnmun yŏmsong　禪門拈頌
sŏnpang　禪房
sŏnsa　禪師
sŏnwŏn　禪院
Sŏnwŏnsa　禪源寺
Sŏsan Taesa　西山大師
Sōto　曹洞
sujwa　首座
Susŏnsa　修禪社
Taegak Kuksa　大覺國師
T'aego　太古
T'aejong　太宗
Ta-hui　大慧
tamsŏn pŏphoe　談禪法會
Tamyang　潭陽
T'ien-t'ai hsiao-chih-kuan
　天台小止觀
toch'ŏpche　度牒制
Tonghak　東鶴
Tongju　洞州
tono chŏmsu　頓悟漸修
Tosŏ　都序

Ts'ao-ch'i　曹溪
Tung-shan-tsung　東山宗
Tz'u-pien　慈辮
Ŭich'ŏn　義天
Ŭijong　毅宗
Wanggŏn　王建
wangsa　王師
Wŏlchŏ Toan　月渚道安
Wŏltam Sŏlche　月潭雪齋
Wŏn'gakkyŏng　圓覺經
Wŏn'gam　圓鑑
Wŏnhyo　元曉
Wŏnmyo　圓妙
Wŏno　圓悟
Yech'ŏn　醴泉

Yi Cha-gyŏm　李資謙
Yi Kyu-bo　李奎報
Yi Sŏng-gye　李成桂
Yŏlbangyŏng　涅槃經
Yŏlbanjong　涅槃宗
yŏmbul　念佛
Yŏndam Yuil　蓮潭有一
Yŏnsan'gun　燕山君
Yose　了世
Yulchong　律宗
Yung-ming Yen-shou
　永明延壽
Yüan-chüeh-ching　圓覺經
yusim　唯心
yu-wei　有爲

182

BIBLIOGRAPHY

A. WORKS OF CHINUL

1.

Works contained in *Hyŏnt'o yŏkhae Pojo Pŏbŏ* 懸吐譯解普照法語 [*Discourses on the Dharma by Pojo*]. Text (*Koryŏguk Pojo Sŏnsa ŏrok* 高麗國普照禪師語錄, ed. by Pang Hanam: Wŏlchŏng Monastery, Kangwŏndo: 1937) and Korean translation by Kim T'anhŏ 金呑虛. Seoul: 1963.

Kwŏnsu chŏnghye kyŏlsa mun 勸修定慧結社文 [*Invitation to the Society for the Cultivation of* Samādhi *and* Prajñā].
Susimgyŏl 修心訣 [*Key to the Cultivation of Mind*]. *T.* 48, No. 2020.
Chinsim chiksŏl 眞心直說 [*Direct Exposition of the True Mind*]. *T.* 48, No. 2019A.
Wŏndon sŏngbullon 圓頓成佛論 [*Treatise on the Complete-sudden Attainment of Buddhahood*].
Kanhwa kyŏrŭiron 看話決疑論 [*Treatise for the Settlement of Doubts on* Kanhwa].

2. Other Works

Kye ch'osim hagin mun 誡初心學人文 [*Admonitions to Beginning Students*]. *T.* 48, No. 2019B.
Hwaŏmnon chŏryo 華嚴論節要 [*Condensation of the Treatise on Hua-yen*]. Ed. by Kim Chi-gyŏn. Seoul: 1972 (Photographic reprint of the original edition. Tokyo: 1968).
Pŏpchip pyŏrhaengnok chŏryo pyŏngip sagi 法集別行錄節要並入私記 [*Condensation with Comments of the Pŏpchip pyŏrhaengnok*]. Contained in *Sajip happon* 四集合本 (ed. by An Chin-ho; Seoul: 1957).

Yŏmbul yomun 念佛要門 [*Essential path of* Yŏmbul]. Contained in *Sammun chikchi* 三門直指 (ed. by Chinhŏ P'algae in 1769; Ŭnjŏk Monastery, P'yŏngan Namdo: 1769). Part of the text is also contained in Nukariya Kaiten, *Chōsen zenkyōshi* (Tokyo: 1930), pp. 191–92.

Yukcho Taesa pŏppo tan'gyŏng pal 六祖大師法寶壇經跋 [*Postscript to the Platform Sūtra*]. Contained in *Hyŏnt'o pŏnyŏk Yukcho tangyŏng* 懸吐翻譯六祖壇經. Text (based upon the edition of Yŏngŭn Monastery) and Korean translation by Kim T'anhŏ. Seoul: 1960.

B. OTHER CLASSICAL WORKS (by title)

Ch'an-men shih-tzu ch'eng-hsi-t'u 禪門師資承襲圖, by Tsung-mi 宗密 Z. 2, 15, V.

Ch'an-yüan chu-ch'üan-chi tu-hsü 禪源諸詮集都序, by Tsung-mi 宗密 T. 48, No. 2015.

Chin'gak Kuksa ŏrok 眞覺國師語錄, by Hyesim 慧諶. Edited by Yi Chong-uk. Poje Monastery, Kaesŏng: 1940.

Ch'ŏnghŏdang chip 清虛堂集, by Hyujŏng 休靜. Myohyangsan edition. Wŏlchŏng Monastery, n.d. (*circa* 1900).

Gen en'yū Kōrai kokubon Rokuso Daishi hōbō dankyō 元延祐高麗刻本 六祖大師法寶壇經. Contained in *Zengaku kenkyū* 禪學研究 23 (1935): 1–63.

Haedong kosŭngjŏn 海東高僧傳, by Kakhun 覺訓. T. 50, No. 2065.

Hsin Hua-yen-ching-lun 新華嚴經論, by Li T'ung-hsüan 李通玄. T. 36, No. 1739.

Hwaŏm ilsŭng pŏpkyedo 華嚴一乘法界圖, by Ŭisang 義湘. T. 45, No. 1887A.

Kanhwa kyŏrŭiron palmun 看話決疑論跋文, by Hyesim 慧諶. Contained in *Han'guk kosŭngjip* 韓國高僧集: *Koryŏ sidae* 高麗時代, Seoul: 1974. Vol. II. pp. 627–28.

Kisillon-so 起信論疏, by Wŏnhyo 元曉. T. 44, No. 1844.

Kuan mi-le p'u-sa shang-sheng tou-shuo-t'ien-ching 觀彌勒菩薩上生兜率天經. T. 14, No. 452.

Liu-tsu ta-shih fa-pao t'an-ching 六祖大師法寶壇經. T. 48, No. 2008.

Mi-le hsia-sheng ch'eng-fo-ching 彌勒下生成佛經. *T.* 14, No. 454.

Mi-le ta-ch'eng-fo-ching 彌勒大成佛經. *T.* 14, No. 456.

Sajip happon 四集合本. Ed. by An Chin-ho 安震湖. Seoul: 1957.

Samguk sagi 三國史記, by Kim Pu-sik 金富軾. Ed. by Chōsenshi gakkai 朝鮮史學會. Seoul: 1928.

Samguk yusa 三國遺事, by Iryŏn 一然. *T.* 49, No. 2039.

Shen-hui ho-shang i-chi 神會和尚遺集, by Shen-hui 神會. Edited by Hu Shih 胡適. Shanghai: 1930.

Sinp'yŏn chejong kyojang ch'ongnok 新編諸宗教藏總錄, by Ŭich'ŏn 義天. *T.* 55, No. 2184.

Sŏn'ga kwigam 禪家龜鑑, by Sŏsan. *Z.* 2, 17, V.

Sŏn'gyosŏk 禪教釋, by Sŏsan. Contained in the *Ch'ŏnghŏdang chip*, facicle 4, pp. 37–43.

Sin'gan hyŏnt'o Sŏnmun ch'waryo 新刊懸吐禪門撮要. Ed. by Kyŏng-hŏ 鏡虛. Pŏmŏ Monastery. Pusan, 1968. Original edition: Pŏmŏ Monastery: 1908.

Sŏnmun pojangnok 禪門寶藏錄, by Ch'ŏnch'aek 天頙. *Z.* 2, 18, V.

Sŏyŏk Chunghwa Haedong Pulcho wŏllyu 西域中華海東佛祖源流, by Saam Ch'aeyŏng 獅巖釆永. Songgwang Monastery, Chŏnju: 1764.

Sung kao-seng-chuan 宋高僧傳, by Tsan-ning 贊寧. *T.* 50, No. 2061

Ta-ch'eng ch'i-hsin-lun 大乘起信論. *T.* 32, No. 1666.

Taegak Kuksa munjip 大覺國師文集, by Ŭich'ŏn 義天. Contained in *Han'guk kosŭngjip: Koryŏ sidae*, Seoul: 1974. Vol. I.

Taesŭng kisillon pyŏlgi 大乘起信論別記, by Wŏnhyo 元曉 *T.* 44, No. 1845.

Ta-fang-kuang fo-hua-yen-ching 大方廣佛華嚴經 80 fascicles. *T.* 10, No. 279.

Ta-fang-kuang yüan-chüeh hsiu-to-lo liao-i-ching 大方廣圓覺修多羅了義經. *T.* 17, No. 842.

Ta-hui p'u-chüeh ch'an-shih yü-lu 大慧普覺禪師語錄, by Ta-hui 大慧. *T.* 47, No. 1998A.

Tongsa yŏlchŏn 東師列傳, by Pŏmhae Kagan 梵海覺岸. Contained in *Pulgyo munhŏn charyojip* 佛教文獻資料集. Seoul: 1972. Vol. I.

Tsu-t'ang-chi 祖堂集. Contained in *CKPN*. Seoul: 1965.

Wŏnhyo chŏnjip 元曉全集. Ed. by Pulgyohak Tonginhoe 佛教學同人會. Seoul: 1973.

C. INSCRIPTIONS AND RECORDS (By Title)

Chogyesan che ise ko Tansoksa chuji Susŏnsa-chu chŭngsi Chin'gak Kuksa pimyŏng pyŏngsŏ 曹溪山第二世故斷俗寺主持修禪社主贈諡眞覺國師碑銘並序. *CKC*, Vol. I, pp. 461–64.

Haedong Chosŏn'guk Honamno Sunch'ŏnbu Chogyesan Songgwangsa Chŭngsi Puril Pojo Kuksa pimyŏng pyŏngsŏ 海東朝鮮國湖南路順天府曹溪山松廣寺贈諡佛日普照國師碑銘並序. *CKC*, Vol. II, pp. 949–53.

Koryŏguk taesŏngil Hŭngwangsa ko kuksa sosi Taegak Taehwasang myojimyŏng pyŏngsŏ 高麗國大聖日興王寺故國師所諡大覺大和尙墓誌銘並序. *CPT*, Vol. II, pp. 314–16.

Kŭmgangsan T'oeŭn Kugil Totaesŏnsa Sŏn'gyo Toch'ongsŏp saja Pujongsugyo kyŏm Tŭnggye Poje Taesa Ch'ŏnghŏdang haengjang 金剛山退隱國一都大禪師禪教都總攝賜紫扶宗樹教兼登階普濟大師清虛堂行狀. Contained in *Ch'ŏnghŏdang chip*, fascicle 4, pp. 44–46.

Mandŏksan Paengnyŏnsa Wŏnmyo Kuksa pimyŏng pyŏngsŏ 萬德山白蓮社圓妙國師碑銘並序. *CKC*, Vol. I, pp. 590–93.

Pyŏksongdang haengjang 碧松堂行狀. Contained in *Ch'ŏnghŏdang chip*, fascicle 3, pp. 31–34.

Sŭngp'yŏngbu Chogyesan Susŏnsa Puril Pojo Kuksa pimyŏng pyŏngsŏ 昇平府曹溪山修禪社佛日普照國師碑並銘序. Contained in *Po*, pp. 139–43.

Sŭngp'yŏng Chogyesan Songgwangsa sawŏn sajŏkpi 昇平曹溪山松廣寺嗣院事蹟碑. *CSS*, Vol. I, pp. 277–79.

Taesŭng Sŏnjong Chogyesan Susŏnsa chungch'anggi 大乘禪宗曹溪山修禪社重創記. *CSS*, Vol. I, pp. 174–77.

Unak Hyŏndŭngsa sajŏk 雲嶽懸燈寺事蹟. *CSS*, Vol. I, pp. 32–35.

D. WORKS ON CHINUL

Eda, Shunyū 江田俊雄. "Chōsen zen no keisei—'Fushōzen' no seikaku ni tsuite" 朝鮮禪の形成―「普照禪」の性格について, *Indogaku Bukkyōgaku kenkyū* 印度學佛教學研究 V, 2 (1957): 351–59.

Han, Ki-du 韓基斗. "Han'guk ŭi Sŏnji" 韓國의 禪旨, *Han'guk Pulgyo sasang* 韓國佛教思想. Iri, Chŏlla Pukto: 1973.

Im, Sŏk-chin 林錫珍. "Pojo Kuksa yŏn'gu" 普照國師研究, *Pulgyo*

佛敎 101–103 (1942–1943).

Kim, Ing-sŏk 金仍石. "Puril Pojo Kuksa" 佛日普照國師, *Pulgyo hakpo* 佛敎學報 2 (1964): 3–41.

Kim, T'anhŏ 金呑虛, trans., *Hyŏnt'o yŏkhae Pojo Pŏbŏ* 懸吐譯解普照法語. Seoul: 1963.

Ko, Hyŏng-gon 高亨坤. "Pojo sisŏl Haedong Chogyejong" 普照始設海東曹溪宗, *Haedong Chogyejong ŭi yŏnwŏn mit kŭ choryu* 海東曹溪宗의 淵源및 그 潮流. Seoul: 1970.

Kokuyaku zenshū sōsho kankōkai, trans., "Kokuyaku Kōraikoku Fushō Zenshi shūshinketsu" 國譯高麗國普照禪師修心訣, *Kokuyaku zenshū sōsho* 國譯禪宗叢書 III (1919): 1–20.

Nukariya, Kaiten 忽滑谷快天. "Chitotsu ga zengaku no dokusō" 知訥が禪學の獨創, *Chōsen zenkyōshi* 朝鮮禪敎史. Tokyo: 1930.

Pak, Chong-hong 朴鍾鴻. "Chinul ŭi sasang" 知訥의 思想, *Han'guk sasangsa* 韓國思想史: *Pulgyo sasang p'yŏn* 佛敎思想篇. Seoul: 1972.

Pak, Sŏng-bae 朴性培. "Pojo—chŏnghye ssangsu ŭi kuhyŏnja" 普照—定慧雙修의 具現者, *Han'guk ŭi in'gansang* 韓國의 人間像, Vol. III: *Chonggyoga, sahoe pongsaja p'yŏn* (Seoul: 1965), pp. 143–54.

Song, Ch'ŏn-ŭn 宋天恩. "Chinul ŭi Sŏn sasang" 知訥의 禪思想, *PHPS*, pp. 477–513.

Tongguk Yŏkkyŏngwŏn 東國譯經院, trans., "Pojo Kuksa chip" 普照國師集, *Han'gŭl taejanggyŏng, Han'guk kosŭng*. Seoul: 1971. Vol. III, pp. 17–493.

Yi, Chong-ik 李鍾益. "Chinul ŭi Hwaŏm sasang" 知訥의 華嚴思想, *PHPS*, pp. 515–50.

———. *Kōrai Fushō Kokushi no kenkyū—sono shisō taikei to Fushōzen no tokushitsu* 高麗普照國師の研究—その思想體系と普照禪の特質. Seoul: 1974 (mimeographed).

———. "Pojo Kuksa ŭi Sŏn'gyo kwan" 普照國師의 禪敎觀, *Pulgyo hakpo* 9(1972): 67–96.

Yi, Chong-uk 李鍾郁, trans., *Wŏnmun kugyŏk taejo Koryŏ Pojo Kuksa pŏbŏ* 原文國譯對照高麗普照國師法語. Seoul: 1948.

E. OTHER WORKS ON KOREAN BUDDHISM

An, Kye-hyŏn 安啓賢. "Han'guk Pulgyosa (sang)" 韓國佛敎史 (上),

Han'guk munhwasa taegye 韓國文化史大系. Seoul: 1970. Vol. VI, pp. 177–267.

Idem. "P'algwanhoe ko" 八關會攷, *Tongguk sahak* 東國史學 4 (1956): 31–54.

Idem. Silla chŏngt'o sasangsa yŏn'gu 新羅淨土思想史研究. Tongguk Taehakkyo Han'gukhak yŏn'gu ch'ongsŏ che ch'ilchip. Seoul: 1976.

Idem. "Yŏndŭnghoe ko" 燃燈會攷, *PKPN*, pp. 501–35.

Idem. "Yŏwŏn kwangye esŏ pon Koryŏ Pulgyo" 麗元關係에서 본 高麗佛教, *Haewŏn Hwang Ŭi-don Sŏnsaeng kohi kinyŏm sahak nonch'ong* 海元黃義敦先生古稀記念史學論叢. (Seoul: 1960), pp. 147–70

Clark, Charles A. "Buddhism," *Religions of Old Korea.* Seoul: 1961 (Reprint of the original edition, New York: 1932).

Cho, Myŏng-gi 趙明基. *Koryŏ Taegak Kuksa wa Ch'ŏnt'ae sasang* 高麗大覺國師와天台思想. Seoul: 1964.

Idem. Silla Pulgyo ŭi inyŏm kwa yŏksa 新羅佛教의 理念과 歷史. Seoul: 1962.

Idem. "Taegak Kuksa ŭi Ch'ŏnt'ae sasang kwa sokchang ŭi ŏpchŏk" 大覺國師의 天台思想과 續藏의 業績, *PKPN*, pp. 891–931.

Ch'oe, Nam-sŏn 崔南善. "Chosŏn Pulgyo" 朝鮮佛教, *Yuktang Ch'oe Nam-sŏn chŏnjip* 六堂崔南善全集. Seoul: 1973, Vol. II, pp. 547–72.

Chŏng, Chung-hwan 鄭仲煥. "Silla ŭi Pulgyo chŏllae wa kŭ hyŏnse sasang" 新羅의 佛教傳來와 그 現世思想, *CKPN*, pp. 173–95.

Dumoulin, Heinrich S. J. "Contemporary Buddhism in Korea," *Buddhism in Modern World.* Ed. by H. Dumoulin and John C. Maraldo. New York and London: 1976.

Eda, Shunyū 江田俊雄. "Chōsen Bukkyō to gokoku shisō—tokuni Shiragi jidai no sore ni tsuite" 朝鮮佛教と護國思想—特に新羅時代のそれについて, *Chōsen* 朝鮮 (April, 1935) pp. 51–67.

Idem. "Shiragi Bukkyō ni okeru Jōdokyō" 新羅佛教に於ける淨土教, *Shina Bukkyō shigaku* 支那佛教史學 III, 3–4 (1939): 145–55.

Idem. "Shiragi no Bukkyō juyō ni kansuru shomondai" 新羅の佛教受容に關する諸問題, *Bunka* 文化 8 (1935): 961–88.

Idem. "Shiragi no Jizō to Godaisan" 新羅の慈藏と五台山, *Bunka*

21 (1957): 562–73.

Idem. "Zenshū toshite no Chōsen Bukkyō no dentō ni tsuite" 禪宗と
しての朝鮮佛教の傳統に就いて, *Bukkyōgaku no shomondai* 佛教
學の諸問題. Ed. by Buttan nisen gohyaku-nen kinen gakkai 佛誕
二千五百年紀念學會 (Tokyo: 1935), pp. 898–914.

Gard, Richard A. "The Mādhyamika in Korea," PKPN, pp. 1153–
74.

Gundert, Wilhelm. "Die Religionen der Koreaner (Der Buddhis-
mus)," *Japanische Religionsgeschichte: Die Religion der Japaner
und Koreaner im geschichtlichen Abriss dargestellt.* Stuttgart: 1943.

Han'guk Pulgyo Yŏn'guwon 韓國佛教研究院. *Han'guk ŭi sach'al*
韓國의 寺刹 (6): *Songgwangsa* 松廣寺. Seoul: 1975.

Han, Ki-du 韓基斗. *Han'guk Pulgyo sasang* 韓國佛教思想. Iri,
Chŏlla Pukto: 1973.

Idem, *Silla sidae ŭi Sŏn sasang* 新羅時代의 禪思想. Iri: 1974.

Han, U-gŭn 韓沽劢. "Yŏmal sŏnch'o ŭi Pulgyo chŏngch'aek" 麗末
鮮初의 佛教政策, *Seoul Taehakkyo nonmunjip* 서울大學校論文集:
Inmun sahoe kwahak 人文社會科學 6(1957): 1–80.

Hatada, Takashi 旗田巍. "Kōraichō ni okeru jiin keizai" 高麗朝に於
ける寺院經濟, *Shigaku zasshi* 史學雜誌 XLIII, 5(1932): 557–93.

Hong, Sun-ch'ang and Tamura Enchō 洪淳昶, 田村圓澄, eds., *Hanil
kodae munhwa kyosŏpsa yŏn'gu* 韓日古代文化交涉史研究. Seoul:
1974. Japanese edition: *Shiragi to Asuka, Hakuhō no Bukkyō bunka*
新羅と飛鳥・白鳳の佛教文化. Tokyo: 1975.

Hwang, P'ae-gang 黃浿江. *Silla Pulgyo sŏrhwa ŭi yŏn'gu* 新羅佛教說
話의 研究. Seoul: 1975.

Im, Sŏk-chin 林錫珍. *Taesŭng Sŏnjong Chogyesan Songgwangsa chi*
大乘禪宗曹溪山松廣寺誌. Songgwang Monastery, Chŏlla Namdo:
1965.

Ikeuchi, Hiroshi 池內宏. "Kōraichō no daizōkyō" 高麗朝の大藏經,
Mansenshi kenkyū 滿鮮史研究: *Chūsei* 中世, Vol. II (Tokyo: 1937),
pp. 483–614.

Imanishi, Ryū 今西龍. "Shiragisō Dōsen ni tsuite" 新羅僧道詵に就
て, *Tōyō gakuhō* 東洋學報 II, 2(1912): 257–63.

Inaba, Seiji 稻葉正就. "Chōsen shusshin sō Ensoku ni tsuite" 朝鮮出
身僧圓測について, *Chōsen gakuhō* 朝鮮學報, No. 2(1951).

Idem. "Ensoku sen Gejinmikkyō-so no Chibetto yaku ni tsuite" 圓測撰解深密經疏の西藏譯に就て, *Ōtani gakuhō* 大谷學報 XXV, 1 (1944): 50–65.

Kanda, Kiichiro 神田喜一郎. "Tō Genju Kokushi shinseki 'Shiragi Gishō Hōshi ni yoseru sho' kō" 唐賢首國師眞蹟「寄新羅義湘法師書」考, *Nanto Bukkyō* 南都佛教 26 (1971): 1–15.

Kim, Chi-gyŏn and Ch'ae In-hwan 金知見, 蔡印幻, eds., *Shiragi Bukkyō kenkyū* 新羅佛教研究. Tokyo: 1973.

Kim, Ch'ŏl-chun 金哲埈. "Koryŏch'o ŭi Ch'ŏnt'aehak yŏn'gu" 高麗初의 天台學研究, *Han'guk kodae sahoe yŏn'gu* 韓國古代社會研究. Seoul: 1975.

Kim, Chong-guk 金鍾國. "Kōrai bushin seiken to sōto no tairitsu kōsō ni kansuru ichi kōsatsu" 高麗武臣政權と僧徒の對立抗爭に關する一考察, *Chōsen gakuhō* 朝鮮學報 21–22(1961): 567–89.

Kim, Ing-sōk 金仍石. "Koguryŏ Sŭngnang kwa samnonhak" 高句麗僧郎과 三論學, *PKPN*, pp. 41–67.

Kim, Sang-gi 金庠基. "Hwarang kwa mirŭk sinang" 花郎과 彌勒信仰, *Yi Hong-jik Paksa hoegap kinyŏm Han'guk sahak nonch'ong* 李弘稙博士回甲記念韓國史學論叢 (Seoul: 1969), pp. 3–12.

Idem. "Taegak Kuksa Ŭich'ŏn ŭi haengjŏk e taehayŏ" 大覺國師義天의 行蹟에 對하여, *Han'guk chŏnsa* 韓國全史: *Koryŏ sidae sa* 高麗時代史 (Seoul: 1961), pp. 168–81.

Kim, Yŏng-su 金映遂. "Chogyejong kwa chŏndŭng t'onggyu" 曹溪宗과 傳燈通規, *Pulgyo sin* 佛教新 43–45(1943).

Idem. "Chogye Sŏnjong e ch'wihaya" 曹溪禪宗에 就하야, *Chindan hakpo* 震壇學報 9 (1938): 145–75.

Idem. "Chosŏn Pulgyo chongji e ch'wihaya" 朝鮮佛教宗旨에 就하야, *Pulgyo sin* 8–9 (1937–1938).

Idem. "Ogyo yangjong e taehaya" 五教兩宗에 對하야, *Chindan hakpo* 8 (1937): 74–101.

Kim, Yŏng-t'ae 金煐泰. "Han'guk Pulgyosa (ha)" 韓國佛教史 (下), *Han'guk munhwasa taegye* VI (Seoul: 1970), pp. 269–364.

Idem. "Silla Chinhŭng Taewang ŭi sinbul kwa kŭ sasang yŏn'gu" 新羅眞興大王의 信佛과 그 思想研究, *Pulgyo hakpo* 佛教學報 5 (1967): 53–83.

Idem. "Silla Pulgyo taejunghwa ŭi yŏksa wa kŭ sasang yŏn'gu" 新羅

佛教大衆化의 歷史와 그 思想研究, *Pulgyo hakpo* 佛教學報 6 (1969): 145–91.

Idem. Sŏsan Taesa ŭi saengae wa sasang 西山大師의 生涯와 思想. Seoul: 1975.

Kuroda, Akira 黑田亮. *Chōsen kyūsho kō* 朝鮮舊書考. Tokyo: 1940.

Kwŏn, Sang-no 權相老. "Chogyejong—Chosŏn esŏ charip han chongp'a ŭi ki sa" 曹溪宗—朝鮮에서 自立한 宗派의 其四, *Pulgyo* 佛教 58 (1929): 2–10.

Idem. "Ch'ŏnt'aejong kwa Sihŭngjong—Chosŏn esŏ charip han chongp'a ŭi ki yuk" 天台宗과 始興宗—朝鮮에서 自立한 宗派의 其六, *Pulgyo* 佛教 60–61 (1929).

Idem. Chosŏn Pulgyo yaksa 朝鮮佛教略史. Seoul: 1972.

Kwŏn, Sang-no. "Chosŏn ŭi Yulchong—Chosŏn esŏ charip han chongp'a ŭi ki sam" 朝鮮의 律宗—朝鮮에서 自立한 宗派의 其三, *Pulgyo* 佛教 56 (1929): 2–14.

Idem. "Han'guk Sŏnjong yaksa" 韓國禪宗略史, *PKPN*, pp. 263–98.

Lee, Peter H. "Fa-tsang and Ŭisang," *Journal of the American Oriental Society* LXXXII, 1 (1962): 56–62.

Idem. "The life of the Korean Poet-Priest Kyunyŏ," *Asiatische Studien* XI, 1–2 (1957/1958): 42–72.

Idem, trans., *Lives of Eminent Korean Monks: The Haedong Kosŭng Chŏn*. Cambridge, Mass.: 1969.

Matsubayashi, Hiroyuki 松林弘之. "Shiragi Jōdokyō no ichi kōsatsu—Gengyō no Jōdokyō shisō o megutte" 新羅淨土教の一考察—元曉の淨土教思想をめぐつて, *Indogaku Bukkyōgaku kenkyū* 印度學佛教學研究 XV, 1 (1966): 196–98.

Mishina, Shōei 三品彰英. "Chōsen ni okeru Bukkyō to minzoku shinkō" 朝鮮における佛教と民族信仰, *Bukkyō shigaku* 佛教史學 4 (1954): 9–32.

Idem. "Shiragi no Jōdokyō—'Sankoku iji' shosai Jōdokyō kankei kiji chūkai" 新羅の淨土教—「三國遺事」所載淨土教關係記事註解, *Tsukamoto Hakushi shōju kinen Bukkyō shigaku ronshū* 塚本博士頌壽記念佛教史學論集 (Kyoto: 1961), pp. 727–45.

Mochizuki, Shinkō 望月信亨. "Gishō, Gengyō, Gijaku nado no Jōdoron narabini jūnensetsu" 義湘・元曉・義寂等の並に十念說, *Chūgoku Jōdo kyōrishi* 中國淨土教理史. Kyōto: 1942.

Motoi, Nobuo 本井信雄. "Shiragi no Gengyō no denki ni tsuite" 新羅の元曉の傳記について, *Ōtani gakuhō* 大谷學報 XLI, 1 (1961): 33–52.

Ninomiya, Keinin 二宮啓任. "Chōsen ni okeru ninnōe no kaisetsu" 朝鮮における仁王會の開設, *Chōsen gakuhō* 朝鮮學報 4 (1959): 155–63.

Idem. "Kōraichō no hakkan'e ni tsuite" 高麗朝の八關會について, *Chōsen gakuhō* 9 (1956): 235–51.

Idem. "Kōraichō no jōgen nentōe ni tsuite" 高麗朝の上元燃燈會について, *Chōsen gakuhō* 12 (1958): 111–22.

Idem. "Kōraichō no saie ni tsuite" 高麗朝の齊會について, *Chōsen gakuhō* 21–22 (1961): 229–36.

Nukariya, Kaiten 忽滑谷快天. *Chōsen zenkyōshi* 朝鮮禪教史. Tokyo: 1930.

Ōya, Tokujō 大屋德城. "Chōsen Kaiinji kyōhan kō—tokuni daizōkyō hohan narabini zōgai zappan no Bukkyō bunkengakuteki kenkyū" 朝鮮海印寺經板攷—特に大經藏補板並に藏外雜板の佛教文獻學的研究, *Tōyō gakuhō* 東洋學報 XV, 3 (1920): 285–362.

Idem. Kōrai zokuzō chōzō kō 高麗續藏彫造攷. 3 Vols. Kyoto: 1937.

Paik, Nak Choon. "Tripitaka Koreana," *Transactions of the Korea Branch of the Royal Asiatic Society* XXXII (1951): 62–78.

Pak, Chong-hong 朴鍾鴻. *Han'guk sasangsa* 韓國思想史: *Pulgyo sasang p'yŏn* 佛教思想篇. Seoul: 1972.

Pang, Hanam 方漢岩. "Haedong ch'ojo e taehaya" 海東初祖에 對하야, *Pulgyo* 佛教 70 (1930): 7–11.

Pratt, James B. "Korean Buddhism," *The Pilgrimage of Buddhism and a Buddhist Pilgrimage.* New York: 1928.

Sakamoto, Yukio 坂本幸男. "Genju Daishi no shokan ni tsuite" 賢首大師の書簡について, *Shohon* 書品 62 (1955): 2–4.

Idem. "Shiragi no Gishō no kyōgaku" 新羅の義湘の教學, *Kegon kyōgaku no kenkyū* 華嚴教學の研究. Kyoto: 1956.

Sŏ, Kyŏng-bo. *A Study of Korean Zen Buddhism Approached Through the Chodangjip.* Seoul: 1973.

Sŏngt'a 性陀. "Kyŏnghŏ ŭi Sŏn sasang" 鏡虛의 禪思想, *PHPS*, pp. 1103–1120.

Starr, Frederick. *Korean Buddhism: History, Condition, Art.* Boston:

1918.

Suematsu, Yasukazu 末松保和. "Shiragi Bukkyō denrai densetsu kō" 新羅佛教傳來傳說考, *Shiragishi no shomondai* 新羅史の諸問題 (Tokyo: 1954), pp. 207–34.

Sugano, Ginpachi 菅野銀八. "Kōrai Sōkeisan Shōkōji jūroku kokushi no keishō ni tsuite" 高麗曹溪山松廣寺十六國師の繼承に就て, *Seikyū gakusō* 青丘學叢 9 (1932): 92–102.

Idem. "Mantokuji shi ni tsuite" 萬德寺誌に就て, *Chōsen* 朝鮮 (Sep., 1928), pp. 79–92.

Sungsan Pak Kil-chin Paksa hwagap kinyŏm saŏphoe, ed. *PHPS.* Iri, Chŏlla Pukto: 1975.

Takahashi, Tōru 高橋亨. "Daikaku Kokushi Giten no Kōrai Bukkyō ni taisuru keirin ni tsuite" 大覺國師義天の高麗佛教に對する經倫に就いて, *Chōsen gakuhō* 朝鮮學報 10 (1956): 113–47.

Idem. Richō Bukkyō 李朝佛教. Tokyo: 1929.

Idem. "Sŭngbyŏng kwa Yijo Pulgyo ŭi sŏngsoe" 僧兵과李朝佛教의盛衰, *Pulgyo* 佛教 4–11 (1924–1925).

Tongguk Yŏkkyŏngwŏn, trans., *HTHK*, Vol. I (Seoul: 1969); Vol. III (Seoul: 1971); and Vol. IV (Seoul: 1973).

Trollope, Mark N. "Introduction to the Study of Buddhism in Corea." *Transactions of the Korea Branch of the Royal Asiatic Society Records* VIII (1917): 1–41.

Yaotani, Takayasu 八百谷孝保. "Shiragisō Gishō-den kō" 新羅僧義湘傳考, *Shina Bukkyō shigaku* 支那佛教史學 III, 1 (1939): 79–94.

Idem. "Shiragi shakai to Jōdokyō" 新羅社會と淨土教, *Shichō* 史潮 VII, 4 (1937): 115–64.

Yi, Chae-ch'ang 李載昌. *Koryŏ sawŏn kyŏngje ŭi yŏn'gu* 高麗寺院經濟의研究. Tongguk Taehakkyo han'gukhak yŏn'gu ch'ongsŏ che kujip. Seoul: 1976.

Yi, Chae-yŏl 李在烈. "Koryŏ ogyo yangjong ŭi sachŏk koch'al" 高麗五教兩宗의 史的考察, *Sahak yŏn'gu* 史學研究 4 (1959).

Idem. "Ogyo yangjong kwa Chogyejong pŏpt'ong" 五教兩宗과 曹溪宗法統, *Pulgyo sasang* 佛教思想 1–6 (1973–1974).

Yi, Chi-gwan 李智冠. *Han'guk Pulgyo soŭi kyŏngjŏn yŏn'gu* 韓國佛教所依經典研究. Seoul: 1971.

Yi, Hŭi-su 李喜秀. *T'och'akhwa kwajŏng esŏ pon Han'guk Pulgyo*

土着化過程에서 본 韓國佛教. Seoul: 1971.

Yi, Hong-jik 李弘稙. "Silla sŭnggwanje wa Pulgyo chŏngch'aek ŭi chemunje" 新羅僧官制와 佛教政策의 諸問題, *PKPN*, pp. 659–79.

Yi, Ki-baek 李基白. "Samguk sidae Pulgyo chŏllae wa kŭ sahoejŏk sŏngkyŏk" 三國時代佛教傳來와 그 社會的性格, *Yŏksa hakpo* 歷史學報 6 (1954): 128–205.

Yi, Nŭng-hwa 李能和. *Chosŏn Pulgyo t'ongsa* 朝鮮佛教通史. 2 vols. Seoul: 1918.

Yi, Sang-baek 李相佰. "Yubul yanggyo kyodae ŭi kiyŏn e taehan il yŏn'gu" 儒佛兩教交代의 機緣에 對한 一研究, *Han'guk munhwasa yŏn'gu non'go* 韓國文化史研究論攷. Han'guk munhwa ch'ongsŏ che ijip. Seoul: 1948.

Yŏ, Tong-ch'an 呂東贊 (Roger Leverrier). *Koryŏ sidae hoguk pŏphoe e taehan yŏn'gu* 高麗時代護國法會에 對한 研究. Seoul: 1970. Contains French extract, pp. 95–117.

Yu, Kyo-sŏng 劉教聖. "Koryŏ sawŏn kyŏngje ŭi sŏngkyŏk" 高麗寺院經濟의 性格, *PKPN*, pp. 605–26.

F. OTHER WORKS

Araki, Kengo 荒本見悟. *Bukkyō to jukyō* 佛教と儒教: *Chūgoku shisō o keisei suru mono* 中國思想を形成するもの. Kyoto: 1963.

Idem. trans., *Zen no goroku* 禪の語録 (17): *Daie-sho* 大慧書. Tokyo: 1969.

Bellah, Robert. "The Contemporary Meaning of Kamakura Buddhism," *Journal of the American Academy of Religion* XLII, 1 (1974): 3–17.

Carman, John B. *The Theology of Rāmānuja: An Essay in Interreligious Understanding.* New Haven and London: 1974.

Chang, Chung-Yuan, trans., *Original Teaching of Ch'an Buddhism: selected from the Transmission of the Lamp* [*Ching-te ch'uan-teng-lu*]. New York: 1969.

Ch'en, Kenneth K. S. *Buddhism in China: A Historical Survey.* Princeton, N. J.: 1964.

Chiba, Jōryū, Kitanishi Hiromu, and Takagi Yutaka 千葉乘隆・北西弘・高木豊. *Bukkyōshi kaisetsu* 佛教史概說: Nihon-hen 日本篇.

Kyoto: 1969.

Chindan Hakhoe 震檀學會. *Han'guksa* 韓國史: *Chungse p'yŏn* 中世篇. Seoul: 1961.

Dumoulin, Heinrich S. J. *A History of Zen Buddhism.* Translated from the German by Paul Peachey. New York: 1963.

Eliade, Mircea and Kitagawa Joseph M., eds. *The History of Religions: Essays in Methodology.* Chicago: 1959.

Geertz, Clifford. *Islam Observed: Religious Development in Morocco and Indonesia.* New Haven and London: 1968.

Gernet, Jacques, trans. *Entretiens du Maître Dhyāna Chen-Houei du Ho-Tsö.* Publications de L'école française d'Extrême-Orient. Hanoi: 1949.

Hakeda, Yoshito S., trans., *The Awakening of Faith [Ta-ch'eng ch'i-hsin-lun].* New York and London: 1967.

Hatada, Takashi. *A History of Korea.* Translated and edited by Warren W. Smith, Jr. and Benjamin H. Hazard. Santa Barbara, Calif.: 1969.

Ha, Tae-Hung and Mintz K. Grafton, trans., *Samguk yusa: Legends and History of the Three Kingdoms of Ancient Korea.* Seoul: 1972.

Hirai, Shun'ei 平井俊榮. "Sanron gakuha no genryū keifu—Kashō ni okeru kanga kyūsetsu o megutte" 三論學派の源流系譜 ― 嘉祥における關河舊説をめぐって, *Tōhōgaku* 東方學 28 (1964): 52–65.

Hu, Shih. "Ch'an (Zen) Buddhism in China, Its History and Method," *Philosophy East and West* III, 1 (1953): 3–24.

Ienaga, Saburo 家永三郎. *Chūsei Bukkyō shisōshi kenkyū* 中世佛教思想史研究. Revised edition. Kyoto: 1955.

Ikeuchi, Hiroshi 池內宏. "Shiragi karō ni tsuite" 新羅花郎について, *Tōyō gakuhō* 東洋學報 XXIV, 1 (1936): 1–34.

Im, Ch'ang-sun 任昌淳. "Songgwangsa ŭi Koryŏ munsŏ" 松廣寺의 高麗文書, *Paeksan hakpo* 白山學報 11 (1971): 31–51.

Im, Tong-gwŏn 任東權. "Han'guk wŏnsi chonggyosa" 韓國原始宗教史 (1), *Han'guk munhwasa taegye* VI: *Chonggyo ch'ŏrhaksa* (Seoul: 1970), pp. 21–114.

Jan, Yün-hua. "Tsung-mi, His Analysis of Ch'an Buddhism," *T'oung Pao* 通報 LVIII (1972): 1–54.

Idem. "Two Problems concerning Tsung-mi's Compilation of Ch'an-tsang 禪藏," *Transactions of the International Conference of Orientalists in Japan* XIX (1974): 37–47.

Jung, Carl G. *Modern Man in Search of a Soul*. Translated by W. S. Dell and Cary F. Bayes. London: 1933.

Kamata, Shigeo 鎌田茂雄. *Chūgoku Bukkyō shisōshi kenkyū* 中國佛教思想史研究. Tokyo: 1968.

Idem. Chūgoku kegon shisōshi no kenkyū 中國華嚴思想の研究. Tokyo: 1965.

Idem. "Nihon kegon ni okeru seitō to itan—Kamakura kyū-Bukkyō ni okeru Myōe to Gyōnen" 日本華嚴における正統と異瑞—鎌倉舊佛教における明惠と凝然, *Shisō* 思想 (Nov. 1973), pp. 62–77

Idem. Shūmitsu kyōgaku no shisōshi teki kenkyū 宗密教學の思想史的研究. Tokyo: 1975.

Idem. trans., *Zen no goroku* 禪の語錄 (9): *Zengenshosenshu tojo* 禪源諸詮集都序. Tokyo: 1971.

Kamekawa, Kyōshin 龜川教信. *Kegongaku* 華嚴學. Kyoto: 1949.

Kamstra, J. H. *Encounter or Syncretism: The Initial Growth of Japanese Buddhism*. Leiden: 1967.

Katsumata, Shunkyō 勝又俊教. *Bukkyō ni okeru shinshikisetsu no kenkyū* 佛教における心識說の研究. Tokyo: 1961.

Kim, Ch'ŏl-chun 金哲埈. *Han'guk kodae sahoe yŏn'gu* 韓國古代社會研究. Seoul: 1975.

Idem. "Silla sangdae sahoe ŭi Dual Organization" 新羅上代社會의 Dual Organization, *Yŏksa hakpo* 歷史學報 1–2 (1952).

Kim, Chong-gwŏn 金鍾權, trans., *Wanyŏk Samguk sagi* 完譯三國史記. Seoul: 1960.

Kim, Hee-Jin. *Dōgen Kigen—Mystical Realist*. Tucson, Ariz.: 1975.

Kim, Sang-gi 金庠基. *Han'guk chŏnsa: Koryŏ sidae sa*. Seoul: 1961.

Koryŏsa, 高麗史. 3 vols. Seoul: Asia Munhwasa, 1972.

Kuksa P'yŏnch'an Wiwŏnhoe 국사편찬위원회. *Han'guksa* 한국사 (7): *Koryŏ musin chŏngkwŏn kwa taemong hangjaeng* 고려무신정권과대몽항쟁. Seoul: 1974.

Kungnip Chungang Tosŏgwan 국립중앙도서관. *Kosŏ mongnok* 고서목록, Vol. I. Seoul: 1970.

Kwŏn, Sang-no 權相老. *Han'guk chimyŏng yŏnhyŏk ko* 韓國地名沿革考. Seoul: 1961.

Liebenthal, Walter, trans., *Chao Lun: The Treatises of Seng-chao*. Second, revised edition. Hong Kong: 1968.

Mishina, Shōei 三品彰英. *Shiragi karō no kenkyū* 新羅花郎の研究. Tokyo: 1943.

Mochizuki, Shinkō 望月信亨. *Bukkyō daijiten* 佛教大辭典. 10 vols. 1954-63.

Nakamura, Hajime 中村元. *Bukkyōgo daijiten* 佛教語大辭典. 3 vols. Tokyo: 1975.

Nakamura, Hajime and Kawada Kumatarō 川田熊太郎, eds. *Kegon shisō* 華嚴思想. Kyoto: 1960.

Ōya, Tokujō 大屋德城. "Gen en'yū Kōrai kokubon Rokuso Daishi hōbō dankyō ni tsuite" 元延祐高麗刻本六祖大師法寶壇經に就いて, *Zengaku kenkyū* 禪學研究 23 (1935): 1-29.

Reischauer, E. O. and J. K. Fairbank. *East Asia: The Great Tradition*. Boston: 1960.

Robinson, Richard H. *Early Mādhyamika in India and China*. Madison, Wisconsin: 1967.

Sakamoto, Yukio 坂本幸男. *Kegon kyōgaku no kenkyū* 華嚴教學の研究. Kyoto: 1956.

Sansom, G. B. *Japan: A Short Cultural History*. Revised edition. New York: 1962.

Sekiguchi, Shindai 關口眞大. *Daruma Daishi no kenkyū* 達摩大師の研究. Revised edition. Tokyo: 1969.

Idem. Zenshū shisōshi 禪宗思想史. Tokyo: 1964.

Idem. "Zenshū to Tendaishū to no kōsō" 禪宗と天台宗との交渉, *Taishō Daigaku kenkyū kiyō* 大正大學研究紀要 44 (1959): 39-75.

Shimada, Kenji 島田虔次. "Tai-yō no rekishi ni yosete" 體用の歴史に寄せて, *Tsukamoto Hakushi shōju kinen Bukkyō shigaku ronshū* (Kyoto, 1961), pp. 416-30.

Suzuki, Daisetsu T. *Essays in Zen Buddhism*. 3 vols. New York, 1961, 1971, 1971 (originally published in London in 1927, 1933, 1934).

Idem. "Zen: A Reply to Hu Shih," *Philosophy East and West* III, 1 (1953): 25-46.

Suzuki, Daisetsu T. *The Zen Doctrine of No mind: The Significance of the Sutra of Hui-neng (Wei-lang)*. New York: 1972. Originally published in London in 1949.

Taehan Min'guk Kukhoe Tosŏgwan 大韓民國國會圖書館. *Han'guk kosŏ chonghap mongnok* 韓國古書綜合目錄. Seoul: 1968.

Takamine, Ryōshū 高峯了州. *Kegon shisōshi* 華嚴思想史. Kyoto: 1942.

Idem. Kegon to zen to no tsūro 華嚴と禪との通路. Nara, Japan: 1956.

Tokiwa, Daijō 常盤大定. *Shina Bukkyō no kenkyū* 支那佛教の研究, Vol. III. Tokyo: 1943.

Ui, Hakuju 宇井伯壽. *Zenshūshi kenkyū* 禪宗史研究. Tokyo: 1939.

Idem. Dai san zenshūshi kenkyū 第三禪宗史研究. Tokyo: 1943.

Unhŏ, Yongha 운허용하. *Pulgyo sajŏn* 불교사전. T'ongdo Monastery, Kyŏngsang Namdo: 1961.

Wach, Joachim. "Verstehen," *Religion in Geschichte und Gegenwart*. 2nd edition. Tübingen: 1931.

Weinstein, Stanley, "Imperial Patronage in the Formation of T'ang Buddhism," *Perspectives on the T'ang*. Edited by Arthur F. Wright and Denis Twitchett. New Haven and London: 1973.

Yampolsky, Philip B., trans., *The Platform Sutra of the Sixth Patriarch*. The Text of the Tun-Huang Manuscript. New York and London: 1967.

Yi, Hŭi-sŭng 이희승. *Kugŏ taesajŏn* 국어대사전. Seoul: 1961.

Yi, Hong-jik 李弘稙. *Kuksa taesajŏn* 國史大辭典. Revised edition. Seoul: 1971.

Yi, Ki-baek 李基白. *Han'guksa sillon* 韓國史新論. Seoul: 1967.

Yi, Pyŏng-do 李丙燾. *Han'guksa taegwan* 韓國史大觀. Seoul: 1964.

Idem. Koryŏ sidae ŭi yŏn'gu 高麗時代의 研究. Han'guk munhwa ch'ongsŏ che sajip. Seoul: 1948.

INDEX

hsü: 19, 60, 67, 98, 99, 125, 171, 175

Chao-chou: 148

Chao-lun: 81

Characteristies: 22, 23, 48, 70, 81, 83, 84, 86, 91, 92, 96, 97, 108, 109, 112, 115, 120, 121, 126, 132, 142, 149, 152, 173; see also Nature

Ch'egwan: 3

Ch'eng-kuan: 58, 59, 77, 94, 109

Chiao: see Kyo

Chih-i: 3, 5

chih-kuan: 58, 102, 131, 132

Chih-yen: 58

Ch'imun kyŏnghun: 125

Ch'ing-yüan: 3, 59

Chin'gak Kuksa: see Hyesim

Chinsim chiksŏl: 48, 53, 68, 134

Ch'oe: brothers, 6; Ch'ung-hŏn, 44–46, 162; family, 41, 45, 46, 161; Hang, 44; U, 44, 162

Ch'oe Sŏn: 9, 44

Chogye: Mountain, 9, 15, 35, 41, 49; Order, 5, 14, 41, 42, 167–70, 173, 178

Chogyejong: see Chogye (Order)

Chonghwi: 12, 14

Chŏng Kwang-u: 11

Ch'ŏngwŏn Monastery: 24, 27

Ch'ŏnt'ae: 35, 42; doctrinal classification, 3; mountain,

5; Order, 4, 28; philosophy, 3, 57, 58; School, 59, 101; teachings, 4, 28

Ch'ŏnt'ae sagyoŭi: 3

Chŏryo: see *Hwaomnon Chŏryo*

Chosŏn Pulgyo Chogyejong: 168

Ch'ungdam: 49

compassion: 23, 43, 46, 136, 140; vow of, 136, 140

concentration: 126, 127

Confucianism: 34

conscience: 17, 28

consciousness: 80–82

contemplation: 3, 4, 37, 48, 51, 92, 108, 131, 142; act of, 49, 51, 58, 62, 63, 72, 90, 91, 117, 126, 146, 154–156

courage: 22, 23, 104, 107, 116

cow-tending: 115

cultivation: 51, 94, 113, 115, 116, 119, 120, 158; act of, 111, 123, 125, 128, 131, 133; carefree, 127; Characteristic-oriented, 126, 130, 157, 158; defiled, 129; essence of, 157; exclusive, 20; gradual, 36, 47, 53, 65, 94, 110–13, 117–20, 122–24, 128, 136, 137, 144, 146, 155, 156, 158, 173; gradual-perfect, 130; Nature-oriented, 127, 130, 133, 143, 157; parallel, 4; paradoxical, 120; 126, 130, 135; path of, 117, 118; perfect, 157;

perfect-gradual, 129; perfuming, 120; Phenomena-accomplishing, 130; positions of, 30, 103, 118, 123, 131; process of, 119, 123, 132, 136, 138, 147; provisional, 143; subtle, 121; sudden, 130; true, 120, 122, 126, 138; undefiled, 136

death: 17, 33, 34; Chinul's, 9, 49, 51, 54, 55; Uich'ŏn's, 5
debasement: self-, 104, 116, 171
defilement: 73, 97, 114, 115, 119–122, 126, 128, 129, 131, 138, 140, 157
delusion: 17, 89, 95, 96, 113, 118, 119, 125, 136
Dharma: 70, 140, 141, 154, 171; as the mind of sentient beings, 70; counterfeit-, 21, 106, 138; degenerate-, 21, 22, 88, 99, 106, 138, 156; discourse on, 48, 54, 90; esoteric transmission of, 51, 62, 93; flavor of, 100; gate of, 65, 125, 153, 158; obtainment of, 137; the objective side of Sŏn, 67; questions and answers on, 54; right-, 21, 106, 138; seal of, 26, 74; separate transmission of, 57, 59, 64, 144; transmission of, 71, 144, 169, 173; true, 71; two aspects of, 65, 70; unchanging, 104
Dharmadhātu: 30, 58, 68, 83,

92, 93, 103, 105, 106, 108, 149, 151–154, 159
Dharmakāya: 68, 70, 95, 105
dharmas: 25, 69, 70, 73, 74, 111, 120, 125, 126, 151, 152, 158
dharmatā: 70, 74
dhyāna: 120, 127; see meditation
Diamond Sūtra: 43, 57, 175
disease: of intellectual understanding, 39, 51, 64, 150, 153, 154; of the students of Kyo, 170–71; of the students of Sŏn, 172; ten kinds of, 171
distraction: 125, 129, 132
dream: 73, 74, 95
dwellings: ten, 106, 123, 124, 132

Eda Shunyū: 8
effect: 102; see also cause
elevation: self-, 116, 117, 172
Empress Wu: 58
Emptiness: 69, 74, 77, 84, 86, 88, 96, 119, 121, 125, 126, 134, 149, 150, 152, 155, 158, 173
enlightenment: 23, 36, 51, 80, 82, 91, 95, 96, 108, 112, 113, 115, 116, 119, 122, 125, 128, 136–38, 147, 148, 154; act of, 136, 138; complete, 69, 96, 117; complete-sudden, 49; entering, 27, 48; esoteric, 94, 110; exoteric, 94, 110; ex-

perience of, 111; great, 140; liberating, 47; mysterious, 152, original, 66; perfect, 157; realization-, 94, 110, 124, 132, 136, 145–47, 156, 157; sudden, 26, 30, 47, 51, 53, 65, 90, 93–101, 109, 111, 112, 114, 115–122, 126, 127, 129; 130, 136, 138, 141, 143, 144, 146, 155–58; thought of, 123, 124, 131; true, 142; two kinds of, 93, 94; underestanding-, 94, 100, 109, 110, 123, 124, 132, 136, 143, 145, 153, 155

Essence: 77, 78, 98, 108, 109, 114, 135; of True Mind, 70–90, 95, 97, 99, 126, 127, 131, 134, 135; and function, 75, 77, 99, 109, 117, 135, 152, 154

evolution: 95, 118, 130

examination: civil-service, 2; monks' examination, 2, 15, 24 33, 165, 166

exclusion: total, 89, 90

experience: 31, 54, 90, 91, 100, 101, 114; enlightenment, 52; liberating, 46; mystical, 39; of final consummation, 39; religious, 24, 37, 53, 101, 114, 147, 150; spiritual, 23

Fa-hsiang: 57

Fa-tsang: 3, 58, 60, 82, 105, 152

face: original, 74, 75

faith: 30, 31, 101–07, 109, 110, 116, 120, 123, 139, 153, 157; and understanding, 107; entrance in, 29; in one's own mind, 100; in rebirth, 52; right, 107; ten, 30, 103, 105, 106, 117, 123, 132

freedom: 38, 40, 43, 55, 85, 152, 156, 158, 159

Function: 77, 96, 97, 99, 104, 109, 118, 121, 123; two kinds of, 87, 135; of True Mind, 70, 79, 81–90, 95–98, 108, 109, 111, 119, 134

grace: four kinds, 16; of the Buddha, 49

genuine teaching in words: 26, 51, 62–63, 94, 100, 110, 143, 143, 152, 153, 157, 171

geomaney: 5

habit: old, 115; defiled, 117

habitual force: 114, 115, 129, 138, 140

Haedong Pulcho wŏllyu: 10

hakchŏng: 11

hangnok: 11, 12

Heart Sūtra: 84

Hsien-shou: see Fa-tsang

Hua-yen: see Hwaŏm

Hŭijong: 9, 11 41, 45, 46, 55

Hui-ko: 72, 78

Hui-neng: 5, 26, 39, 50, 59, 62, 110, 111, 125, 145, 148

Hŭngch'ŏn Monastery: 165,

170, 171
Hung-chou Sect: 87, 97–100
Hŭngdŏk Monastery: 165
hwadu: 148–150, 151, 153, 156, 158; see also *kŏan* and Sŏn (*kanwha*)
Hwaŏm: contemplation, 31, 58; doctrine, 25, 27, 59, 107, 108; doctrinal classification, 3, 60, 102, 117; enlightenment, 49; monastery, 3; philosophy, 57, 58, 82; *Sūtra*, 3, 27–29, 105, 106, 147, 151, 171, 175, 176; teaching, 28, 29; thought, 51, 101, 109
interfusion: of sentient beings and Buddhas, 107–09
Hwaŏmnon Chŏryo: 10, 27, 48, 64, 101, 156, 171 175–177
Hyesim: 9, 45, 51, 55, 162, 176
Hyŏndŭng Monastery: 10

ideal: 16, 18, 23, 24, 33, 36, 161, 163
ignorance: 96, 114, 115, 123, 149, 153; fundamental, 113; secondary, 113
illumination: 51; internal, 23, 48, 141; inward, 78, 91–93, 100, 108, 110
Im Ki-san: 11
impediment: of Principle, 114; of Phenomena, 114
inclusion: total, 89, 90
intellectual understanding: 40,

66, 100, 149, 151, 153, 156, 171; disciple of, 145; disease of, 39, 51, 64, 150, 153, 154; genuine, 64; master of, 39, 144, 148
invasion: Mongol, 6, 162

Kamakura: 20, 143, 162
Kamata Shigeo: 61
kangwŏn: 176, 177
Kanwha kyŏrŭiron: 51, 64, 147, 150, 155, 156, 172
karma: 17, 114
Kasong: 52
Kilsang Monastery: 36, 39, 41
Kim Kun-su: 8, 9
Kim Pu-sik: 6, 8
Kisillon: see *Taesŭng kisillon*
knowing: and being, 112; and doing, 113, 114, 116, 118, 122–24, 130, 132, 136, 141, 146, 157–59; as the Essence of True Mind, 72–77, 80, 86, 87, 91, 121, 126; clear 100; order of 67; spiritual, 99, 110, 145
kŏan: 38, 39, 176; see also *hwadu*
Kobong: 171
Kŏjo Monastery: 32, 33, 35, 36, 39
Kongjŏnje: 163
Koryŏ: Buddhism, 2, 3, 8, 14, 16, 18, 24, 28, 31, 33; bureaucracy, 6; dynasty, 2, 5;

economic order, 163; monasteries, 2, 7, 18–20, 34, 44, 45; monks, 21, 44, 45; society, 2, 8, 21, 34
kugye: see precepts
Kukch'ŏng Monastery: 4
Kumārajīva: 81
kusan: see Nine Mountains
kwan (*kuan*): see contemplation; see also *kyo*
Kwangjong 61
Kwanŭm: 78
Kwŏnsu chŏnghye kyŏlsamun: 10, 12, 15, 19, 20, 21, 33
Kye ch'osim hagin mun: 43, 47, 113, 176
Kyo: 1, 3, 23, 31, 51, 52, 61–63, 68, 101, 103, 144, 147, 172–75; and *kwan*, 3, 4, 19; separate transmission outside of, 57, 59, 64, 94, 155; students of, 116–17, 143, 147, 155, 157; see also Sŏn
kyŏgoesŏn: 173
kyogwan kyŏmsu: 3, 19
Kyŏlsamun: see *Kwŏnsu chŏnghye kyŏlsamun*
Kyŏngdŏk chŏndŭngnok: 176
Kyŏnghŏ: 177

Laṅkāvatāra Sūtra: 57
letters: 46, 47, 51, 52, 148, 155; *Dharma* master of, 91; nonestablishment of, 144; nonreliance on, 49, 57, 59
liberation: 54, 118, 135, 156,

173; by removal of impediments, 113; of Self-Nature, 113; source of, 118
Lin-chi: 37–38, 135, 165, 170
literature; Buddhist, 3, 54, 177; Mahāyāna, 125; *Prajñāpāramitā*, 150; Sŏn, 48
Li T'ung-hsüan: 10, 30, 31, 49, 51, 62, 64, 102, 103, 105, 109, 146
Lotus Sūtra: 101, 171, 176

Mādhyamika: 69
malpŏp: see degenerate-*dharma*
maṇi jewel: 86, 96–98
master: authentic, 148; of Sŏn, 36, 40; permanent, 15, 46, 47; Sŏn, 26, 39, 46, 47, 49, 52, 53, 63, 67, 68
Ma-tzu Tao-i: 1, 59, 87
meaning: understanding of, 90
meditation: 17, 48, 49, 51, 125, 127, 155, 158, 172, 176; hall, 23, 176; see also *dhyāna*
merit: 20; transference of, 141; worldly, 17–18
mind (Mind): 24, 31, 33, 57, 66–71, 74, 78, 79, 95, 106, 110, 119, 121, 138, 139, 141, 149; as Buddha, 28, 30; cultivation of, 48, 88, 92, 119; cultivators of, 99, 109, 116, 119; deluded, 80, 81, 134; direct pointing to, 57, 66; disease of, 81; essence of,

91; great, 49;–ground, 66, 68, 76, 92, 125; illuminating, 90, 91; mirror of, 49; mysterious, 69; nature of, 89; one, 70, 134, 149, 152, 154, 156, 174; one's own, 88, 92, 93, 104, 105, 108–10, 117, 139, 156, 172, 173; original, 78, 116, 117; pure, 72–74; realize, 51, 62, 63, 91; reflect, 51; school of, 27, 66; students of, 153, 154; transmission of, 72; see also body

Mind-Nature: 22, 23, 26, 34, 80, 86, 89, 120, 121, 126, 127, 129, 149

Mind-only: 138, 139, 141

Mind-seal: silent transmission of, 73

mirror: 110, 111, 119, 139; for the act of contemplation, 62, 91; of mind, 49; spiritual, 69

Moguja: 11, 35, 115, 136

Mo-ho chih-kuan: 58

monk-license: 164

monk-soldiers: 45

monks: 16, 17, 34, 44, 71; goal of, 18

Mt. Kong: 32, 35, 39

Mt. Sagul: 12, 14

Mt. Songgwang: 36, 41

Munjong: 3, 7, 22

Myoch'ŏng: 5, 6

mysteries: 89; myriad, 72–74, 77, 87

Nan-yüeh: 59

National Academy: 11

Nature: 16, 23, 57, 65, 66, 74, 78–80, 83, 86, 88, 89, 95–97, 104, 108, 109, 112, 125–127, 129, 140, 142, 153, 172, 173; and Chracteristics, 65, 68, 70, 88, 90, 93, 96, 99, 104, 117, 120, 152, 173; enlightenment –, 75, 85; original, 95; path of, 117–118; pure, 96; school of, 120; sea of, 108, 137; seeing into, 26, 48, 57, 66, 95, 110, 117, 129, 136, 137, 172; True, 25, 66, 85, 143, 154

Neo-Confucianism: 164

Nine Mountains: 1, 4, 42

nirmāṇakāya: 68

nirvāṇa: 68, 82, 84, 102, 103, 114, 119, 122, 131, 132; see also *saṁsāra*

Niu-t'ou Sect: 88, 97–100

no-mind: 134, 136, 137, 157; study of, 157, 158

no-thought: 121, 146; cultivation of, 121, 126, 130, 133, 134, 157; enlightenment of, 122

nonaction: 115, 122, 129

nonbeing: 81, 97, 98

nonexistence: 114, 148

nongjang: 163

nonobstruction: between Nature and Characteristics, 90; between Phenomena and

precepts: 25, 34, 42, 43, 120, 142; five, 142; of *pigu* (*bhikṣu*), 12; of *sami* (*śrāmaṇera*), 12
Principle: 25, 82, 89, 105, 112, 113–15, 117, 158; and Phenomena, 25, 70, 82, 112, 114, 117, 122, 125, 141, 152
P'u-chi: 59
Puhyu: 166, 168, 170
Pure Land: 21, 57, 92, 106, 138–141, 172, 176
Pure Rules: 44, 59
Puril Pojo Kuksa: 11, 55
purity: by removal of dirt, 113; of Self-Nature, 113
Puyong Yŏnggwan: 166, 169, 173, 174
Pyŏgam Kaksŏng: 174, 175
Pyŏkkye Chŏngsim: 167, 169
Pyŏksong Chiŏm: 167, 171, 169, 173, 175
Pyŏnyang Ŏn'gi: 173–75

Queen Munjong: 166
quiescence: 23, 96, 133, 158; and knowing, 126, 129, 131, 133; and wakefulness, 132, 150; as the Essence of True Mind, 74–77; empty, 99, 135

reality: inner, 78; nature of, 69; timeless, 106; true, 173; ultimate, 25, 48, 65, 67, 69, 91
realization: sudden, 89

rebirth: 139, 141, 142
recitation: of the name of the Buddha, 92, 139, 142
religion: history of, 24; state, 2, 14
repentance: according to Principle, 113; through Phenomena, 113
revolution (mental): 95, 118, 120, 130

sagyokwa: 176
saint: mind of, 81
sajip: 171, 175
sajipkwa: 175
salvation: 14, 20
samādhi: 10, 15, 19, 52, 76, 116, 125, 142, 149, 158; and *prajñā*, 10, 15, 19–21, 23, 24, 35, 36, 43, 75, 76, 106, 124–33, 136, 137, 140, 142, 143, 146, 150, 158; of Self-Nature, 75, 76, 125, 158
śamatha-vipaśyanā: 131, 132; see also *chih-kuan*
sambhogakāya; 68
Samguk Sagi: 6, 8
samikwa: 175
saṁsāra: 17, 82, 84, 114, 119, 125, 140; and *nirvāṇa*, 82, 84, 114, 119
saṅgha: 2, 4, 7, 17, 18, 20, 24
Sangch'ong: 170
Sangdangnok: 52
Sangmujuam: 37, 38
San-lun: 57

207

Sejong: 164, 165, 168
self: 69, 102, 159; authentic, 75; true, 26, 84, 95, 107
Self-Nature: 25, 26, 72, 85, 87, 103, 108, 113, 115, 118, 126, 128, 129, 158
Seng-chao: 81
Shen-hsiu: 59, 88, 110, 119
Shen-hui: 26, 39, 50, 51, 58–60, 61, 63, 72, 73, 76, 77, 87, 88, 91, 97–99, 144, 148
shih-li wu-ai: see nonobstruction between Phenomena and Principle
shih-shih wu-ai: see nonobstruction between Phenomena and Phenomena
Shih-t'ou: 59
śīla: 116, 125; see also precepts
Silla: Buddhism, 1, 2; culture, 1; politics, 1
Sin Hyewŏl: 177
Sixth patriarch: see Hui-neng
Sŏchang: 175
Society for the Cultivation of *Samādhi* and *Prajñā*: 10, 20, 32, 33, 37, 41
Society for the Cultivation of Sŏn: 9, 37, 41–47, 52–55, 159, 161–163, 170
Sŏn: 24, 26–28, 31, 38, 40, 46, 48, 49, 57–61, 144, 147, 153, 157, 172, 174, 178; act of, 65–67, 90, 93, 95, 101, 109, 116, 158, 159; and Hwaŏm,

29, 53; and Kyo, 2, 4, 7, 8, 19, 28, 34, 47, 52, 54, 59–61, 64, 68, 101, 192, 117, 164–66, 170, 172, 174, 175; beginning of, 53, 65, 90, 94, 159; exotericization of, 91; gate of, 152, 154, 173; history of, 62; *hwadu*, 64, 94, 143, 148, 150–52, 155, 171, 172; idiotic, 19, 51, 62; instruction in, 53; intellectual, 144
Sŏn'ga kwigam: 171, 173
Songgwang Monastery: 9, 170, 174
Song Man'gong: 177
sŏn'gyo yangjong: 164, 165
Sŏn'gyosŏk: 172
Sŏnjong: 168
Sŏnmun ch'waryo: 177
Sŏnmun yŏmsong: 175
sŏnwŏn: 176
Sŏnwŏnsa: 162
Sŏnyo: 171, 175
Sŏsan: 166–69, 171–74, 177
soul: 78, 79, 80, 83
Southern Ch'an: see Southern Sect
Southern Sect: 57–59, 60–63, 101
śrāvakas: 71, 102, 119
state: and Buddhism, 2; power, 54; protection, 18; welfare of, 7
Subhuti: 71
Suchness: 25, 68, 69, 79, 84, 85, 97, 115, 129, 142, 151

suikwa: 176
sŭngkwa: see examination (monks')
śūnyatā: see Emptiness
Susimgyŏl: 47, 48, 53, 78
Susŏnsa: see Socriety for the Cultivation of Sŏn
Susŏnsa Chungch'anggi: 9, 45, 47
Suu: 36, 37, 39

Ta-ch'eng ch'i-hsin-lun: see *Taeesŭng kisillon*
T'aego Pou: 167, 169
taegyokwa: 176
Taesŭng kisillon: 70, 71, 82, 113, 175
Ta-hui: 37, 39, 40, 51, 54, 62, 64, 115, 143–150, 175
Takahashi Tōru: 170, 172–73
tamsŏn pŏphoe: 15
Tao: 15, 35, 51, 155, 156; commitment to, 42; discussion of, 42; exoteric transmission as, 155; fit in with, 129, 146; great, 68, 71; origin of, 102; place of, 174; respect for, 46; unity with, 144, 157
Taoism: 34
Tao-sheng: 112
tathāgatagarbha: 69, 70, 82, 84
teaching: complete, 147, 152–54, 172; complete-sudden, 103; expedient, 120, 153; five, 151; perfect, 102; sudden, 59,

60, 100, 117, 147, 151, 152, 155, 172
theory: 54, 100, 113; and practice, 100, 113
thoughts: 85, 89, 115, 119, 121, 133, 151; deluded, 74, 95, 115, 120; quiet, 120; illusory, 128; nonexistence of, 121
Three Jewels: 140
three learnings: 24, 43, 125, 126
three realms of existence: 16
Thusness: 68, 69
T'ien-t'ai: see Ch'ont'ae
T'ien-t'ai hsiao-chih-kuan: 58
Ti-lun: 57
time: 118, 123; transcending of, 106
Tonghak Monastery: 177
Tongsa yŏlchŏn: 10, 12
Tosŏn: 10
transmigration: see *saṁsāra*
transmission: exoteric, 152, 153, 155
Treatise on Hua-yen: 10, 29–32, 43, 53, 62–63, 101, 114, 136, 138
Tripiṭaka: 48, 71
True Mind: 48, 66–91, 93, 95–97, 119, 121, 126, 127, 131, 133, 143, 144, 159; the auxiliary of, 137; the primary of, 137; two aspects of, 70, 71, 76
truth: 77, 93, 151; four noble, 102; lower level of, 67; unity with, 150; world of, 90

Yüan-chüeh-ching: see *Wŏn'-gakkyŏng*

Yung-ming Yen-shou: 61, 71, 139